TRAVEL Writing

TRAVEL *Writing*

Leromi Publishing

© 2006 by LEROMI PUBLISHING

All rights reserved. No part of this publication may be reproduced, stored in a retrieval system, or transmitted in any form or by any means, electronic, mechanical, photocopying, recording, or otherwise, without the prior written permission of the copyright owner.

Leromi Publishing
P.O. Box 40484
Denver, Colorado 80204
Phone: (303) 271-3532

Printed in the United States of America
10 9 8 7 6 5 4 3 2 1

ISBN 978-0-97-135859-1

Library of Congress Control Number: 2005911169

JENNY ELLIOTT-BENNETT received her bachelor of arts honors degree from Plymouth University and her master of arts degree from the University of the West of England. She has been analyzing various literatures of travel since her undergraduate days and has produced dissertations for both of the above degrees on the subject of travel: *Goût du Gouffre: The Female Voice from Foreign Lands* and *Modernism and the Genre of Travel*, respectively. Apart from traveling, Elliott-Bennett has taught English as a Foreign Language at various European establishments intermittently for five years and has studied at the Teikyo Transatlantic Study Centre in Maastricht. Her current research interests include: Moorish versus Christian Spain in travel, religious and crime texts, the literature of (un)holy wars and crusades, literature of the sea, and island literature.

Sentence Number	Small Points / Specific Points	Big Picture / General Points
1.	_____	_____
2.	_____	_____
3.	_____	_____
4.	_____	_____
5.	_____	_____
6.	_____	_____
7.	_____	_____
8.	_____	_____
9.	_____	_____
10.	_____	_____

Final Step: If you have more lines, please continue on another sheet of paper. Add your name to the Instructor Comment Sheet for Writing Assignment Two in appendix 5 and staple it to this sheet with the ten or more lines on which you identify small, specific points and the big picture, general points. Then turn in these two sheets to your professor.

CONTENTS

ACKNOWLEDGMENTS	xi
FOREWORD	xiii

SECTION I   1
An Introduction to Travel Writing

CHAPTER 1   5
The Exciting World of Travel Writing—James Poynter

CHAPTER 2   19
Toward a Definition of Travel Writing—Jon Volkmer

CHAPTER 3   31
The Diversity of the Literary Genre of Travel—
Jenny Elliott-Bennett

CHAPTER 4   43
A History of Travel Writing—Karen Carmean

CHAPTER 5   69
Travel Writing Brought Up-to-Date—Amanda Castleman

SECTION II   77
Starting Out—Five Approaches

CHAPTER 6   79
Selecting and Narrowing Travel Article Ideas—Sue Rumbaugh,
Amanda Castleman & James Poynter

CHAPTER 7   101
Your Travel Journal—The Tool for En Route and Destination
Pieces—Twila Papay

CHAPTER 8   125
Press Trips—Katherine Lemmon

SECTION III — 143
Aiming for the Best

CHAPTER 9 — 145
Quality Travel Writing—Sue Rumbaugh

CHAPTER 10 — 155
Toward Excellence in Travel Writing—Thomas Swick

SECTION IV — 173
Developing and Honing the Article

CHAPTER 11 — 175
Query Letter or Phone Call—James Poynter

CHAPTER 12 — 193
Travel Writing Styles and Types— Amanda Castleman

CHAPTER 13 — 211
The Process—James Poynter, Amanda Castleman & Sue Rumbaugh

CHAPTER 14 — 231
Provide Photos—Amanda Castleman

CHAPTER 15 — 251
Other Photo Sources—James Poynter

SECTION V — 255
Travel Books

CHAPTER 16 — 259
Guidebook Writing—Andrew Hempstead

CHAPTER 17 — 283
How-To Travel Books—James Poynter

SECTION VI — 301
Making Travel Writing Profitable for You

CHAPTER 18 — 303
The Business of Travel Writing—James Poynter

CHAPTER 19 — 321
Advance and Make Top Money—James Poynter

APPENDICES — 327

APPENDIX 1 — 327
The Chronological List

APPENDIX 2 — 333
Writer's Guidelines for Selected Magazines That Buy Travel Articles

APPENDIX 3 — 345
Travel Article Leads

APPENDIX 4 — 351
Resources

APPENDIX 5 — 353
Instructor Comment Sheets

INDEX — 393

TO

DR. TWILA YATES PAPAY
Without whose encouragement this book would never have been written

and

ROBERT AND NILI POYNTER
Whose wedding was the happiest day of my life

ACKNOWLEDGMENTS

The contributors to this book are many. I am deeply indebted to all of them. When Leromi Publishing almost gave up on publishing the book, Twila Papay provided such strong encouragement, the project participants took heart and moved forward again with renewed efforts. Her strong verbal kick in the rear is much appreciated.

Every quality book is a compromise. Otherwise, they would take ten years or more to come off the press and would be thousands of pages long. However, the contributing authors of this book have done an excellent job of keeping to their subjects, honing the verbiage, and providing excellent copy. Thanked for this are Karen Carmean with Converse College in South Carolina; Amanda Castleman, a travel writer who writes both articles and guides for European, American, and sometimes other publishers; Jenny Elliott-Bennett with Sheffield Hallam University in the United Kingdom; Andrew Hempstead, a Canadian travel writer who specializes in guidebooks; Katherine Lemmon, a prolific freelance writer specializing in travel with over five hundred articles published; Dr. Twila Papay with Rollins College, both a travel writer and an educator who specializes in travel writing; Sue Rumbaugh, MPM who both teaches travel writing at Carlow College in Pittsburgh and is a freelance writer; Tom Swick, travel editor for the *South Florida Sun Sentinel*; and Dr. Jon Volkmer, who teaches travel writing at Ursinus College in Pennsylvania.

Quality books are also a reflection of the behind-the-scenes specialists. Migual Mosqueda is thanked for his initial development of the book cover concept. Also thanked is Andy Selutin, who took the concept and produced the cover the book now so proudly wears.

Good readers and reviewers, like good authors, can elevate the quality of a book, especially a source book, to the highest degree possible. Thanked for doing a top-quality job on this book are three exceptional individuals. Melanie McDaniel provided an important first review of the rough manuscript and made several beneficial change suggestions. Later manuscript reviews and change suggestions were made by Tilar Mazzeo, president of the International Society for Travel Writing, and Dr. Russ Pottle, president of the Society for American Travel Writing. Both provided comprehensive reviews and made valuable improvement suggestions.

Dr. Pottle also authored a cogent and a motivating foreword. His intimate and extensive background in and knowledge of travel writing combined with his experience in introducing newcomers to the field is clearly reflected in the guidance he provides to readers.

Sherry Roberts with The Roberts Group is a true miracle worker. She is a top-rate book interior designer, editor, proofreader, and indexer. There is little (or nothing) she cannot do to make a book look great and flow easily. Without her expertise this (and many other books) would not come close to reaching their full potential. Her efforts are always appreciated.

Mike Daniels with Sheridan Books made a number of beneficial suggestions. These have not only added to the image of the book, but they have also kept the book within the forecasted budget. Publishers are fortunate when they get a printing expert like Mike to guide them.

Family members can often make or break an author, an editor, and/or a publisher. The support of family members is very much appreciated. Without Nili and Robert Poynter, this book would be far less than it is. Bill Poynter has encouraged and contributed ideas over the more than three years since the book idea was initiated. Sue, Lewis, and Michael Poynter have also provided their support. But of special interest are the grandchildren, Andrew and Matthew Poynter. These young guys have wanted to distribute manuscript pages in many directions, scatter computer disks, and eat author photos—but Lewis, their father, has done an excellent job of discouraging that.

FOREWORD

The novelist and critic Nicholas Delbanco says that "all writing is travel writing"—that writing about a voyage into one's own mind, soul, or past is like writing about a voyage across the sea.[1] However, for many readers, and for an increasing number of writers, travel writing still describes a physical voyage, a new place, an exotic destination, an unfamiliar culture. For these people, particularly for writers who want to jump into the travel game, *Travel Writing* is an exciting resource.

Travel Writing is a professional textbook, a guide to learning about travel writing as a craft and a career. If you are a budding travel writer, there is much to think about. What are your interests? Where do you want to go? Do you want to write short articles or a book? Do you want to make a living at this, or do it on the side? There is also much to do. You must identify an audience for your writing. You must plan your itinerary and organize your writing process. You must take notes efficiently, learn to keep a journal, learn about photography, learn the travel writing market, remember to keep lists and receipts. And then there is the networking. It can all seem overwhelming.

Written by working travel writers and academic professionals, *Travel Writing* helps students sort out these questions and demands. Chapters welcome students to the profession of travel writing and show them its nuts and bolts. These days, there are other ways to start work than jumping ship in the South Pacific, as Herman Melville did over a century ago. Publishers print resort reviews, destination pieces, industry and trade articles, "how-to" volumes, and guidebooks. Writers can work in press trips, as columnists for magazines, or as literary freelancers. Many chapters in *Travel Writing* acquaint students with these points of entry into travel writing. Others offer frank advice on backing student writing with sound commercial sense. Want to sell your latest travel piece?

---

1. Nicholas Delbanco, "On why all writing is travel writing," *Harper's Magazine* 309.1852 (September 2004): 91-96.

The chapter called "Query Letter or Phone Call?" shows how. Want to know what it means to sell the rights to that latest travel piece? A clear explanation is included in the chapter, "The Business of Travel Writing." Read further in that chapter and you will find suggestions about purchasing the right printers, file cabinets, and fax machines.

Most important for any student of travel writing, *Travel Writing* provides a sequence of nineteen assignments that enables each student to conceive and produce a finished "spec" article, complete with photographs, that can be sold to newspapers or magazines. Assignments guide students in finding out what kind of travel writers they are. They provide direction for understanding the basics of travel writing, finding a writer's voice and style, selecting article ideas, and working with a traveler's journal. Like assignments in all good writing textbooks, these in *Travel Writing* help writers draft the article, target an audience, and polish prose. But they go beyond the usual learning process in showing students how to pair photos with an article and even how to package and submit the text and pictures. Talent helps a writer, as the chapter entitled "Toward a Definition of Travel Writing" points out. But there is no substitute for hard work and good organization in putting out a solid, salable article. The sequence of assignments in *Travel Writing* encourages students to make the best of these efforts.

For teachers in classrooms or professional workshops, *Travel Writing* offers an exciting opportunity to engage in dialogue with students about theory and practice in the profession. Two chapters offer extended definitions and histories of travel writing, situating students' efforts in a long literary and commercial tradition. Other chapters provide material for workshopping drafts of travel pieces or discussing various approaches to telling a travel story. The chapter, "Selecting and Narrowing Travel Article Ideas," is not simply the explanation of a step in producing a travel piece. It is an exploration of where story ideas come from and how they can be expressed in different forms, including poetry. Regardless of its focus, each chapter is accompanied by review questions that aid students in remembering important concepts and incorporating new ideas into their own writing. And each assignment contains forms for instructor feedback on student work, ensuring that a teacher's professional insight accompanies each student's journey through the assignment sequence.

Foreword

Travel writing sounds like a dream job. But it is also a craft and a profession. *Travel Writing* gives prospective writers a clear and helpful guide through it.

Russ Pottle
President, Society for American Travel Writing

SECTION I

AN INTRODUCTION TO TRAVEL WRITING

The introduction offers five chapters that provide the reader with a strong initial understanding of travel writing. In chapter one, "The Exciting World of Travel Writing," the reader discovers why travel writing is exciting, why it is a field that many aspire to, and why most active travel writers would never trade their vocation for any other. It explains the many different hats (roles) of travel writers and it provides eleven different kinds of travel writing a person entering the field can choose as a specialty.

The second chapter, "Toward a Definition of Travel Writing," helps the reader to get a handle on just what travel writing is all about. It provides a historical overview of travel writing and gives the reader a map of the world of travel writing.

The third chapter is an introduction to some parameters of travel writing. This chapter helps the reader more easily identify what travel writing is and what it is not.

The fourth chapter is a history of travel writing. Here the reader learns how the field started in a relatively narrow framework or set of guidelines. Then it shows how travel writing has exploded in both the volume of articles and books published on travel and in the scope of what those in the field consider to be travel writing.

The fifth chapter brings the reader up-to-date. It identifies issues, but it concentrates on where travel writing is today—and where it seems to be going.

These five chapters should help to provide the "setting" for travel writing so that the student of the field or the aspiring travel writer will have a better understanding of what professionals in the field mean when they say they do travel writing.

JIM POYNTER has authored or coauthored seven travel books, with his first book being published in 1969. He has also written numerous articles for both trade and consumer magazines, and, for two years, he authored a weekly travel column for a major international newspaper. He has been a full-time faculty member at Metropolitan State College in Denver for twenty-three years and has taught travel writing courses in the continuing education programs of the University of Texas–Austin and the University of Wisconsin–Madison. As this book goes to press, Poynter is scheduled to teach travel writing courses in the continuing education programs of California State University–San Bernadino and Loyola Marymount University in Los Angeles.

CHAPTER 1

The Exciting World of Travel Writing

James Poynter

Travel writing can be an exotic, exciting, and adventuresome way of life. Experienced travel writers can and frequently do take one international trip after another. This week you might trek across Antarctica. After resting a bit, you might find yourself on a luxury cruise between the United States and England. While in Europe, you visit some of the world's top ski resorts, and then it is on to adventures in North Africa, Asia, and South America. This is a life many dream of, but it is a life that travel writers live. As a part-time freelance travel writer, I have worked in more than sixty countries in the world, but my life, although exciting and interesting, pales in comparison with those of some travel writers. Your life becomes what you make it. You can travel almost constantly, writing as you go, and seeing the best that the world has to offer. Alternatively, if you prefer, you can stay at home most of the time, taking a journey to an exotic part of the world now and then throughout the year, doing most of your actual writing in your office at home. Or you can do anything in between. Many of us turn down far more trip offers than we take—simply because there isn't time to do it all. But isn't it nice to be able to choose to travel or not to travel, to decide where you want to go and what you want to write about?

Travel writing is unlike any other kind of writing, because most travel writers do a lot of traveling. In just a few years, the chances are good, if you are a travel writer, that you will have flown on many kinds of jets, prop planes, and tiny two- or three-seat planes; trekked in countries on just about every continent; ridden on horses, camels, donkeys, elephants, and a variety of other animals; sailed the seas in luxury cruise ships, yachts, houseboats, barges, ferries, dhows, and many other sea-going craft; traveled on a variety of trains and in a wide variety of vehicles; and traversed the globe in many other ways as well.

YOU MAKE IT HAPPEN

Sound exciting? It is. And this exciting occupation can be yours. It really is an attainable lifestyle for just about anyone over eighteen years old, in reasonably good health, and with a reasonably good education. It takes setting your mind to it and taking the steps needed to accomplish it. This book will tell you how to do it, but only you can make it happen. In other words, you have to do it.

A TRAVEL WRITER WEARS MANY HATS

Many travel writers chafe at the fact that they can't just write. They say, "I am a good writer. That's all I want to do." But the system is not set up that way. As a freelance travel writer, you do need to write. After all, writing is what you sell. But if you are to make a good living as a travel writer, you will need to sell a substantial amount of travel writing. And that requires you to be more than just a writer.

Businessperson, Salesperson, Bookkeeper, and Office Manager

Successful travel writers also are businesspeople. After all, if you don't sell what you write, you will just be a traveler who likes to write and probably a person who keeps journals of his or her trips. There is nothing wrong with that as long as you have money from some other source. But you will not be considered a travel writer unless you sell what you write. Therefore, at the very least you need to be a salesperson. Much of this book is devoted to how to sell what you write. Some travel writers say they expend more effort in selling what they write than they do in writing what they sell. Unfortunately, for many who are new to travel writing selling their work is their biggest job. As in some other fields, however, travel writers frequently develop a "following." Once this has been done, selling becomes easier—you can pick up the phone and pitch a story idea to an editor who has previously purchased your articles or books, or you can send the editor finished articles and be assured that she or he will be receptive to your work and eager to see if it will "fit" in a near-future Sunday travel section.

Once you do start selling your writing, you will be expected to pay taxes on your earnings. Therefore, you will need to be a recordkeeper in general and a bookkeeper in specific. This means that you will need an office—even if it is just a corner in one room of your house. And you will need to manage that office, paying bills when they are due, collecting when money owed to you is slow to come in, handling incoming and outgoing telephone calls, and taking care of the other duties that come with running *your* travel writing business.

Dictator, Transcriber, and Polisher
Most travel writers handle their own content production. This means that the travel writer creates the article or book from his or her thoughts, impressions, and experiences and transforms it into hard copy and electronic copy for use by an editor. Many writers take notes while in the field, but eventually they transform those notes into articles and books and most do it all themselves. I once received a substantial amount of money in advance for a book and said to myself, "I don't need to transcribe my chapter drafts from dictation. I have the money to hire someone to listen to the tapes, put the information on disks, and provide me with both hard and electronic copy. I will need to do a second and perhaps a third draft, but I will be able to simply hand off taped chapter drafts and then polish the material I get back from the part-time clerical person." It sounded good, but when I got the first few

sheets of transcription back I realized that I, like most travel writers, substantially edit my tapes as I transcribe them. Now, like most travel writers, I transcribe my tapes, edit my writing, and polish the material. In other words, as a travel writer, the probability is that you, too, will be a dictator (dictating information into a recorder), transcriber, and polisher.

Mystery Shopper, Critical Evaluator, and Reviewer
Travel writers are expected to be brutally honest about their subject. Readers expect articles to be positive and to say good things about the location, the flora and fauna, the lodging facilities, restaurants, transportation, and other elements of the article or book. However, readers want to know the negatives as well. As an editor is reputed to have said, "Only heaven is heaven." In other words, no place on earth is perfect, so don't suggest that it is. Always find and report on at least one little flaw. You can rave about the hotel, point out the wonderful views from every room, the perfect service, the spaciousness, the decorations, the considerable comfort of the beds, the well-appointed bathrooms, and so forth. But don't forget to mention that noise from the hotel elevators invade every room even though the builder seemed to have tried to make the rooms soundproof. You are expected to review everything and to be a critical evaluator.

Shopping is a major concern for travelers, and even those who do not buy lots of keepsakes will still pay for hotel rooms and meals. Therefore, be a mystery shopper. Report on the good buys and the rip-offs. And even though your five-star hotel in downtown Athens has a five-star restaurant attached to it, report on the fact that the reader can get an even more authentic shwarma at a fraction of the cost just six blocks away in a restaurant crowded with locals. While you might prefer the air-conditioned gourmet restaurant in your hotel where the menu is in English and the waiters speak your language better than you do, your readers may very well want to go native—especially when it means they get a huge savings.

A Sensual Writer
As a travel writer, you will want to stay in touch with all of your senses. Paint a word picture and help readers sense that they are there. Describe

the smooth touch of polished oak, the seeming unreality of a morning sunrise as it brings a soft glow to a waking village, the aromas of the spice market, the tangy taste of exotic fruits, and the steady background reminder of the noise of your clacking rail car as it progresses across the plains. Travel writers bring the reader to the scene by sensing and sharing tactile feelings, subtle tastes, gentle aromas, a full range of sounds, and all that the eye takes in. We are able to give the gift of our travel through every sense with which our bodies perceive.

Psychologist, Anthropologist, and Sociologist
Readers want to know the interesting twists. So you owe it to yourself—and to your readers to learn about and report on such things as the "sweeps" along some popular Latin American beaches where groups of twenty or more young people line up and walk down the beach picking up purses and pickpocketing wallets. This doesn't mean you would advise readers not to go to the beach. It simply means that you warn them so that they can take precautions and leave most of their valuables and money in the hotel safe.

In a story about travel to Japan, you might want to caution your readers not to make direct eye contact and to bow instead of shaking hands. Being aware of these cultural differences might make the difference between an enjoyable trip and one that is less pleasurable than it could have been.

You should do your research so that you can tell the reader that the original people of the Middle Eastern country of Iran were blond with white skin and blue eyes, that the word "aryan" is synonymous with the word "Iran" in the native language, and that tourists are likely to encounter some natives who look much more like Scandinavians than bronze-skinned Arabs.

Tidbits of anthropology, psychology, and history can add spice to your article. You will be able to give the reader something unexpected and something uniquely interesting.

Photographer and Documenter
As a travel writer, you will be expected to provide photographs and to document the facts that you report. Few newspapers will run a story without appropriate photographs, and the photos must bear appropriate

captions. Most magazine editors will also expect photographs. However, book editors vary in terms of expected photos. Some books, especially coffee-table books, will have many photos, and the travel writer is usually expected to provide all of them. Some "how-to" books require no photos. Most books lie somewhere between these two extremes. It will help a lot if you can take the photos yourself, but using tourist bureau, vendor, and other "stock" photos often works out well.

In addition to providing photos, many editors will want to know your source for every fact presented in your article or book. In many cases, this will mean getting the information on site and getting it verified on site. In some cases, however, the tourist board of the country will be able to provide you with confirmations for your facts and the needed documentation and document verification.

WHAT KIND OF TRAVEL WRITING DO YOU WANT TO DO?

The kind of travel writing you choose to do will depend on two people: you and your editor. Cath Urquhart, travel editor for *The Times* in London, says, "What I am interested in is something that's new or different or changing or emerging. And that is always a result of what people are doing."[1] While Urquhart's sentiments are echoed by many travel editors, each editor is different, and it behooves a travel writer to understand clearly what the editor wants. Editors for publications change, and new editors are likely to have a different set of wants and preferences than those of their predecessors. Therefore, even though you may have a written contract that spells out what is expected of you, if there is a change of editors, always go to the new editor and make sure that there has not been a change of expectations. Fortunately, most will honor contracts that have already been written—and signed. But some editors will want all articles and books that have not yet been received when they take over to reflect the preferences of the new editor. It is a good idea to always ask.

You, the travel writer, may choose the kind of writing you prefer to produce. Fortunately, there are many types from which to choose.

---

1. Barry Turner, ed., *The Writer's Handbook* (London, UK: Macmillan Publishing, 2004), 14.

Destination Pieces
Destination pieces are what most people think of when they think of travel writing. These are articles for newspapers or magazines that usually run from two hundred words to two thousand words, and generally they are intended to make the reader want to go to the destination and to give the reader a feel for the destination.

Industry or Trade Articles for the Travel Industry
Industry or trade pieces are articles written for those who are working in the travel industry. They can and frequently do include destination pieces, but the orientation is toward those who are selling the destination. For example, an article on small inns in the Caribbean will include information about how much commission is paid, how the travel agent or tour planner can contact the inn or its representative, what type of clients the inn would appeal to, and so forth. In other words, it can be similar to a destination piece, but it is oriented toward those who are working in the industry. Some trade pieces are much more businesslike. For example, an article might relate to client documentation requirements in each of the South American countries, or it might compare service to and commissions paid by tour companies specializing in tours of southern Italy. Or you might write about the difficulty in finding top-quality step-on guides in Bosnia.

Fewer travel writers target the trade press for articles than those who do destination pieces for the leisure travel public. Therefore, the competition is far less, the pay is frequently much better, and in many cases state and national tourist bureaus are much more willing to get airline tickets and hotel rooms for travel writers when their writing might well result in many travel agents sending clients to their destination or their destination being included in the tours of a number of tour companies. In addition, trade pieces can often be written on spec (speculation), while simultaneously undertaking work on a contracted destination piece.

Trade Articles for Professionals
A little known area of trade travel writing pieces are those articles that are written for businesspeople in industries outside of the travel industry. Specializing in writing travel articles for executives working in

specific professions is an area where there is little competition. All of the major professions and many of the associations representing people in jobs not normally considered professions have trade publications. A large number of them have their own magazine that is sent to all of their members each month. Many of the editors of these association publications want to include travel articles, especially articles that are geared specifically toward their members. In addition, of course, for many of the industries (professions) there are magazines that are not affiliated with their associations. These, too, can be good publications for targeted articles. For example, an article titled "The Bangkok Furniture Show" might well be marketed to *Furnishings Digest*, *Furniture Style Magazine*, or *Home Furnishings Retailer*. This article would not only discuss the annual furniture show itself, but it would also describe hotels and restaurants that are near the Bangkok convention center (where the show is held). It would probably stress the fact that a buying trip to the show could be considered a business expense and that direct deals written between the furniture retailer in the United States and the furniture manufacturer in Asia could result in a substantial savings compared with buying at the furniture shows or furniture wholesale outlets in the United States.

Cruise Articles
Cruise articles, although they usually do not relate to specific destinations, are treated much like destination articles. Most are about specific ships or specific cruise lines. They can be "roundup" (survey) articles. For example, they might present a comparison of the cuisine served aboard different cruise vessels. Alternatively, an article could relate to a single aspect on a single ship. One example might be "Gambling aboard the largest cruise ship" or "The largest casino afloat." The numbers of people who are taking cruises are increasing considerably, and, therefore, the number of cruise articles being purchased and run are increasing rapidly as well.

Tour Articles
Considering the large number of people who take tours, the small number of tour articles in both newspapers and magazines is surprising. Nevertheless, there is a market for articles related to tours, and the

writers who specialize in writing about tours can usually place their articles with both the consumer press and the trade press.

Specialty Tour Articles

Specialty tours are growing rapidly, and articles relating to them are selling briskly. Some say that specialty travel is the most rapidly expanding segment of the travel industry. The nice thing about specialty tours is that almost every specialty has publications that are oriented toward it. For example, if you want to write about bicycle tours, there are a large number of bicycling magazines to which you can submit your article concepts. The same is true for almost any other specialization. The *Specialty Travel Index* lists more than a hundred travel specializations. Each of the specializations is a potential for travel articles. In addition, in almost every specialization area, there are magazines and sometimes newspapers that cater to the people interested in that specialization. These, of course, are excellent target buyers for specialty travel articles.

Reviews or Roundups

Reviews are sometimes called "roundups." They are comparisons of facilities in an area that caters to tourists. For example, consider the following article titles: "The Bed and Breakfasts of Connecticut," "Cairo Hotels," or "The Ethnic Restaurants of Los Angeles." Not all reviews are comparisons, however. For example, when a new airport opens, many publications will run an article discussing the major features of the airport. The same can be true for a new sightseeing facility or a new ground transportation possibility. A travel writer might, for example, write about taking a train to and from Manhattan after arriving at any of the major three airports serving New York City. Alternatively, an article might be written about just riding the Sky Train from JFK airport to and from downtown New York City.

How-to Travel Articles and Books

How-to pieces are growing in popularity in newspapers, magazines, and books. Frequently, these have the words "how to" in their titles. Examples include "How to Pack," "How to Travel with Children," "How to Travel with Pets," and "How to Select a Cruise." However, sometimes they do not have the words "how to" in the title. For example, this book is essentially a book on how to be a successful travel writer. Some travel writers find they do well writing nothing but "how-to" pieces.

Humorous Travel Writing
Humor is hard to write, and few writers are able to do a good job writing travel humor. However, when a well-written humorous travel article or book hits the market, it often sells well. If you are able to do it, you should rapidly find a lucrative market as many magazine, newspaper, and book editors are actively looking for quality humorous travel writing.

Guidebooks
Visit your local bookstore, and you will find a vast range of guidebooks. Each book had at least one author. Breaking into guidebook writing can be challenging, but the chapter on guidebook writing in this book will help you get a good start.

Other Areas of Travel Writing
While these are the main areas of travel writing, there are many other areas as well. Scriptwriting for radio and television travel pieces is growing in popularity. Writing contract articles for state and national travel offices has been lucrative for some travel writers for many years. And there are certainly many other travel writing markets. This book will introduce you to many opportunities. It is suggested that you dip in and try your hand at several types of travel writing. You won't know what you are best at or what you will like best until you try it.

THE TRAVEL WRITING WORLD IS YOURS
One of the nice things about travel writing is the wide variety of opportunities. Most who enter the field are surprised at the considerable range of specializations travel writers have available to them. If you target several of the less competitive areas of travel writing, you will be surprised at how fast you can get your work published and how rapidly you can move into making a good annual income from travel writing—even if you only do it on a part-time basis.

End-of-Chapter Questions

1. Are experienced travel writers often able to take frequent international trips?
2. Does a travel writer need to be a businessperson?
3. Since, as a travel writer, you will be expected to pay taxes on your earnings, you will need to be a recordkeeper in general and what in specific?
4. Was it an editor or a travel writer who is reputed to have said, "Only heaven is heaven"?
5. What kind of picture should travel writers paint?
6. According to the author, tidbits of what three things can add spice to your article?
7. Who said, "What I am interested in is something that's new or different or changing or emerging. And that is always a result of what people are doing"?
8. What kind of travel pieces are what most people think of when they think of travel writing?
9. Why are the number of cruise articles being purchased and published increasing?
10. Is the field of scriptwriting available to travel writers?

WRITING ASSIGNMENT ONE

ARE YOU A DESCRIPTIVE OR A FACTUAL TRAVEL WRITER?

Assignment Introduction

What kind of travel writer are you—factual or descriptive? Most travel writers tend to be predominantly descriptive or predominantly factual. This does not mean that there is not at least a little bit of both in just about every piece of travel writing. However, most travel writing is either predominantly descriptive or predominantly factual, and most travel writers reflect the same tendencies. Know yourself! As travel writers, we need to know ourselves and to know both our own preferences and our unique abilities.

What about you? Answer the following questions, and you will be able to come up with at least a tentative determination of whether you are predominantly a descriptive travel writer or predominantly a factual travel writer.

Assignment Activity

Think about a public place with which you are familiar. Pretend that you have relatives coming to visit and that the relatives have indicated to you that they would like to consider visiting this public place. They ask you to write to them about this place because they are considering spending a little bit of their time during their stay in your city visiting that place. They have little time, so they have to be selective as to how they spend it.

Time yourself. For three minutes write about this public place. As you write, concentrate on getting as much on paper as possible and don't pay attention to grammar, punctuation marks, or spelling. Your writing will need to be good enough that you can go back and read it and understand what you were writing, but like most of our first drafts, this exercise is about getting as much down on paper as possible.

When you are finished, answer the following questions:

1. How many descriptive words did you use? Use your own judgment as to whether or not a word is "descriptive."
   Answer: _____ words

2. How many factual words did you use? Again, use your own judgment as to whether or not the word is a word relating to one or more facts.
    Answer: _____ words

3. Did the factual words exceed the descriptive words by at least 20 percent?
    Answer: Circle the appropriate word—A) Yes or B) No

4. Did the descriptive words exceed the factual words by at least 20 percent?
    Answer: Circle the appropriate word—A) Yes or B) No

If either your descriptive words or your factual words exceeded the other by at least 20 percent, then you are probably predominantly that type of writer. It is not recommended that you try to change. Rather, it is recommended that you keep this tendency in mind and plan your marketing and your writing accordingly.

Final Step: Add your name to the Instructor Comment Sheet for Writing Assignment One in appendix 5, staple it to this sheet with your answers to questions one through four, and send or give these two sheets to your professor.

JON VOLKMER is professor of English and director of creative writing at Ursinus College in Collegeville, Pennsylvania. He is the author of the travel memoir, *Eating Europe: A Meta-Nonfiction Love Story* (Parlor Press), and of more than a dozen travel articles for *The Philadelphia Inquirer, The South Florida Sun-Sentinel,* and other newspapers and magazines. His two-part feature on St. Croix was listed among the notable travel writings of 1999 in *Best American Travel Writing 2000*. As a scholar, he has presented papers on travel writing at conferences around the country. In addition to his work in the field of travel writing, he is widely published in a variety of genres. His poetry, essays, and short fiction have appeared in such journals as *Parnassus, Literal Latte, Prairie Schooner, Texas Review, Seattle Review, Painted Bride Quarterly, The South Dakota Review, Hellas,* and *Poet Lore*. He is a past winner of the Thomas Wolfe Fiction Award, has been nominated for a Pushcart Prize in nonfiction, and served as 2002 poet laureate for Montgomery County, Pennsylvania. He is the author of a textbook, *The Fiction Workshop Companion,* and of a collection of poetry, *Art of the Country Grain Elevator*, featuring photography by Bruce Selyem (Bottom Dog Press). He holds a PhD in literature from the University of Nebraska, an MA in creative writing from Denver University, and a BA in English from the University of Colorado.

CHAPTER 2

Toward a Definition of Travel Writing

Jon Volkmer

INTRODUCTION

In the challenge of finding a serviceable definition, "travel writing" is quite a lot like "classical music." Both of the phrases are used by many different people to mean many different things, and the answer depends, at least in part, on how much of a specialist one is. In common usage, any music old or orchestral is called classical. Others associate it with the Western tradition, while still others define it in opposition to popular music. Musicologists make it a capital C and reserve the phrase for music of the Classical period in Europe, roughly 1730–1820, coming after the Baroque and before the Romantic.

In a similar vein, travel writing in its most common usage refers to writing *for* travelers: short, first-person destination accounts and guidebook installments. These are the writings one is likely to find in newspaper travel sections and on the travel shelf at the bookstore—and is what might more precisely be called "tourisitic writing." The travel shelf at most bookstores has overflowed in recent years, giving rise to step-shelves with names such as "literary travel" or "travel memoir." Here we find more sustained narratives, book-length, often with loftier artistic ambitions. As was the case with musicologists, we have reached the domain of the specialists. Writers, editors, and scholars might well emulate the capitalization trick, where travel writing crosses over from the travel section to the more prestigious book review neighborhood of the newspaper. Indeed, there is a widespread belief that the U.S. and Anglophone literary world is now enjoying an age of especially successful, robust, and varied literary travel books, so perhaps this is the classical age of travel writing. The remainder of this chapter will examine that claim, explore some problems of genre definition, set minimal criteria for literary travel writing in the contemporary setting, and present a cartographical compendium of travel writing through the ages.

"THE CURRENT RENAISSANCE"

There is evidence to support the idea that travel writing is flourishing with exceptional vitality in our own time. Literary historians of the future may well refer to the late twentieth and early twenty-first centuries in terms of a renaissance, or even a classical period, since such terms are already being applied. A meteoric rise in the sales of travel narrative books has been accompanied by a great expansion of serious scholarship on travel writing. Travel scholar David Espey, speaking at a 1999 travel writing conference at the University of Pennsylvania, chronicled the surge, and named two works that might be credited with jump-starting the interest:

> *We like to speculate on when the current renaissance in travel writing started—perhaps with the success of Paul Theroux's* The Great Railway Bazaar? *(1975) . . . In the fifteen years after 1975,*

> *four times as many travel books were published as in a similar period before, and the increase continues. In the realm of travel writing criticism, Paul Fussell's* Abroad: British Literary Traveling Between the Wars *(1980) may hold a similar position. Searching under the critical category, "Literature of Travel," I found only fourteen books between 1935 and 1980. Since 1980, there have been 133 full-length studies of travel writing, not to mention a multitude of journal articles.*[1]

In addition to Theroux, a list of leading figures of the current renaissance in literary travel writing would include such names as Bill Bryson, Tim Cahill, Bruce Chatwin, Robyn Davidson, Patrick Leigh Fermor, William Least Heat-Moon, Pico Iyer, Jan Morris, Mary Morris, Dervla Murphy, V.S. Naipaul, Redmond O'Hanlon, Jonathan Raban, Thomas Swick, and Colin Thubron.

The wealth of books has been accompanied by a somewhat more recent boom in multi-author anthologies. Travelers' Tales, Inc., founded in 1993, alone publishes dozens of anthologies. Since the turn of the millennium, Houghton Mifflin has attempted to seize the high ground with its "Best American Travel Writing" annual anthology.

The publishing bonanza has been matched by an explosion of populist initiatives on the Web, as thousands of people every day post pictures and accounts of their own journeys on personal Web sites and blogs. Indeed, the two worlds are bleeding into each other—at the Web site of travel publisher Lonely Planet, it's sometimes difficult to tell the books from the blogs. The Web introduces other problems to the definition of travel writing. Critic Patrick Holland goes so far as to argue that the distinction between real and virtual travel is becoming obsolescent, as

> *Travel—as actual practice, as a mode of being in the world, as a metaphor—is increasingly mediated as a* virtual *experience, accessed as readily—if not more readily—in virtual modes than through physical or conventional textual contact; similarly, actual*

---

1. David Epsey, "Paul Fussell's Abroad and the Scholarship of Contemporary Travel," Conference Director's Address, Conference on Travel Writing, University of Pennsylvania, June 1999.

destinations evolve into paradigmatic spatial configurations (see Italo Calvino, Invisible Cities*).*[2]

But aside from such metaphysical concerns, basic questions remain in attempting to define literary travel writing, both in the current age and across the span of history. Current travel writing shares or overlaps generic affiliations with a host of other kinds of writing, including humor, environmental, political, war, sports, adventure, and pilgrimage, to name a few. One might ask if it is possible to distinguish "travel writing" from writing that happens to contain accounts of travel. The next section lists four minimal criteria which might be said to apply to distinguish contemporary literary travel writing as a genre.

A SET OF CONTEMPORARY CRITERIA

1. Travel Writing Begins in Ephemera

Details are essential. The small, closely observed physical objects of place and real moments of time occupy the foreground of the narrative, as related by an identifiable, usually first-person traveler. The universal, the timeless, the metaphorical, and the allegorical—the traditional Big Ideas—these must wait on the particulars, must grow out of them. Of course, narrative that adjusts or invents the circumstances to meet the needs of theme or plot is fiction, as opposed to the "found" realism of nonfiction. This generic distinction remains necessary despite the tricks, gimmicks, lies, and subterfuges which have been invented to undermine it. Travel writers and editors agree that the momentary, passing observations of place, person, and circumstance are the building blocks of travel writing.

2. Travel Writing Makes the Understanding of Person a Function of Observation of Place

Travel writing is a humanistic enterprise. At the most fundamental level, it moves toward a deeper understanding of the human condition or conditions. A distinguishing characteristic, however, is the primacy of place. Travel writing asserts that some measure of understanding may

---

2. Patrick Holland, "The Futures of Travel Writing" (abstract), Conference on Travel Writing, University of Pennsylvania, June 1999.

be achieved by focusing attention first on the environment, the background, the situation, in the most literal senses of those terms. The real estate agent's mantra is relevant: if you wish to know about a person or people, the three things to focus on are *location, location, location*. In some relatively rare instances of adventure travel narrative, the only person to be understood may be the self, the one who is climbing the mountain or crossing the desert. But even a book such as Robyn Davidson's *Tracks: A Woman's Solo Trek Across 1,700 Miles of Australian Outback* features many human interactions; it would be a short book without them.

3. Travel Writing Depends Upon an "Otherness" Created by the Dissociation of Place

Just as one's eyes cannot focus on an object too close, one must obtain some distance to distinguish the features of place. Virtuality and reality may at some point converge, as Holland suggests, but at this time it is still true that travel writing is not possible without actual physical travel from point to point being involved, referenced, or described in the narrative. However, details of the journey do not in themselves constitute travel writing any more than the continuous video streaming from a Web cam constitutes a motion picture. The physical displacement must create and sustain a necessary double consciousness: the new, the unknown, the mysterious is processed through the lens of what is known and familiar. The failure to recognize this necessity is responsible for one of the most common misunderstandings about travel writing. When would-be travel writers imagine themselves as recorders rather than as processors of information, they are committing a failure of imagination, and the writing usually fails as well.

4. Travel Writing Is the Genre of the Epitomic Moment

Another way to map the spectrum of travel writing is from the informational to the inspirational. At one end is the most didactic travel text of all, the map, and closest to it are directories and then guidebooks. At the other end are travel books such as Phil Cousineau's *The Art of Pilgrimage: The Seeker's Guide to Making Travel Sacred*, where the actual narratives are submerged in an assemblage of pious quotations and exhortations about the spirituality of it all. Somewhere in the middle, along about Rick Steves, there occurs a basic shift between guidebook, with its emphasis on the reader's impending journey, and memoir, in which the reader relives the author's experience. To make that experience come alive for the reader, the writer must have a talent for recognizing, seizing, constructing, and showcasing certain moments among the ephemera as the epitome of the journey. These moments of interpersonal connectedness or disconnectedness manage to put a finger directly on some nerve, to illustrate in some way the glories and the impossibilities of understanding across the barrier of otherness. The novelist seeks to construct epiphanic or epitomic moments. For the nonfiction writer, the power of *selection* and *(re)construction* becomes paramount. As noted travel writer and editor Tim Cahill puts it:

> One way to write is to simply chronicle events. This sometimes constitutes a failure of imagination. The events will work themselves into a story if you think about them enough. It is like holding up a prism to the sun: turn it just the right way and a rainbow of light pours through. So, a word of advice: a person's journal is the raw material. A story is made from these events. Use the journal to craft the story. Don't submit a travel journal.[3]

As much as anything else, contemporary nonfiction travel writing is about recognizing the moment that is the epitome of everything the writer has experienced on the journey and presenting that moment to the reader. These four criteria are present in, and necessary to, the kind of first-person, nonfiction, essay-narrative writing that gets its most serious treatment as a form of contemporary literature.

A HISTORICAL OVERVIEW

Of course, travel writing was not invented by Paul Theroux in 1975. Accounts of travel abound from the inception of the written word, so that any endeavor to fashion a broader, more historical definition of travel writing quickly becomes a problem of delimitation rather than inclusion. Attempts to unravel the literal from the metaphorical frustrate at every turn. Adam and Eve must leave the Garden. Shakyamuni travels the Middle Way and becomes the Buddha. Gilgamesh travels to

---

3. Tim Cahill, interview with Rolf Potts, *Rolf Potts' Vagabonding*, www.rolfpotts.com/writers/cahill.php.

the Great Cedar Forest and Mashu's Twin Mountains on his quest for the secret to life everlasting. The history of writing is the history of travel writing.

Among mythic travelers, it is perhaps Odysseus who best embodies the paradox inherent in travel and offers a fascinating journey through the literary ages as well. In *The Odyssey*, he is devoted to Penelope and Patria. He wants nothing more, Homer tells us, than to return home. But along the way he sleeps with a nymph and a witch, goes poking around the Cyclops' den, and lingers over dinner with the Phaeacians. And then there's that business with the Sirens. It would have been so much simpler to plug his own ears with wax. But history's first tourist cannot resist going out of his way to experience what he knows he will never find at home. Dante, in the midst of his own pilgrim journey, has no patience for such follies. He puts Odysseus in the eighth circle of hell, from which the erstwhile hero relates the thin details of his final trip: he could not be happy at home in Ithaca, so he sails to the end of the world, falls off, and dies. Tennyson, apologist for empire builders, revisits Dante's Odysseus with manly admiration, emphasizing the striving and seeking. It remained for James Joyce to knock Odysseus off the epic pedestal and, as Leopold Bloom, subject him to tawdry commonplaces and countless indignities of travel around dear dirty Dublin. The travels of Odysseus take another poetical and tropical turn in Derek Walcott's *Omeros*.

As is already apparent, generic distinctions are troublesome as well. While most contemporary readers assume that travel writing must be nonfiction, they may not realize that the dichotomy between nonfiction and fiction emerged and evolved over the course of centuries. Travel writing predates the term "nonfiction," showing up in myths, religious tracts, epic poems, fables, romances, lyric poems, and novels.

In addition to the Odyssean cycle and other works already mentioned, works that might be said to sit among the pantheon of travel writings include, to name a few, Chaucer's *The Canterbury Tales*, Cervantes' *Don Quixote*, Lord Byron's *Childe Harold's Pilgrimage*, and Twain's *Innocents Abroad*, not to mention all the great works from the history of exploration and conquest, from Marco Polo or Bernal Diaz to Lewis and Clark.

THE MAP: THE WORLD OF TRAVEL WRITING

Rather than an attempt to catalogue and/or categorize travel writing through the ages, this chapter takes a cue from cartography and concludes with a visual chart of the history of travel writing (see the map enclosed in your shrink-wrapped travel writing package). Maps and charts are indispensable to travelers. If one is unable to find an omnibus definition of travel writing, it might be possible to make some navigable sense of the world of travel writing in spatial terms.

Observations and Explanations Concerning the Map

"The World of Travel Writing" refers, obviously, to the Western heritage and in particular to the Anglo-American world. A more comprehensive chart inclusive of worldwide conceptions of travel writing is beyond the scope of this chapter and the expertise of its author.

The vertical coordinate begins at the bottom with the closest portable analog to place; that is, cartography, the map. The movement toward the top of the map takes us from nonfiction to fiction, with a floating island for poetry, through the speculative and the philosophical, and finally to fantasy.

The horizontal coordinate covers the most of known history, but, like the famous *New Yorker* cover, shows our own place and the places nearest to us in much greater detail. Thus, the twentieth century takes up half the map, and the nineteenth another quarter. It would be fair to object that a great age of travel writing, eighteenth century, gets unfairly lumped in with all that precedes it, but space limitations apply.

Space limitations also constrict the amount of information. This version features titles of works only and usually only one title per author, no matter how impressive the oeuvre. The titles are intended to be *representative*, not exhaustive, as are the works. For a chronological list of titles and authors on this chart, see appendix 1. For a more inclusive chronological list of travel works, see, for example, *The Cambridge Companion to Travel Writing*.

The chart's bifurcation into "fiction and nonfiction" is problematic. Prior to the eighteenth century, the distinction between fiction and nonfiction becomes less and less meaningful. Poetry is represented as floating in space above the bifurcation.

The prominence of the fiction space at the center of the chart represents a general critical contention that the last half of the nineteenth century and the first half of the twentieth constituted something of a Golden Age for the travel novel. The last quarter of the twentieth century, by comparison, is commonly considered to be a time of pre-eminence for the first-person nonfiction travel book whose many permutations often overlap with other genres.

CONCLUSION

As problematic as these forays toward a definition of "travel writing" have been, the questions promise to become more difficult in years to come. The age of the printed word, as a more or less discreet medium since the invention of moveable type, is coming to a close. As digital media and the World Wide Web overtake print as the dominant means of information exchange, terms such as "publication" and even "writing" splinter into new species and subspecies, and commerce and art will continue their endless interweavings. The only things that are sure are that people will continue to travel, and that accounts of travels will continue to be made and shared, and that occasional gestures will be made toward summary, categorization, and definition of that practice.

End-of-Chapter Questions

1. What kind of travel writing is one likely to find in newspaper travel sections?

2. Why might this be considered the classical age of travel writing?

3. On what list would one find such names as Jan Morris, Tim Cahill, Pico Iyer, and Colin Thubron?

4. What is one of the four criteria which might be said to apply to distinguish contemporary literary travel writing as a genre?

5. What occupies the foreground of the narrative in travel writing?

6. Is a travel writer a recorder or a processor of information?

7. According to Volkmer, for what must the travel writer have a talent?

8. Do accounts of travel go back to the inception of the written word?
9. Must travel writing be nonfiction?
10. Does the chart, "The World of Travel Writing" depict the entire "world" of travel writing or just a part?

WRITING ASSIGNMENT TWO
SMALL POINTS—BIG PICTURE

Assignment Introduction

As human beings, when we talk with other people about our travel experiences, we tend to move between the specific and the general, sometimes concentrating on the specifics and sometimes on the general points. A well-written travel piece will usually do the same thing.

Assignment Activity

Go back to what you wrote in Writing Assignment Number One. Spend some time with it and rewrite it in such a way that you feel it makes sense and is the beginning of a travel article. After you have finished working with it, then read it with an eye toward your ability to identify small points and the big picture. Then using the lines below for each sentence, identify words that relate to the small points that were used in the sentence and the words that related to the big picture. There may be some sentences where you have no small points, and that is okay. There may be some sentences where you have written nothing regarding the big picture, and that too is okay. The probability is that one or the other, and sometimes both, will be in the majority of all sentences.

CHAPTER 3

The Diversity of the Literary Genre of Travel

Jenny Elliott-Bennett

THREE TYPES OF CREATIVE TRAVEL WRITING

This chapter addresses the diversity of the content, in terms of both textual form and subject matter, of literary travel texts. It is first necessary to make the basic distinction between the three general types of "creative" travel publications (as opposed to philosophical tomes or theoretical critiques) that are usually grouped under the broad "travel writing" banner: travel literature, travel writing, and guidebooks. There is a distinction to be made between different types of travel publications just as there is a distinction to be made between the traveler and the tourist; travelers explore countries, cultures, minds, and bodies, whereas tourists generally lack the quest instinct and have a herd mentality. Further, travelers seek to encounter the foreign, whereas tourists seek to find the familiar in unfamiliar surroundings. Travel literature can be seen as the publication counterpart of the traveler. Such books are written in an almost scholarly style (Ernest Hemingway or Evelyn Waugh, for example) and are concerned with all the travail in travel, all the incidental experiences and fallout of the act, as well as the foreign and foreignness and the alien topography and geography.

Travel writing is not literary in the traditional sense, and it can not be considered "writerly" in style. It can be most readily described as travel literature's touristic counterpart. It is domestic, mainstream, and geared for tourists. It usually is concerned with city-break packages, brief lines on historical points of interest, and the proximity of the accommodation to the beach.

If a publication is not a guidebook and not travel literature, it occupies the middle ground and can be classed as travel writing. This distinction follows the codification of a high/low culture divide.

Travel writing and tourism are obviously both hugely valid in their own terms, as a type of writing and a leisure pursuit respectively, and both greatly benefit a country's economic revenue via cultural commodification. However, for this chapter it is necessary to realize that tourism is a false act of travel. Learning gives over to leisure, experiencing to consuming, and it can only generate a pseudoblepsis of the visited city or country. For this chapter, and following high/low culture tensions, travel literature is academically astute, as opposed to today's ubiquitous, comparatively lowbrow travel writing publications.

LITERARY TRAVEL IS NOW SPLIT

Traditionally, the genre of literary travel was governed by (what we now see as) stereotypically romanticized notions of the transcendence of being, in both the literal and metaphorical senses. The romantic still remains a significant influence on the style of travel literature, but the genre has evolved in line with industrialization, sprawling urbanization, war and the modern human condition, and thus the center of interest has become split between the external world and the self.

BOTH MEASURED AND BOUNDLESS

The genre is as measured or as boundless as the journeys (real or make-believe) it can describe. This boundless scope can incorporate any and all other genres in its unequivocally hybrid nature. The fundamental characteristics of such genres of writing as the short story, the novel or novella (according to textual length, speed of plot development, narrative technique), poetry, and the properties of factual and fictional writing (independently or in cohesion in the generic mode of faction) are all inherent and intrinsic to the literary genre of travel. All subcategories of fiction are appropriate, as are all types of factual information. A document of travel, the nonwritten artifact, or an excerpt from a historical text can all be utilized. Often included are details of the acquisition of symbolic objects (traditionally the putative reasons for making a journey), and pictures or sketches of these prizes.

AN EASILY CORRUPTIBLE GENRE

Travel literature is the most easily corruptible genre. It is and can be an amalgamation of all forms of art and all forms of literature that have been previously established academically. It is truly "literature's red-light district".[1] The fundamental feature pertaining to the content, form, and style of travel literature is that it is "collective and incremental rather than singular and aesthetic."[2]

BASED ON THE THEORY OF DIFFERENCE

The point of traveling is to encounter differences, indeed "it is the very otherness of the visited country (including its people) that makes the journey valuable."[3] These travel publications, therefore, are based upon the theory of difference. The raison d'être of the act extends to the textual representation. It is chaotic in the sense that traditional generic assumptions and rules pertaining to the practice of writing methods

---

1. Patrick Holland and Graham Huggan, *Tourists with Typewriters: Critical Reflections on Contemporary Travel Writing* (Michigan: The University of Michigan Press, 1998), 216.
2. Steve Clark, ed., *Travel Writing and Empire: Postcolonial Theory in Transit* (London: Zed Books Ltd, 1999), 1.
3. Mark Cocker, *Loneliness and Time: British Travel Writing in the Twentieth Century* (London: Secker, 1992), 47.

and styles are here exploded. As an always impure, mixed genre, travel literature deforms and subverts traditional, teleological, and chronological methods of narration and storytelling. It has a mosaic structure, with, for example, the seemingly random use of stream-of-consciousness juxtaposed with frequent digressions and insertions of factual information (such as historical references or map coordinates). It might even dispense with punctuation in order to decimate the innate hierarchics which occur in books and magazines; the lack of quotation marks, for instance, de-prioritizes speech, and makes it only as important as everything else that is written rather than more so.

AN AUTOBIOGRAPHICAL PERSPECTIVE

Usually it is an autobiographical perspective that is taken in literature of this kind. First-person narratives are thus the most common to the genre, and this encourages the confessional and introspective aspects of the writings. As with autobiography, travel literature can be a patchwork of material history, anecdote, script, cultural analysis, dialogue, and asides. Publications range from cultural critique to aesthetic interpretation. Travel literature goes further, however, as it crosses methodological, theoretical, disciplinary, cultural, textual, literal, and figurative boundaries. Travel, typically a topos of liberation, can provide the subject around which to create wholly liberated and informal literature that does what it likes when it likes.

FORM VERSUS PLOT

Dense, meandering chapters contrast with clipped subchapters or even single words used as paragraphs, and the capitalization or mispunctuation of bits of writing result in the form of the travel writing competing with the plot for primacy. Travel literature is meta-fictive. Fact and fiction blur. The use of classical intertext or historical perspectives is common, as is the inclusion of alternative (nontextual) insertions that decimate the textual form. Both physical and intangible artifacts of travel experiences can be put into the writing: quotes, pictures, documents, tickets, characters, smells, memories. The genre is essentially humanist and all encompassing regarding what it can accommodate and relate of human experience. Because travel literature utilizes so many forms of information and can appear as so many configurations of generic forms itself, these articles and books force us to rethink our assumptions about seemingly straightforward terms, such as traveler, tourist, map, boundary, border, and liberty.

AN AMORPHOUS GENRE

Travel literature has the capacity to utilize and explore any subject or issue, though the most common and significant to the genre are culture, nationality, geography, identity, sociology, history, and gender. Under these broad headings, the travel writing can consider the global, racial, political, continental, national, regional, personal, class-related, religious, psychological, and linguistic perspectives. As might be expected, methodological and theoretical boundaries (for example postcolonialism and feminism) are crossed while innumerable subjects and issues are analyzed via this amorphous genre.

EVERYTHING CAN BE OBJECTIFIED AND SUBJECTIVIED

The hybrid nature of travel literature enables the highly effective representation of intercultural exchange. To locate meanings (of various kinds) in the disorder of the foreign is a primary objective. These texts are narratives of encounter, and, as such, everything can be objectified and subjectified at the author's will.

A THEME OF LOSS

The death or rejection of the familiar in order to bear the experience of the "other" is commonly encoded or propounded as necessary, and this death or rejection gives rise to the lateral theme of loss. This theme of loss can be compounded by the use of the past tense, if an author is recounting a trip made in the past and therefore looking back upon a lost time, and by the inclusion of memorial sites in both the literal and psychological terms (i.e., the architectural tributes to or symbols of a nation's loss, or sites once seen but now remembered). Ideas of permanency and impermanence are questioned in this literature, the transient and in-transient nature of the traveler and the place. To express these issues, texts do not adhere to a singular tense or employ traditional teleological and chronological methods of narration and storytelling. Technical corruption and experimentation, the insertion of foreign words and phrases and linguistic innovation are all devices by which authors represent the dysfunctional reality of operating in an unfamiliar environment and their subsequent loss of control over their situation.

TRAVEL WRITING IS AN EXTENSION OF THE TRAVELER

All writing is an extension of its author to some degree, but travel literature is wholly an extension of the traveler. Foreign landscapes cannot be immediately understood and so are shaped, mapped, and recorded by the personality that is crossing them. The author is mediating between the reality of travel and the reader's experience of it, and, therefore, the author's psychology completely determines the metaphorical, mental, and physical route the reader follows. The literature reflects the many varied aspects of that traveler's humanity. The act of travel creates the destabilization of the self, and the literature can reflect all the psychological, physical, and geographical aspects of this destabilization, so that to travel becomes an exploration of the physical and mental self and of the external world. People are complex, and their complexities are magnified and protracted when they are uncomfortable and unstable. One of the most disruptive acts we can inflict upon ourselves is to uproot ourselves from our normal, habitual, and safe existences and place ourselves in unfamiliar territory. Travel literature is a highly impure generic mode that reflects the disorder, disunity, and the destabilizing effect of the act of travel, and the multifarious disturbing repercussions of encounters with the foreign and foreignness.

Travel is a relatively obscure, impostor genre in terms of the degree of analytical attention and subsequent academic mapping it has received; it is an extension of the traveler as obscure and an impostor in the foreign place. As such figures, we must be aware that to the denizens of whichever place we are visiting, we are the strangers, and they will project on to us their ideas of who we might be. We are a fiction to them, and it is interesting to contemplate that it may be that "to understand ourselves as fictions, is to understand ourselves as fully as we can."[4]

---

4. Jeanette Winterson, *Art Objects, Essays, on Ecstasy and Effrontery* (London: Pandora Press, 1989), 60.

The Diversity of the Literary Genre of Travel

There comes a point in every journey, when one has been away from "home" for long enough, that one becomes clearly conscious of one's own "otherness," as perceived by an "other." This experience of the "other" is synonymous with gaining access to oneself. Edward Said argues that the construction of identity involves "establishing opposites and 'others' whose actuality is always subject to the continuous interpretations and reinterpretation of their differences from 'us'."[5] In traveling, we might seek to lose ourselves in a foreign abyss or to construct an identity for ourselves in opposition to what we find around us in unfamiliar places, for perhaps the easiest way to determine what you *are* is to observe that which you know that you are not.

That travel makes us self-aware is an ancient doctrine. This kind of conscious clarity facilitates the kind of writing that authors such as the modernist Hilda Dolittle is associated with: self-analysis through her own writings as she explored language and meaning. The loss of normalcy and familiarity experienced by travelers upon leaving "home," which often spurs the characters to introspection and creates tension and conflict, is successfully represented through the disjointed text that is common to travel literature. Travel forces you to learn, on a multitude of personal, social, geographical, and historical levels and provides opportunities for revelation. Once unbounded by its own personal traditions of existence, the psycho-physical spiritual organism of the traveler is altered en-route, and all these stages of alteration and the resulting altered aspects of the personality are documented in a variety of literary techniques, styles, and methods.

AN EXAMPLE OF THE LITERARY GENRE OF TRAVEL WRITING

An excellent example of the literary genre of travel writing is Robert Byron's *The Road to Oxiana* written in 1937.[6] Oxiana is the region pertaining to the Oxus river, the ancient name for the Amu Darya river, which forms part of the border between Afghanistan and the former Soviet Union. Borders of this kind and others, both physical and nonphysical, fashion the plot. Narratological, methodological, theoretical, and literary borders are also traversed. Byron applied

---

5. Edward W. Said, *Western Conceptions of the Orient* (London: Penguin, 1978), 187.
6. Robert Byron, *The Road to Oxiana* (1937) (London: Penguin Group, 1992).

modernist techniques to the genre of travel literature. His narrative is expressionistic and fragmented, and his text appears dense as in the style of the decadent writing of the 1890s.

The book is comprised of five parts, and, as a frontispiece, each part has a map showing the region that is covered therein. *The Road to Oxiana* is in diary form, and to enforce this the contents page is termed "Entries." Each new entry within the book first notes the place and date; once he has left the continent of Europe, Byron also gives the height above sea level. Paragraphs and subsections vary considerably in length; for example, compare those on pages 198–199 with page 332, sometimes capturing a scene or meeting, his thoughts or feelings in a few words, sometimes verbosely re-presenting them. He blends objective experience with subjective associations; facts mix with emotions. An impressive and varied array of lists, signs, notices, and official documentation is transcribed into the book, including letters to and from various Islamic governors, such as those on pages 191 and 290. Byron even goes so far as to insert something of a postscript into the middle of part five (page 231), which he added two years after this journey was made. He also inserts postscripts to individual paragraphs, such as on page 61, simply heading them up as "Later."

There is a play-script quality to several of Byron's pages, where he records the action through methods that appear as a director's speech and action instructions, such as "(*mf*)" for makes face, "(*pp*)" for pregnant pause, "(*puffing furiously at his cigarette*)" and block capitals to indicate verbal volume (pages 140 and 185). All this is loosely threaded together with Byron's narration, which itself changes intermittently from first to third person and from present to past tense. His text is indexed like an academic textbook and also has footnotes, so that we are at once in possession of an autobiography, a historical and political tome, a travel novel, and a factual record.

Ostensibly, Byron made the journey to Persia in order to see the Gumbad-i-Kabus, an eleventh century burial column. The actual experience of traveling, however, soon usurps the importance of the original, precise objective. The book celebrates the realities and revelations of travel, while the original goal takes second place as the singular end that vaguely guides the trip. The teleological aim loses its urgency and becomes merely the propulsion to keep traveling, the act of which becomes the real focus of the story.

It is interesting to note that, in line with the distinctions made here previously, Byron expounds the type of traveler a person must be in order to experience travel in a true and sincere sense, i.e., not an observer of the rules, "laden with medicines," but a drinker and a reader (page 276).

TRAVEL WRITING IS THE BROADEST LITERARY GENRE

The literary genre of travel is not modeled on a singular prose form, and it does not have firmly fixed boundaries. It cannot be easily limited in order to aid the process of academic definition. It is the broadest literary genre and certainly is potentially all encompassing regarding what it can reflect and re-present of human experience and existence. In such ways, it is boundary-less; the genre explicates its own modus operandi: the navigation and exploitation of, and reaction to, all conceivable systems of boundary, imposed or absent. The point of such literature is to examine and explore every issue that can be raised against every type of boundary; not least the geographical but also boundaries pertaining to time in all its psychological manifestations; the boundary between the physical and mental self; between people, societies, and cultures, their pasts and their presents. Boundaries are employed to stabilize, and, when they are challenged, we are left with profound destabilization. Destabilization is a powerful notion and an uncomfortable reality that requires artistic expression through representative methods. The main method in terms of literature, as has been discussed here, is the use of the highly impure generic mode of travel literature.

End-of-Chapter Questions

1. Two of the three general types of "creative" travel publications are guidebooks and travel writing. What is the third general type of "creative" travel publication?

2. Is travel writing literary in the traditional sense?

3. Is travel literature the least corruptible genre?

4. According to Clark, what is the fundamental feature pertaining to the content, form, and style of travel literature?

5. Is travel literature meta-fictive?

6. Can everything be objectified and subjectivied in travel writing?

7. Three devices are identified in this chapter whereby travel writing authors represent the dysfunctional reality of operating in an unfamiliar environment and their subsequent loss of control over their situation. Two of these are chronological experimentation and the insertion of foreign words and phrases and linguistic innovation. What is the third device?

8. What completely determines the metaphorical, mental, and physical route followed by the reader of a travel article according to the author of this chapter?

9. What does travel make us be, according to an ancient doctrine?

10. Is travel writing a genre that is boundary-less?

WRITING ASSIGNMENT THREE
ARTICLE ANALYSIS

Assignment Introduction

Now you are beginning to get the basics of travel writing. You understand the basics of descriptive versus factual writing and writing about the general versus the specific.

Assignment Activity

Take a trip to your library. Select at least three of the current issues of travel magazines. We suggest *National Geographic*, *Budget Travel*, and *Islands*. Skim through the articles in all three publications until you find an article that you like and that you feel represents good travel writing. You can claim that it is good travel writing simply because you enjoy reading it. Choose the article that you like best and then fill in the following information about the first paragraph in the article. You may have to look at the first two paragraphs as some first paragraphs are short.

1. Right away did you have a sense that you were there? _____

2. If so, what about that paragraph gave you the sense that you were there? _____

3. If you did not get a sense that you were there, what do you feel that the author did to substitute for that sense and draw the reader into the article? _____

4. How many descriptive words did you find in the first one or two paragraphs? _____

5. How many factual words did you find in the first one or two paragraphs? _____

6. List the small or specific points that were made in the first one or two paragraphs. How many were there? _____

7. List the big picture or general points that were made in the first one or two paragraphs. How many were there? _____

8. There were probably transition words or phrases. What were they and how many of them were there?
Number: _____
Words or Phrases:

_____ _____ _____ _____ _____
_____ _____ _____ _____ _____
_____ _____ _____ _____

Final Step: Add your name to the Instructor Comment Sheet for Writing Assignment Three in appendix 5 and staple it to the sheet on which you have answered the eight questions above. Then turn in these two sheets to your professor.

KAREN CARMEAN is the Charles A. Dana Professor of English at Converse College in Spartanburg, South Carolina. After earning her BA and MA degrees from the University of North Texas in English literature, she completed her PhD in contemporary literature at Auburn University. During her teaching career, she has taught a variety of courses in the humanities, including travel literature. Prior to settling into her teaching career, she served in the office of a U.S. senator as educational adviser and as fiction editor of *The Washington Book Review*. Carmean is the author of *Toni Morrison's World of Fiction*, *Ernest J. Gaines: A Critical Companion*, and *Robert Shaw: More than a Life*. Her critical and review essays have appeared in *The Canadian Journal of American Studies*, *Critique: Studies in Modern Fiction*, the *New Orleans Review*, and *The Washington Book Review*. Currently, she is compiling material for a critical exploration of women travel writers.

CHAPTER 4

A History of Travel Writing

Karen Carmean

IMAGINATION: THE START OF TRAVEL WRITING

Travel writing may first begin as an exponent of the imagination. Perhaps that is why it remains the most varied of literary genres. In an essay, "Travel Narrative and Imperialist Vision," Mary Louise Pratt has described travel writing as a "polyphony," that is as a genre consisting of many voices and not appropriated by professionals.[1] In fact, many travel writers never imagined being "professional" at all; they simply

---

1. Mary Louise Pratt, *Imperial Eyes: Travel Writing and Transculturation* (London and New York: Routledge, 1992), 216.

have written of their travels because they thought their adventures would appeal to others: family members, friends, people curious about "exotic" places. Pratt further compares travel literature to "a street corner," which is "continually crisscrossed by all manner of people,"[2] an apt description for the variety of people who have ventured into this polyphonic and polymorphic genre. That travel literature has attracted nonprofessionals as well as professionals from a variety of interests, cultural perspectives, disciplines, social categories, physical abilities, and limitations has enriched and enlarged the genre beyond all boundaries.

EARLIEST TRAVEL WRITING FOUNDED IN METAPHOR AND STRUCTURE

From our earliest recorded documents, travel has provided both metaphor and structure in works, beginning with Homer's *Odyssey* (ninth century BCE). While this indeed may qualify as myth, fiction, and epic poem, the *Odyssey*, Menippus of Gadara's *A Journey to the Underworld* (third century BCE), and Lucian of Samosata's story of a trip to the moon (*True Story*, c.120–90) underscore human curioity about unknown places as well as imaginative adventures. Fantastic journeys have taken readers into magical lands (*Orlando Furioso*, *The Land of Magic*), utopian societies (*Gulliver's Travels*), psychic landscapes (*The Drowned World*, *Labyrinths*, *Dreams*, *Time Trips*), invisible cities (*Invisible Cities*), toward spiritual salvation (*Pilgrim's Progress*), and inside the human body (*Fantastic Voyage*).[3] As fascinating and as influential as these narratives are, they lack a factual basis. But as it turns out, travel writing based on actual experience—however embroidered by imagination, prejudice, faulty memory, lack of language skills, interpreters, health, and religious zeal—may be just as varied as the human imagination.

THE FIRST TRAVEL WRITERS

Herodotus, in the fifth century BCE, is generally credited with being the

---

2. Ibid., 216.
3. Roger Cardinal, "Fantasy Travel Writing," *Literature of Travel and Exploration: An Encyclopedia*, Ed. Jennifer Speake, 3 vols. (New York and London: Fitzroy Dearborn, 2003). I am deeply indebted to the many contributors to these volumes whose scholarship greatly eased my labor. Subsequent citations will include author, section title, work title, and editor.

first travel writer, as well as Western culture's first historian. Traveling for information to include in his history, Herodotus made a lengthy journey into Egypt, Ethiopia, and present-day Libya; his work continues to give readers significant ethnographic information. While Herodotus was seeking information, other early travel writers were traveling for their faith. Although their writing concerns itself with pilgrimage, it also contains significant information about the countries through which they traveled. Two fourth century writers, Fa-Hsien, a Chinese Buddhist monk and translator, and Egeria, a Spanish nun, took long journeys for the sake of their faith. Walking from Central China through the Gobi Desert to India, Fa-Hsien eventually returned to his monastery with books of the Buddhist Canon. His autobiographical account of his journey was an essential part of his pilgrimage. Egeria's account of her trip to the Holy Land was intended for her religious community. Using a Latin Bible as a guidebook, she spent four years on an extended journey that stretched from Egypt to Galilee.

Two Arabic writers, motivated by diplomacy and trade, also contributed to the genre. Ibn Fadtan left an account of his tenth century diplomatic mission. Nasiri Khusro's eleventh century travelogue offers a vivid testimony of the religious, political, and intellectual ferment of the Islamic Mediterranean world in *Sefer nameh*. Ibn Jubaya's twelfth century narrative notes the conditions of Muslims in Christian environments on the heels of the Crusades.

A Franciscian friar who was later beatified, Odoric di Pordenone, was a traveler with few equals. Living on bread and water and wearing a hair shirt, this wandering ascetic traveled through the Middle East, India, Southeast Asia, and China between 1318 and 1330. His travel narrative astounded many readers who found his accounts fantastic. From Kublai Khan's palace to the fishing cormorants of southern China, Odoric's *Travels* provided both inspiration for and plagiarism by later travel writers. Thus while many may believe Marco Polo to be the first Western traveler to China, he was preceded by Odoric as well as several papal legates. However, thanks to a term in a Genoa prison with a well-known writer of romances named Rustichello as a roommate, Polo managed to write his account with more than usual flair. His *Travels* gained both renown and a wide audience, in part because Rustichello brought a variety of literary conventions to Polo's story, making it one of the most read travel narratives in literature.[4]

FIFTEENTH-CENTURY TRAVEL WRITING

During the fifteenth century, people continued to travel for trade, diplomatic, and religious purposes. The world seemed to have expanded. Ships became ever more sea-worthy, navigational equipment more sophisticated, charts and maps more accurate, and navigational techniques improved—all enabling us to add to our growing information about the world. Several travelers also infused their accounts with personal interests, enlarging the genre still further. A fifteenth-century merchant named Cyriaco D'Ancona added his archeological interests in Greco-Roman antiquities to his account, including descriptive notes and drawings. Portugal's Prince Henry the Navigator significantly increased voyages of discovery through his extensive patronage and intellectual passion. A pragmatist, he worked with shipbuilders to create the Portuguese caravel, which would venture in search of "new" lands looking for new trade markets. He also added increased knowledge of geography to the genre. European explorers owed a great debt for the advances Henry promoted through his keen intellectual interests as well as his personal fortune. A virtual explosion of exploration occurred after Henry, resulting in expanded discoveries as well as accounts of these journeys. Willen Lodewycksz, a Dutch merchant, published an elaborate description of his voyage following the Portuguese route via the Cape of Good Hope to Asia in 1597, an account that became a sailing manual, a merchant's guide, and a descriptive narrative.[5]

SIXTEENTH-CENTURY TRAVEL WRITING

Sixteenth-century travelers practically covered the globe. Indeed, the

---

4. Klaus Karttuner, "Herodotus"; D.P.M. Weerakkody, "Fa-Hsien"; Rene Gothoni, "Egeria"; James E. Montgomery, "Ibn Fadlan"; Nabil Matar, "Khusro, Nasiri"; Yehoshua Frenkel, "Ibn Jubaya"; Paul Smethurst, "Odoric Di Pordenone"; and Nicholas Frankopan, "Marco Polo," *Literature of Travel and Exploration: An Encyclopedia*, Ed. Jennifer Speake.

5. John V. Fleming, "D'Ancona, Cyriaco"; Maria Laura Pires, "Henry the Navigator"; and Vibke Roeper and Diederick Wildeman, "Lodewycksz, Willen," *Literature of Travel and Exploration: An Encyclopedia*, Ed. Jennifer Speake.

first circumnavigation account of Ferdinand Magellen's voyage around the world was written by one of the seventeen survivors who returned (Magellan was not among them, needless to say). *A Short Voyage around the World (1519–1522): An Account of Magellan's Expedition* was included in Richard Eden's *The Decades of the Newe World; or, West India . . . by Peter Martyr of Angeleria, 1555*. This age of exploration, exploitation, and colonization was driven by such figures as Sir Walter Raleigh, who added a new dimension to travel literature: marketing. Unable to find the riches he sought, Raleigh shifted his strategy to make the Americas appear almost irresistible by proposing colonization. Captain John Smith in his nine books similarly enhanced his claims of the New World, making it far more welcoming in terms of climate, soil richness, and indigenous residents than it was in reality.

Far less mercenary in motivation was Lodovico de Vartheme, an Italian whose love of travel, first-person point of view, wit, and, imagination made his *Travels* one of those exceedingly rare books remaining in print almost continuously since 1510. Leo Africanus possibly provided one of the most significant cultural links between Africa and Europe in his "Descrittiona dell'Africa," a manuscript included in *Navigazione e viaggi* [Navigations and Travels] in 1550, twenty-four years after it was written. Part geographical description and part autobiography, Africanus' *Description* offered significant information about life in North and West Africa. In China, Father Matteo Ricci brought to his memoir, *China in the Sixteenth Century, The Journals of Matteo Ricci 1583–1610*, not only his observations of customs but also illustrations, anecdotes, and transcripts of Chinese tales.[6] Clearly, the genre was developing in highly idiosyncratic ways.

SEVENTEENTH-CENTURY TRAVEL WRITING

By the seventeenth century, travel writing was the second most popular form of literature after theology. William Dampier's *A New Voyage 'Round the World*, published in 1697, was free of missionary, mercantile,

---

6. David Judkins, "Circumnavigation Narratives"; John Holmes, "Raleigh, Walter"; Alan J. Silva, "Smith, John"; Joan Pau Rubies, "Varthema, Ludovico de"; Oumelbanine Zhiri, "Leo Africanus"; and Horacio Araujo, "Ricci, Matteo," *Literature of Travel and Exploration: An Encyclopedia*, Ed. Jennifer Speake.

or political motivations. Instead, it celebrated travel for its own sake. Along the way, it recorded Dampier's adventures aboard a privateer (also known as a pirate ship) as it raided Spanish ships and settlements for booty. Possibly the first professional travel writer, Fynes Moryson constructed a massive *An Itinerary* (1617), which was published in three volumes recounting his extensive trips through Europe. William Lithgow, an intrepid Scot, saw and lived his life as a journey in his account of a forty-thousand-mile-long trip through Europe, Asia, and Africa in *The Total Discourse of Rare Adventures and Painful Peregrinations of a Long Nineteen Years Travayles* (1632). Lithgow's travelogue added a new element to travel narrative—torture techniques—as he was especially interested in the policies and practices of the Spanish Inquisition.

One of the first guidebooks also appeared in the seventeenth century, when Thomas Coryate published his guidebook to fifty cities in 1608. He not only included illustrations and historical data but also practical advice regarding prices, food, and local customs. Another influential contributor to travel writing was the Marquise de Sevigne, who recorded her extensive European travels and love of art in a series of letters, mostly addressed to her daughter.[7] Moving beyond limited aristocratic social circles, the Marquise influenced subsequent writers, especially women, who emulated both her sense of adventure as well as her style.

EIGHTEENTH-CENTURY TRAVEL WRITING

Whether or not the Marquise's letters influenced Lady Mary Wortley Montague in the eighteenth century may be a matter of conjecture, but certainly Lady Mary's series of letters, written for publication and collected and published under the title *Embassy To Constantinople* in 1763, have been profoundly influential to travel writing. Accompanying her husband when he assumed duties as British ambassador to Turkey, Lady Mary believed her account of Turkey and Turkish culture would "embellish a worn-out Subject with a variety of fresh and elegant

---

7. Carl Thompson, "Dampier, William"; Andrew Hadfield, "Moryson, Fynes" and "Lithgow, William"; Michael Strachan, "Coryate, Thomas"; and Maryanne Cole, "Women Travelers, 1500–1800," *Literature of Travel and Exploration: An Encyclopedia*, Ed. Jennifer Speake.

A History of Travel Writing

Entertainment."[8] Indeed it did. Taking advantage of her gender, Lady Mary took her readers into the harems and women's baths, where no man had ventured. But rather than making Turkish women objects of her scrutiny, Lady Mary had the women examine her, a turn notable for its lack of cultural superiority. Lady Mary's acute observations, combined with wit and graceful writing, made her account an enduring addition to an increasing genre.

Captain James Cook—possibly the most famous explorer and traveler of all time—stood out in the eighteenth century for his many contributions to the genre of travel writing. A lieutenant with an excellent record of making accurate charts, Cook was sent by the British government and the Royal Society with a famous astronomer, Joseph Banks, to chart a rare astronomical event. Cook also had secret orders to find "new territories."[9] His voyage to Tahiti initiated the first of three journeys, which increased both geographical and ethnographical knowledge. So extensive were Cook's "discoveries" that, by the time he was killed in Hawaii, only Antarctica remained the last undiscovered place on earth—and Cook came close there, too. Cook's journals, published and republished, related a wealth of information—from making landfall in Australia and circumnavigating both islands of what became New Zealand to exploring the islands of the South Pacific. His mathematical skills, genuine interest in indigenous inhabitants, remarkably unprejudiced accounts, and sheer endurance ushered in a new dimension in travel writing—scientific travel.

SCIENTIFIC TRAVEL AND TRAVEL WRITING

While scientific travel might not precisely begin in the eighteenth century, it certainly gained prominence, largely due to improving transportation as well as changes in the education of wealthy young European men. The Grand Tour became a standard of "finishing" a young man's education, particularly in England, as young men were

---

8. Mary Wortley Montagu, *Letters from the Levant, during the Embassy to Constantinople, 1716–1718, 1838*; reprinted, 1971.

9. David Judkins, "Circumnavigation Narratives," *Literature of Travel and Exploration: An Encyclopedia*, Ed. Jennifer Speake. Readers may revisit Captain Cook's voyages with Tony Horwitz in *Blue Latitudes: Boldly Going Where Captain Cook Has Gone Before* (New York: Henry Holt and Company, 2002).

sent, often with a tutor or traveling companion, to gain knowledge and social skills by seeing the world. In the case of Edward Clark and his wealthy pupil John Morton Cripps, the journey became more about science and collecting than social polish. Their travels through Greece, Turkey, Cyprus, and the Holy Land resulted in a huge collection of artifacts, including minerals and plants, leading to a career in mineralogy for Clark. Another scientific adventurer traveled to write a history of world agriculture. Arthur Young might not be well known as a travel writer, but his five books speak of his charm and intellectual depth. Unwilling to settle for fast, often superficial, observations, Young stayed in places long enough to examine both himself as well as his hosts. Young did not merely observe; he reflected and learned.[10] Future travel writers will similarly linger for long periods as they absorb and learn to grasp subtleties of varied cultures and cultural practices.

FICTION AND TRAVEL WRITING

As travel became more common and nonfiction writing developed into a profession, a number of writers, perhaps better known for their fiction, also contributed to travel writing: Henry Fielding, Daniel Defoe, Tobias Smollett, Lawrence Sterne, and Samuel Johnson brought their various idiosyncratic talents to the genre, improving the characterization of the traveler and celebrating travel as an end in itself. In the American colonies, Sarah Kemble Knight's *The Journal of Mme. Knight (1724–1725)* recorded important historical data of New England and New York, including geographical details, street names, descriptions of buildings, and other physical details.[11] Additionally, Knight's journal described gender roles. Casting herself as a bold social critic, Knight gave an accurate picture of the colonial Northeast—including inedible food, peculiar people, bad weather, and surprising adventures. Knight's wit and energy celebrated the joy and surprise of travel.

---

10. Katherine Edgar, "Clarke, Edward Daniel," and Christopher Smith, "Young Arthur," *Literature of Travel and Exploration*, Ed. Jennifer Speake.

11. Christopher K. Brown, "Knight, Sarah Kemble," *Encyclopedia of Travel Literature* (Santa Barbara, Denver, and Oxford: ABC-CLIO, 2002).

A GROWING VARIETY OF TRAVEL WRITING

Near the end of the eighteenth century, one of the legends of travel literature emerged. Mungo Park, a Scottish physician, was commissioned by the British Africa Association to investigate the commercial navigation of the Niger River in East Africa. Park's accounts of his adventures when he was captured by the King of the Ludamar and endured fever, near starvation, fatigue, and additional hardships were so well crafted that he inspired later adventurers. While his objective was commercial, Park included valuable information regarding a variety of cultural groups, natural science, and geographical data in his *Travels in the Interior of Africa* (1799).[12] While Park was roaming deep into the interior of Africa, Xavier de Maistre composed a different type of travelogue, *Voyage Around My Room* (1794), a forty-two-day exploration of his own bedroom.[13] These extremes seem to gauge the variety of travel writing, as it ranged in both breadth and depth. By now, this genre included spiritual travel, military adventures, buccaneer adventures, political and diplomatic missions, commercially inspired journeys, scientific travel, circumnavigation accounts, imperialist narratives, colonist narratives, guidebooks, and travel for its own sake.

NEW APPROACHES TOWARD TRAVEL WRITING

Alexander Kinglake, a British travel writer, historian, and lawyer, has often been credited with transforming travel writing to a more personal, often ironic, genre. His *Eothen; or, Traces of Travel Brought Home from the East* (1844) influenced subsequent travel writers, including Robert Curzon, Robert Burton, Charles M. Doughty, and T.E. Lawrence.[14] However, as already indicated, he was not the first to imbue his adventures with irony, wit, and personal observations. Perhaps the quality of his writing contributed to his influence. Whatever the case, Kingslake pointed toward a direction which travel writing increasingly followed, as more—and more diverse—people traveled the globe and wrote of their personal journeys. New world travelers could find

---

12. Robert Fraser, "Park, Mungo," *Literature of Travel and Exploration: An Encyclopedia*, Ed. Jennifer Speake.

13. Xavier de Maistre, *Voyage autour de ma Chambre* [*Voyage Around My Room*], 1794.

14. William Baker, "Kingslake, Alexander," *Literature of Travel and Exploration: An Encyclopedia*, Ed. Jennifer Speake.

practical advice in Sir Francis Galton's *The Art of Travel* (1860), which was full of helpful tips on diverse subjects such as medications and communications. With most of the Earth already "discovered," travelers began inventing new approaches with respect to both travel and its representation in writing.

NATIONAL CONCERNS LINKED TO SCIENTIFIC INQUIRY

At the peak of its imperialist power, England produced a number of hardy explorers and travelers who ventured to most corners of the globe. These trips frequently linked commercial and/or strategic national concerns to scientific inquiry. Such was the case of the survey vessel *Beagle*. Charles Darwin's five-year-long circumnavigation aboard the *Beagle* between 1831 and 1836 altered both Darwin as well as modern science. A meticulous observer and recordkeeper, Darwin kept a logbook as well as a scientific notebook. Additionally, he wrote detailed letters to his family and friends in the scientific community, which were published in their own right after his return. Darwin also integrated and edited his writing into *Journal of Researches* (1839, 1845), known as *The Voyage of the Beagle*. This work, especially in its 1845 edition, added scientific observations and speculations that stirred controversy.

Unlike Darwin, who delighted in natural beauty and abhorred the abuses of colonialism in South America, John Hanning Speake embodied a stereotypical British imperialist. Partnered with Robert Burton to "discover" the source of the Nile, Speake treated Africa as a competitive sport, seeing his accomplishments as representatations of British imperialist supremacy. Travel, for Speake, was a marathon, proving survival of the fittest through actions such as battling rhinos with swords. Another major figure in the exploration of Africa, Henry Morton Stanley, characterized Africa as a paradise ready for commercial development and conversion.[15] His lecturing in England spurred additional expeditions to establish settlements and inspired additional adventurers looking for a challenge and writing of their daring.

---

15. David Amigoni, "Darwin, Charles"; Greg Garrett, "Speake, John"; and Beau Riffenburgh, "Stanley, Henry Morton," *Literature of Travel and Exploration: An Encyclopedia*, Ed. Jennifer Speake.

ARCTIC ADVENTURES

The Arctic offered a climactic challenge adding to the variety of travel literature. Beginning in the nineteenth century and positively flourishing in the twentieth, polar adventures have claimed a number of observant, talented writers. Predictably, exploration began with mercantile and cartographic interests, as people were encouraged to find a northwest passage. William Scoresby's *Account of the Arctic Regions* (1820) was a standard travel narrative many consulted. John Rae, a Scottish physician and explorer, published a rather dull account in his historically significant *Arctic Correspondence* (1853), but his choice of living among the Inuit and adopting their techniques set an unexpected standard of developing relationships with indigenous people. Arctic exploration inspired a number of accounts as parties went in search of the missing Franklin expedition in 1844. Americans became increasingly involved with the Arctic, some following Rae's example by hiring Inuit guides (Charles Francis Hall and Isaac Hayes).

Surviving this harsh climate—even with Inuit assistance—proved difficult for many parties, which fell apart due to drinking, drifting, and disease (scurvy, in particular). Fridtjof Nansen, a Norwegian neurologist, oceanographer, and explorer, brought a new level of organization and knowledge to polar exploration. After leading an expedition across the Greenland ice cap, he decided to push further north. To do so, however, Nansen had to calculate how to design a ship to survive ice movement. In 1893–1896 the ship *Fram* pushed exploration and Arctic narratives to a new level of adventure.[16] Since Nansen, and particularly since the conclusion of World War I, Arctic exploration has been attempted by men and women using all manner of techniques and technologies, from dog sleds to airplanes. Alone and in groups, these hardy adventurers can provide us with narratives of adventure, survival, and contemplation.

FEMALE TRAVEL WRITERS

Changing technology and fewer travel hazards proved to benefit all travelers, especially women travelers, who made impressive gains as

---

16. Sarah Moss, "Arctic," and William Barr, "Nansen, Fridtjof," *Literature of Travel and Exploration: An Encyclopedia*, Ed. Jennifer Speake.

writers. Catharine Maria Sedgwick's *Letters from Abroad to Kindred at Home* (1841) showed her personal growth through travel. Mary Wollstonecraft Shelley used her *Rambles in Germany and Italy in 1840, 1842, and 1843* (1844) not only as reflection upon her own adventures but also as a frame for *Frankenstein*. Georges Sand (Amandine Aurore-Lucile Dudevant) wandered about Europe dressed as a man and demanded the same freedom that men enjoyed. Her *Lettres d'un Voyageur* (1837) detailed her self-examination. So inspirational were these accounts that travel seemed to offer more than just growth; travel was considered a means to improved health. After surviving an operation for a spinal tumor, Isabella Bird was given 100 pounds by her father with permission to stay away as long as the money lasted. Little did he suspect that she could make this sum go as far and as long as she did, for Bird booked passage to Australia and New Zealand. During her often hazardous journey, she discovered important facets of herself, recovered her health through exercise, and did not look toward home except in her letters to her sister, which formed the basis of her travel books. Bird journeyed from the Pacific to the U.S. Rockies (where she climbed Pikes Peak in a dress during a blizzard and took a solo winter journey of six hundred miles on horseback), and later went to Canada, Japan, Malaya, Korea, Northern India, Kurdestan, Persia, and China. When she was seventy, Bird made a thousand-mile ride across Morocco.[17] Her observations and insights made a significant contribution to the variety of travel writing.

The United States began turning out its share of women travel writers, beginning with Anne Newport Royall (1769–1854), the first successful newspaperwoman in this country. When, at age fifty-four, she lost access to her husband's estate, Royall became self-supporting by writing. Her accounts made no attempt to clean up social, political, or environmental conditions as she saw them; thus, her work brought her both fame and infamy. Nancy Prince, a free woman of color, became one of the first African-American travelers to actually have a choice of international travel (slave narratives relate tales of involuntary travel).

---

17. Jennifer Hayward, "Women Travelers, Nineteenth Century," and Cicely Palmer Havely, "Bird, Isabella L.," *Literature of Travel and Exploration: An Encyclopedia*, Ed. Jennifer Speake.

Accompanying her husband, who was attached to the Czar of Russia's court, Prince moved to Russia and wrote an account of her life and involvement with missionary work. An early advocate for women's rights in the United States, Emma Hart Willard traveled to France and Great Britain to observe country women, not the socially elite. Willard was interested in exchanging ideas with people of other cultures, an element often missing in male-authored travel narratives of the time.[18]

As women traveled to more and more remote places during the nineteenth century, they increasingly brought their own observations of people and places, which differed from those of many male writers. Women writers seemed to view their host cultures as neither "alien" nor "other." Indeed, they came to see that cultural stereotypes presented in accounts they studied before their journeys proved both limited and limiting. Anna Leonowens, whose experience as a governess gained fame for its portrayal in the film *The King and I*, moved beyond autobiography into philosophical meditation, adventure, and travelogue in her four books on Siam and India. Mary Kingsley's accounts of her travels in Africa reversed typical notions of personal conquest to those of normalcy as she lived among various groups. Kingsley remained a proper Victorian lady in dress and demeanor, even as she slogged through rivers in a heavy skirt. Her sense of humor as well as her genuine love of adventure brought fresh perspective to African travel. Isabelle Eberhardt (1877–1904) changed both her costume and religion to report on Algeria from a wholly different perspective. After converting to Islam, Eberhardt, disguised as a man, traveled alone across the desert. Her *In the Shadow of Islam* and *Passionate Nomad: The Diary of Isabelle Eberhardt* enriched travel writing, adding doubled perspectives in her dual gender and religious roles.[19]

Annie Smith Peck, a middle-aged classics teacher, discovered personal delight in mountain climbing. Undaunted by age, gender, or altitude, she became the third woman in the nineteenth century to scale the Matterhorn. Her subsequent notoriety (she wore pants) seemed

---

18. Christopher K. Brown, "Prince, Nancy" and "Willard, Emma Hart," *Encyclopedia of Travel Literature* (Santa Barbara, Denver, and Oxford: ABC-CLIO, 2002).

19. Jennifer Hayward, "Women Travelers, Nineteenth Century"; Lila Marz Harper, "Kingsley, Mary Henrietta"; and Nina Allen, "Women Travelers, Twentieth Century," *Literature of Travel and Exploration: An Encyclopedia*, Ed. Jennifer Speake.

unearned. Thus, she decided to tackle a more difficult ascent in Mexico. Peck ultimately sponsored and led nine expeditions to Mexico, Bolivia, and Peru. An intrepid mountaineer, she brought a new dimension of adventure into women's travel accounts.[20] Some years after Peck set an altitude record, Fanny Bullock Workman not only set a new one but also staked her claim for women's right to vote atop several mountain peaks. Workman, along with her husband William, also rode bicycles through Algeria (*Algerian Memories: A Bicycle Tour over the Atlas to the Sahara*, 1895) and later India (*Through Town and Jungle*, 1904). Nellie Bly, a journalist, challenged Jules Verne's fictional travel record in *Around the World in Eighty Days* (1873) and even broke his daunting time limitation by taking a whirlwind trip recounted in *Nellie Bly's Book: Around the World in Seventy-two Days* (1890). Somehow during her publicity stunt, she managed to write not only about the landscapes and climates but also shared characteristics of the world's inhabitants.[21]

ANTARCTIC TRAVEL WRITING

Early in the twentieth century, polar exploration moved south to Antarctica. Colder and windier than the Arctic, Antarctica provided one of the last unexplored land masses on Earth. Robert Falcon Scott's two expeditions in 1901 and 1911 provided Scott with a sense of mission which, despite his failed objectives, he transformed into a noble sense of heroic sacrifice while writing. His diaries, published and republished, elevated him to mythic status. Ernest Shackleton's name may not have Scott's mythic ring, but his leadership during his second journey to reach the South Pole in 1914 inspired awe as he transformed his long, excruciating venture into a spiritual triumph. Roald Amundsen, who actually was first to reach the axis of rotation a month ahead of Scott, romanticized his experiences, too, although the British, in particular, chose largely to ignore his account. The last of the four explorers of the Heroic Age of Antarctic exploration was driven by purely scientific impulse. Douglas Mawson, an Australian geologist, wanted to "reduce this

---

20. Elizabeth Fagg Olds, *Women of the Four Winds* (New York: Houghton Mifflin, 1985).

21. Karen M. Morin, "Workman, Fanny Bullock," *Literature of Travel and Exploration: An Encyclopedia*, Ed. Jennifer Speake. Christopher K. Brown, "Bly, Nellie," *Encyclopedia of Travel Literature*.

land to terms of science," although he acknowledged its mystery and allure.[22] These four men, who ventured into the unknown with no maps, primitive clothing and equipment, limited or no polar experience, elementary communication, remote chance of rescue, undisclosed health problems, and largely untested leadership skills have inspired hundreds of accounts as subsequent travel writers have ventured south. Ernest Shackleton's *South* has remained in print since its first publication in 1919, a rather remarkable feat given the radical changes in the publishing business and mass-market entertainment.

While polar accounts have always been popular, the 1990s experienced an explosion of publications. Mawson's *The Home of the Blizzard*, written during his 1912–1913 sledge journey, was republished in 1990. *The South Pole: An Account of the Norwegian Antarctic Expedition in the Fram, 1910–1912* by Roald Amundsen was reprinted in 2001, and *The Worst Journey in the World* by Apsley Cherry-Gerrard was reissued in 2002. Accounts of Scott have long been set before the public, including Susan Solomon's 2001 *The Coldest March*. Solomon, a meteorologist with Antarctic experience, mined Scott's diaries and researched and collected scientific data to address the issue of Scott's poor choices (or leadership or luck) with regard to the role weather played in his last journey.

There are narratives of personal experiences, too. Reinhold Messner's *Antarctica: Both Heaven and Hell* was published in 1991 as were Will Stegner's *Crossing Antarctica* and Paul Brown's *The Last Wilderness*. Ranulph Finne's *Mind Over Matter*, published in 1993, tells the story of his manhauling a sledge in an unsupported crossing of the continent. Sara Wheeler's *Terra Incognita* (1999) presents a personal exploration of the history, literature, and social customs of the continent as well as the self.

BICYCLE TRAVEL WRITING

Antarctic exploration challenged both human endurance as well as technology, as various experiments with ponies, dogs, and motorized vehicles failed to meet climactic demands. However, improving

---

22. Sara Wheeler, *Terra Incognita: Travels in Antarctica* (New York: The Modern Library, 1999).

technology throughout the twentieth century has since eased many of travel's physical demands and simultaneously offered new challenges. Bicycles offered an independent mode of transportation as well as increasing speed and flexibility as they were modified during the late nineteenth century. Adventurers quickly saw opportunities for new physical challenges, which they often translated into narrative accounts. Initially, physical hardships were part of the challenge. Karl Kron's *Ten Thousand Miles on a Bicycle* (1887) and Thomas Stevens' *Around the World on a Bicycle* (1887–1888) were two of the first cycling travel adventures. Bernard Newman has written an extensive body of travelogues—some eighteen works—recounting his cycling journeys from Albania and Tunisia through the Middle East to Rome and the Pyrenees. Like Newman, other cyclists have challenged themselves as well by cycling daunting terrain, and lived to write about it. Dervla Murphy's *Full Tilt: Ireland to India with a Bicycle* (1965) is only one of several lengthy cycling journeys, as is Betinna Salby's *Riding the Desert Trail* (1988), which is her story of cycling from the Nile delta to the Mountains of the Moon in Uganda. Several men and women have cycled around the world, some in record time as in Nick Sander's *The Great Bike Ride: Around the World in Eighty Days* (1988).[23] From ordinary trips to exotic locales, riding tricycles to racing bikes, bicycle adventures continue to propel both young and old to investigate their world and its varied people.

AUTOMOBILE TRAVEL WRITING

Terrain opened further with the development of the automobile and a highway system to accommodate this liberating mode of transportation. Initially available only to the wealthy, the automobile quickly acquired both popularity and an increasing variety of users. Arthur Jerome Eddy constructed one of the first travel accounts in *Two Thousand Miles on an Automobile* (1902). Women quickly adopted this new form of transportation, often writing of their motor trips through western Europe, the Balkans, the United States, and Mexico. Edith Wharton

---

23. Nicholas Oddy, "Bicycles," *Literature of Travel and Exploration: An Encyclopedia*, Ed. Jennifer Speake.

24. Merrill Distard, "Motorcars," *Literature of Travel and Exploration: An Encyclopedia*, Ed. Jennifer Speake.

became an early adventurer in her *A Motor-Flight Through France* (1908).²⁴ Since Wharton, numerous writers have taken to the highways (some of which exist only on maps and not in reality) of the world to recount their adventures. Among the most famous of road books is Jack Kerouac's partly autobiographical travelogue, *On the Road* (1957), in which he celebrated the freedom of self. John Steinbeck, wanting to get in touch with his own country, took his poodle Charley on a thirty-state adventure in *Travels with Charley: In Search of America* (1962). William Least Heat-Moon, finding himself without a job, packed his camper and took to the highways of America in search of places lost to the rush of interstate traffic in *Blue Highways* (1982). Taking an opposite tact, Larry McMurtrey traveled interstates exclusively in *Roads*, as he investigated communities and people along its routes. North to south, east to west, fast to leisurely, alone, with animal friends, with families, or with other companions—travelogues by automobile adventurers assume shapes as different as their writers can make them. Road trips seem to offer time for contemplation, opportunities to connect with the reality of ordinary places and people, and sufficient distance from personal cares to re-evaluate personal direction and objectives.

RAILROAD TRAVEL WRITING

Travel by railroad appeals to many travelers who, free from the labor of pedaling or driving, may view and meditate on the landscapes through which they travel. One of the most ardent and prolific of train travelers is Paul Theroux, whose many journeys focus less on the landscape than on the people he meets. As he travels through Asia in *The Great Railway Bazaar: By Train Through Asia* (1975), Theroux writes, "I sought trains; I found passengers."²⁵ To Theroux, trains reflect culture. His vivid accounts of the characters he meets on the Orient Express, the Khyber Mail, and the Trans-Siberian express, and particularly the Vietnamese trains still in service reflect a good deal about the hardiness of various cultures. From *The Old Patagonian Express: By Train through the Americas* (1979), *Riding the Iron Rooster: By Train through China* (1988), to *The Kingdom by the Sea: A Journey around the Coast of Great Britain* (1988),

---

25. Paul Theroux, *The Great Railway Bazaar: By Train through Asia* (New York, 1975), 12.

Theroux has influenced other travelers by train, including Eric Newby (*Big Red Train Ride*, 1978), Stuart Stevens (*Night Train to Turkistan: Modern Adventures along China's Ancient Silk Road*, 1988), and Mary Morris (*Wall to Wall: From Beijing to Berlin by Rail*, 1991).[26]

AIR TRAVEL WRITING

Air travel, like land travel, developed rapidly during the twentieth century. The world's first air-passenger service began operating in Florida in 1914, only eleven years after the Wright brothers' first flight in 1903, and demonstrates just how quickly this form of travel assumed a role in human transport. Charles A. Lindbergh recorded the first transatlantic flight in *We, Pilot and Plane* (1927), and Amelia Earhart quickly followed with her *20 Hrs. 40 min: Our Flight in the Friendship: The American Girl, First across the Atlantic by Air, Tells Her Story*, in 1928. Like automobiles, however, air travel was restricted to mainly the wealthy or to those who used this technology for competition or entertainment. Before World War II, airplanes in the United States were used primarily for mail service. Thus, there is a surprisingly small body of aviation adventures. Graham Coster has collected aviation stories in *The Wild Blue Yonder: The Picador Book of Aviation* (1997) and Jimmy Buffet, perhaps better known for his songs than his writing, has left an entertaining account of his seaplane Caribbean adventures in *A Pirate Looks at Fifty* (1998).[27]

OUTER SPACE TRAVEL WRITING

Adventures in space, unlike air adventures, have flourished since the Soviet Union's first successful launch and recovery of Yuri Gargarin in 1961. To promote its scientific superiority, the U.S.S.R. made Gargarin's story, *Road to the Stars* (ed. by N. Kamanin, translated by G. Hanna and D. Myshne, 1962) available quickly. The United States, feeling the Cold War challenge, accelerated its own space program to put Alan Shepherd in space in 1962 and John Glenn into successful earth orbit the following year. The first launches attracted international

---

26. Simon Ward, "Trains," *Literature of Travel and Exploration: An Encyclopedia*, Ed. Jennifer Speake.

27. Elizabeth E. Wein, "Airplanes," *Literature of Travel and Exploration: An Encyclopedia*, Ed. Jennifer Speake.

attention, as television networks broadcast lengthy countdowns to a rapt public. The first astronauts were encouraged to relate their space adventures as part of a publicity campaign. *We Seven, by the Astronauts Themselves* (1962) became a best-selling book. Astronaut stories, however laden with technical details and limited by military restrictions, were snapped up by a proud U.S. public, which saw space pioneers as heroes.[28] Subsequent generations of space travelers have also written their accounts, although these travelers are not graced with the heroic aura granted to the first generation in space. Like air travel, space travel has become almost commonplace, and public interest has waned in the late twentieth century. Space travelers, however, continue to write their accounts.

UNDERWATER TRAVEL WRITING

Another form of space travel involves undersea exploration, best known because of Jacques Cousteau, whose six books (beginning with *The Silent World* in 1952), television documentaries, and films take readers into the ocean's depths and educate them about how the world's oceans contribute to sustaining life. Robert Marx keeps his readers underwater in *Deep, Deeper, Deepest: Man's Exploration of the Sea* (1998) as he explores the sea bottom. There are, naturally enough, books written by passionate deep sea divers, beginning with Guy Gilpatrick's *The Compleat Goggler* (1938) as well as adventures in undersea exploration with Walter G. Olesky's *Treasures of the Deep: Adventures of Undersea Exploration*, focusing on treasure hunting with a variety of scientists. Robert D. Ballard has assembled an anthology of pieces focusing on underwater exploration in *The Eternal Darkness: A Personal History of Deep-Sea Exploration* (2000).[29]

AROUND THE WORLD IN SPACE AND TIME

The fluid environment of the sea is not limited to water, as readers may find in Richard Fortney's *Earth: An Intimate History* (2004). Fortney takes readers around the world to see both space and time. As a

---

28. Robert A. Taylor, "Space Travel and Exploration," *Literature of Travel and Exploration: An Encyclopedia*, Ed. Jennifer Speake.

29. Gabriel E. Abad, "Undersea Exploration," *Literature of Travel and Exploration: An Encyclopedia*, Ed. Jennifer Speake.

geologist, he guides readers to see the earth's surface and then leads them through layers of sandstone, gneiss, granite, and other rocks to look at the earth's development. Readers will discover that, even as we travel the globe, it travels, too.

TRAVEL WRITING RELATING TO UNUSUAL AND SLOWER MODES OF TRAVEL

Other twentieth-century travel writers have turned their backs on technology to embrace early modes of transportation in their unique journeys. Twenty-year-old Mary Bosanquet covers three thousand miles on horseback in *Canada Ride* (1938). Forty years later, Robyn Davidson follows her passion for camels to take an 1,800-mile journey from Alice Springs to the coast of Australia in *Tracks* (1978). Along the way, Davidson encounters physical, emotional, and psychological barriers that have little to do with the demands of either her witty camels or demanding terrain.

Travel by boat has remained a popular form of transport, one demanding new angles of narration. Joshua Slocum was the first to complete a solo circumnavigation which he recounts in *Sailing Alone Around the World* (1898).[30] Testing his theory that Polynesia might have been populated by people from the Americas, Thor Heyerdahl, a Norwegian explorer, ethnologist, and environmentalist built a boat of reeds, which he named *Kon Tiki*, and sailed from South America to the Polynesian Islands.[31] Jonathan Raban, one of the best-known contemporary travel writers, playfully takes on the allure and culture of boats in *Coasting* (1986). Joe Kane's *Running the Amazon* (1990) recounts a source-to-mouth adventure by foot, raft, and kayak from its frozen headwaters in the mountains of Peru to its tropical flat water of the Amazon in Brazil. In addition to daunting physical challenges, this trip offers opportunities to observe political and national differences, which Kane shapes into a commentary and astute observations of colonial legacies along the Amazon. Edward A. Gargan's purpose for traveling the length of the Mekong in *The River's Tale* (2002) is more consciously

---

30. David Judkins, "Circumnavigation Narratives," *Literature of Travel and Exploration: An Encyclopedia*, Ed. Jennifer Speake.

31. Marcia B. Dinneen, "Heyerdahl, Thor," *Literature of Travel and Exploration: An Encyclopedia*, Ed. Jennifer Speake.

exploratory of colonial legacies than is Kane's. From Tibet, where China has made a concerted effort to destroy culture through its systematic elimination of Buddhism, through Burma/Myanmar, Laos, Thailand, and Cambodia to Vietnam, where legacies of French and U.S. presence continue to influence cultures, Gargan provides an astute commentary of colonialism's lingering effects.

AFRICA AND TRAVEL WRITING

In a similar manner, African nations continue to struggle with their own complex political histories and with the effects of colonial occupation. Because of its vastness and its special challenges, Africa beckons divergent writers, some following the footsteps of Mungo Park and others venturing into unknown territory. In 1934, novelist Graham Greene, suffering a severe case of burnout, organized a trip to Liberia. His was an odd choice for someone who was afraid of birds, cared nothing for flora or fauna, and was not keen on exercise. Before leaving England, Greene claimed to have already titled his book *You Can Keep Africa*.[32] But his finished travel book, *Journey Without Maps*, added immeasurably to the variety of travel literature as well as to Greene's fiction. Liberia, at that time, was quite literally unmapped. Even lifetime residents of Monrovia, its capital, had traveled no further than thirty miles inland. Greene traveled with that most important of all guides, an open mind, which could see how shabby "civilization" had made Freetown and Monrovia. He turns his back on the worn veneer of civilization to discover something more basic and authentic: a felt life without the complications of thought. Greene's book is notable for its depth. Ann Jones, a more recent traveler to Africa, has composed a travel book remarkable for its breadth. *Looking for Lovedu* (2001) is a road book, a travelogue in which readers may join Jones and Kevin Muggleton in a driving trip through most of Africa. Along the way, readers can view the variety of African nations and cultures, gain a sense of the legacies of colonialism, and investigate the roles of gender in travel and labor. In between these two books are literally hundreds of personal experiences, for Africa has inspired numerous written accounts, from Isak Dineson's

---

32. Russell Sherry, *The Life of Graham Greene: Volume I: 1904–1939* (New York: Viking, 1989), 512.

Out of Africa and Beryl Markam's *West with the Night* to Edward Hoagland's *African Calliope: A Journey to the Sudan* (1979), Evelyn Waugh's *A Tourist in Africa* (1960), and Sekai Nzenza-Shand's *Songs to an African Sunset: A Zimbabwean Story* (1997).

WRITING ABOUT LESS-FREQUENTED PLACES

With much of the world traveled, some writers have sought less frequented places, resulting in expanding the dimension of travel literature. Robert Byron, who ventured into Central Asia shortly before World War II, brought new writing techniques to his *The Road to Oxiana* (1937); many writers consider his work to be among the best travel narratives ever written. Byron's unique combination of history, official documents, dialogues, and anecdotes present readers with a veritable collage of information.[33] Central Asia continues to attract exceptional travel writers, including Colin Thubron, who visits the five republics, all in a state of political, economic, and cultural flux following the collapse of the Soviet Union in *The Lost Heart of Asia* (1994). Finding herself teaching journalism in Kyrgyzstan on a Fulbright Scholarship, Elinor Burkett takes it upon herself to visit cultures closed to Americans in *So Many Enemies, So Little Time: An American Woman in All the Wrong Places* (2004). She flies to Afghanistan even as the Taliban are vacating Kabul, visits Iraq before the United States begins bombing, and enters Iran to discover how attitudes are shifting with political tides. These writers all bring personal insights into countries not traveled, countries that increasingly play significant roles in world events.

THE EFFECT OF CULTURE AND ECOTOURISM ON TRAVEL WRITING

Already a hybridized form of literature, travel adventures continue to develop in idiosyncratic ways. Some travelogues, such as Norman Lewis' *A Dragon Apparent: Travels in Indo-China* (1951) are prophetic of events that will develop into a prolonged conflict. Others, like Rebecca West's *Black Lamb and Grey Falcon* (1941) are meditations on human destiny. Travel writers are generally outsiders who use their position to

---

33. Chris Hopkins, "Byron, Robert," *Literature of Travel and Exploration: An Encyclopedia*, Ed. Jennifer Speake.

examine varied perspectives. V.S. Naipaul, a Trinidad-born Indian, uses his position as an outsider everywhere to examine the cultures he visits from a keen analytical perspective. His examination of Islamic cultures in *Among the Believers* (1982) and *Beyond Belief* (1998) can give readers an understanding of often conflicting claims among the Islamic faithful. Another gifted travel writer, Jan Morris, brings her dual experience as both male and female into her insightful travelogues. James Humphrey Morris established himself as a major travel writer in the 1960s by traveling to all five continents and writing with a sense of history that infuses his sense of the present. His *Cities* (1963) focuses on the urban environments of seventy major cities. But his most difficult journey is related in *Conundrum* (1972), in which he crosses sexual boundaries.[34]

As human population has increased, placing strains on the earth's environment and resources, more and more writers are seeking to preserve both the few remaining wild spots as well as their fragile wildlife populations. William Karesh's *Appointments at the Ends of the World* (1999) gives a close look at a wildlife veterinarian who makes jungle calls—from endangered okapi in Congo to peccaries in Costa Rico to orangutans in Borneo. Karesh shows his readers physical and emotional depredations inflicted upon landscapes and animal populations by economic concerns and ignorance. Peter Matthiessen travels the world to tell the story of cranes in *The Birds of Heaven* (2001). Accompanied by ornithologists and self-confessed "craniacs," Matteissen shows how fifteen varieties of cranes struggle to survive in a rapidly developing world. Some travel writers scramble to the most inaccessible places remaining on earth, where small populations have changed little over the centuries. Tim Flannery in *Throwim' Way Leg* (1998) has journeyed to the far reaches of Borneo, where cannibalism is still practiced, as a means of both exposing and protecting a cultural group endangered by encroaching development.

THE BENEFITS OF TRAVEL WRITING

Throughout the world, travel writers bring special powers of observation,

---

34. Paul Smethurst, "Morris, Jan," *Literature of Exploration and Travel: An Encyclopedia*, Ed. Jennifer Speake.

characterization, and narration to their adventures, preserving times and events as only writers can. Travel writers inform and delight, opening intellectual doors that many cannot envision. They bring their individual insights to bear on past and current historical and cultural events from a position that manages to suggest both interior understanding and exterior objectivity. Travel writers will venture where few might ever think to go, opening cultural doors for readers. In bringing personal dislocations into readers' intellects, travel writers enrich our understanding of place, history, language, political movements, and cultures. Several manage to teach readers geology, physics, mathematics, botany, zoology, and mechanics. Depending on the writer, readers come to a wider understanding of both ecology and economics. Indeed, as a distinct genre, travel literature offers readers the widest range of information available outside an encyclopedia. With increasing attention given to cultural studies, travel literature may play another important role. In its transmigration from act to word and from there across genres, physical borders, historical times, events, cultures, and languages, travel literature comes close to the epitome of postmodern literature.

End-of-Chapter Questions

1. What is the possible reason (given by Carmean) why travel writing remains the most varied of literary genres?
2. From our earliest recorded documents, travel writing has provided two things in works. One is metaphor. What is the other?
3. Who is credited with being the first travel writer?
4. Did Ferdinand Magellen write about his voyage around the world in the sixteenth century?
5. What person made many contributions to the genre of travel writing but was also considered possibly the most famous explorer and traveler of all time?
6. Who wrote *The Voyage of the Beagle*?
7. What woman wrote four books about Siam and India (her work as a governess was the basis for the film *The King and I*)?

A History of Travel Writing

8. Which continent did Susan Solomon's 2001 book, *The Coldest March*, discuss?

9. What famous author felt that trains reflect culture, saying, "I sought trains; I found passengers."?

10. Is *Tracks* a book about rail travel in Africa?

WRITING ASSIGNMENT FOUR
THIRD-PERSON WRITING

Assignment Introduction

Readers want to have the feeling that they, not you, are there. Therefore, third-person writing, rather than first-person writing, is usually far more effective. It is usually not hard to convert first person to third person, but the reader needs to sense that the writing was in third person originally. Although it is usually better to write in third person originally, it is possible to change a first-person narrative to a third-person narrative.

Assignment Activity

Go back to what you wrote in writing assignments one and two, and convert it to third person. If you make the conversion by simple substitutions for the words "I" and "me," your written piece will most likely be third person, but it is unlikely that it will be smooth. Therefore, do it in steps.

The first step is to convert from "I" or "me" and similar nouns and pronouns into third person. Then, let your material sit for at least two days without looking at it. Next, read what you have written in third person and smooth it out, making it sound as if it were written in third person originally. You might want to do a couple of drafts until you are comfortable that your piece now reads smoothly and easily and is in third person.

Final Step: Add your name to the Instructor Comment Sheet for Writing Assignment Four in appendix 5 and staple it to your third-person rewrite. Then turn in these two sheets to your professor.

AMANDA CASTLEMAN is a freelance journalist, specializing in travel, sports, the environment, and women's issues. Her articles have appeared in the *International Herald Tribune, Wired, Salon, Italy Daily, The Athens News, Guardian,* and *Mail on Sunday* as well as on MSNBC and the U.K.'s BBC. She teaches travel writing through Writers.com. She also is a regular contributor to *The Seattle Post-Intelligencer, Moviemaker,* and *Road and Travel.* Castleman has worked on ten books, including the *Rough Guide to Italy, Michelin's Green Guide to Italy, Time Out Athens, Rome in Detail,* and *Where to Eat and Stay in France* (DK Eyewitness). Currently, she is drafting the *Rome and Central Italy Adventure Guide.* Her most impressive award is first place for In-depth News/Feature Writing from the Columbia Scholastic Press Association.

CHAPTER 5

Travel Writing Brought Up-to-Date

Amanda Castleman

WHAT IS TRAVEL WRITING?

"Travel writing is something everyone seems to do, when e-mailing a friend or writing a fifth-grade assignment on 'what I did on my summer vacation.' It is hard to do well precisely because it is easy to do passably," warned Pico Iyer, one of the genre's most eminent authors.[1]

"We travel, initially, to lose ourselves," he famously announced.

---

1. Pico Iyer and Jason Wilson, eds., *The Best American Travel Writing 2004* (Boston: Houghton Mifflin, 2004), xxiv.

"And we travel, next, to find ourselves."² Travel writing should record these revelations, he counseled, in "a parallel journey, matching the physical steps of a pilgrimage with the metaphysical steps of a questioning (as in Peter Matthiessen's great *The Snow Leopard*) or chronicling a trip to the furthest reaches of human strangeness (as in Oliver Sacks' *The Island of the Colorblind*)."³

At its finest, travel writing stretches for profound insight and illumination, ranking it among the most literary of nonfiction techniques. However, this genre is broad and multifaceted, ranging from brusque newspaper articles on cheap airfares to five-star resort reviews and wild yarns, such as Bill Bryson's *Walk in the Woods*, an account of his inept attempt to hike the Appalachian Trail. Writers employ a variety of "voices," depending on the publication and assignment.

CONTROVERSY

Susan Spano once branded her colleagues an "odd lot" in "So You Want to Be a Travel Writer," a 2005 *Los Angeles Times* article. "Most of them—myself included—have scant preparation and back into the profession, which is an illegitimate child in the world of letters. There's no graduate program culminating in a master's degree in travel arts. Journalists consider it frivolous and easy. Poets and novelists look at it as slumming," she complained.⁴

Professors Patrick Holland and Graham Huggan echoed the same sentiment. "Travel writing, as a genre, has always had a mixed reception, being seen by some as essentially frivolous or morally dangerous," they wrote in *Tourists with Typewriters*.⁵

Some critics attack subsidized trips: this conflict of interest prohibits objective reporting, they argue. Others dismiss "holiday write-ups" as fluff, frequently crafted by hobbyists. Dismissive reactions are common, despite evidence that readers want more travel coverage, according to

---

2. Don George, ed., "Why We Travel by Pico Iyer," *Salon.com's Wanderlust: Real Life Tales of Adventure and Romance* (London: Macmillan, 2001), viii.

3. Ibid., xviii.

4. Susan Spano, "So You Want to Be a Travel Writer?" *Los Angeles Times*, May 22, 2005: L.7.

5. Patrick Holland and Graham Huggan, *Tourists with Typewriters: Critical Reflections on Contemporary Travel Writing* (Ann Arbor: The University of Michigan Press, 2000), viii.

"Impact Study 2000," conducted by Northwestern University's Readership Institute.[6]

However frowned upon, the genre is booming. Glossy magazines stock the shelves, as major metropolitan papers introduce new travel sections, even in the wake of September 11, 2005[7]—and the resulting worldwide tourism slump.[8] From television shows to blogs and bestsellers, travel is a hot topic in the shrinking global village. Scholars, commissioning editors, and writers themselves are slowly beginning to commit more thought, care, respect, and resources to the art of travel (case in point: the eponymous book by pop-philosopher Alain de Botton,[9] not to mention the watershed of *Tourists with Typewriters*, the first extensive survey of contemporary travel writing).

BOOKS

"While travelers have been sending back personal dispatches from the road for centuries, the first-person narrative—shaped like a work of fiction with a beginning, middle, and end—has really come into its own only in the last fifty years or so," pointed out Lonely Planet's Global Travel Editor Don George, also the author of *Travel Writing*.[10]

Paul Theroux's first travel book, *The Great Railway Bazaar*, published in 1953, marked a turning point in travel writing. The curmudgeonly bestseller was "a pivotal part of a widespread movement that liberated travel writing from the confines of pure guidebook writing, and began to equate first-person narrative with literary art," George said.[11]

---

6. Readership Institute, "Impact Study 2000" (Evanston, IL: Northwestern University, 2000), www.readership.org/content/editorial/feature-style/main.htm.

7. "In 2005, the world's travel and tourism industry is expected to generate 3.8% of GDP and 74,223,000 jobs, while the broader travel and tourism economy is expected to total 10.6% of GDP and 221,568,000 jobs. Looking ahead, the forecast for travel and tourism demand is expected to total 5.4% real growth in 2005, and 4.6% real growth per annum between 2006 and 2015," according to Oxford Economic Forecasting, *World Travel & Tourism: Sowing the Seeds of Growth* (economic report) (London: World Travel & Tourism Council, Tourism Satellite Accounting, 2005), www.wttc.org/2004tsa/frameset2a.htm.

8. Mary Williams Walsh, "Many Once-Thriving Cities Are Suddenly Hurting," *The New York Times*, September 30, 2001.

9. Alain de Botton, *The Art of Travel* (London: Penguin, 2002).

10. Don George, *Travel Writing* (London: Lonely Planet, 2005), 11.

11. Ibid., 12.

Other contemporary authors have gained literary laurels: Bruce Chatwin's *In Patagonia*, Pico Iyer's *Video Night in Kathmandu*, Tim Cahill's *Pass the Butterworms*, Peter Matthiessen's *The Snow Leopard*, and nearly all of Jan Morris' entire catalogue, especially *Journeys*. Peter Mayle's 1989 memoir, *A Year in Provence*, sold over a million copies, was translated into seventeen languages, and became a popular British TV serial.[12] *Under the Tuscan Sun* by Frances Mayes won similar commercial success and a silver-screen debut. Bill Bryson's popularity has grown so monumental that he tackled *A Short History of Nearly Everything* in 2004.

Guidebooks too have their superstars. Arthur Frommer and Rick Steves, among others, have spun themselves into multimedia franchises. Even group-authored travel tomes enjoyed a boost: sales swelled 23 percent to $222 million from 1997–2000, then diminished slightly post-9/11.[13]

Nevertheless, as of 2005, Lonely Planet sold six million copies a year, dominating a quarter of the estimated English-language market.[14]

Armchair anthologies are another growing venue for both new work and reprints. Travelers' Tales is a leader with more than sixty titles in print. The imprint ranges from anecdotes (collected by country or region) to advice compilations such as Mary Beth Bond's best-selling *Gutsy Women: Travel Tips and Wisdom*.

Major publishing houses—such as Vintage, Random House, Broadway Books, and Crown Journeys—are best approached through agents, who generally represent established authors with book proposals (twenty to sixty pages) or new talent with finished manuscripts. Some travel writers prefer to skirt the system and self-publish, keeping a larger share of the profits. Tom Brosnahan led the charge with his 2004 memoir *Turkey: Bright Sun, Strong Tea*. But he built on a stellar reputation, having sold nearly four million guidebooks worldwide in twelve languages for imprints such as Berlitz, Frommer's, and Lonely Planet.

---

12. Patrick Holland and Graham Huggan, *Tourists with Typewriters: Critical Reflections on Contemporary Travel Writing* (Ann Arbor: The University of Michigan Press, 2000), 1.

13. Justin Pritchard, "Guidebook sales rebound slowly," Associated Press, March 19, 2002.

14. Tad Friend, "The Parachute Artist," *The New Yorker*, April 18, 2005.

"Publishing your own guidebook profitably can still be done today, but it's far more difficult," he cautioned on Writers Website Planner, an advice archive he maintains online. "Well-known series grew up with world tourism, expanding the load on bookshelves in tandem with the increase in the number of travelers. Now the bookshelves are stuffed with good titles, the long post-oil-crisis economic boom is over, terrorism threats are crimping world tourism, and competition for readers is fierce."[15]

ONLINE

Go web, Brosnahan urged his colleagues. Sites with "evergreen" content—long-lasting information that doesn't require continual updating—can attract considerable attention. For example, his TurkeyTravelPlanner.com Web site anticipates two million visitors from 160 countries in 2005.

The devil is in the details, he wrote: "You will have to spend some time organizing and optimizing your content. You can't just put an article or book text online and expect it to earn much money for you. You may have to work nearly full-time on your Web site for a year or more to get it to the 'take-off' point."[16] Web and marketing savvy are essential, as revenue is drawn from advertising, affiliations, content licensing and resales, and consulting services.

A blog, on the other hand, usually requires less infrastructure, but more ongoing work. Commentary and Web links intermingle in a sort of online diary, which often relies on automated publishing systems like blogger.com.

Even the venerable Arthur Frommer admitted: "The blog has come to travel. Just as political writers have created their own Internet sites for daily comments (a Web log, or "blog"), distinguished travel guidebook writers are now writing about their own geographical specialties online."[17] Several of the best double as industry watchdogs: Carl Parkes'

---

15. Tom Brosnahan, "What's Wrong With Print?" Writers Website Planner, Concord, MA: Travel Info Exchange, Inc., www.writerswebsiteplanner.com/problem_print.html.

16. Ibid., www.writerswebsiteplanner.com.

17. Arthur Frommer, "Guidebook writers' blogs get you the picture quicker," *San Francisco Chronicle*, April 11, 2005.

www.travelwriters.blogspot.com, Jen Leo's www.writtenroad.com, and Rolf Pott's www.vagablogging.net.

Professional travel writers typically avoid posting their work on user-written sites—such as VirtualTourist.com, TripAdvisor.com, WikiTravel.org, and BootsnAll.com—which provide neither pay nor prestige.

ELECTRONIC

Venice in Context gathered a handful of awards in 2003–2004: two audio CDs accompanied each guidebook. Buyers could follow twelve walking tours via Walkman or MP3 player. Emerging technologies also include podcasts, PDAs, and cell-phone downloads.

PRINT MEDIA

Newspapers and magazines remain the heartland of travel writing for the time being, however. Most major dailies have travel pages or special weekly sections. Some pool content into shared online portals such as www.thisistravel.co.uk, affiliated with the UK's *Daily Mail* and *Evening Standard*. Writers should always negotiate extra pay for electronic archives (in fact, an $18 million class-action suit was being settled in 2005 on behalf of freelancers whose stories appeared in online databases without their consent).[18]

Magazines—especially glossies like *National Geographic Traveler*, *Travel and Leisure*, *Condé Nast Traveler*, and airline publications—continue to attract top talent. The industry even produced fresh blooms in the wary post-9/11 period. In June 2003, *travelgirl* became the first national U.S. launch after the New York terrorist attacks. Mixing glamour and globetrotting, the quarterly magazine targets women, who make 75 percent of travel decisions.[19]

START THE WRITING PROCESS

Thus far you have learned much about travel writing. In the next few chapters, you will learn how to start your own travel article. First comes

---

18. www.freelancerights.com.
19. Wendy Guarisco, *travelgirl* launch press release, www.travelgirlinc.com/press.html, June 2001.

the article idea. Several chapters will discuss how good travel article ideas are formed and developed. A variety of suggestions are presented. When you have finished these chapters, you should have a good grasp on one or more travel article ideas about which you plan to write.

End-of-Chapter Questions

1. According to Pico Iyer, why is travel writing hard to do well?
2. What is our initial reason for traveling, according to Iyer?
3. On what do the "voices" of a travel writer depend, according to Castleman?
4. Who branded travel writers as an "odd lot"?
5. Is travel writing booming or decreasing?
6. What publication was the first extensive survey of contemporary travel writing?
7. In 1953, a turning point in the history of travel writing was marked by the publication of Paul Theroux's first travel book. What is the title of that book?
8. What is the name of one of the superstars of guidebook writing?
9. Do book proposals for anthologies normally run from one hundred to three hundred pages?
10. Do professional travel writers typically post their work on user-written Web sites?

WRITING ASSIGNMENT FIVE
POSTCARD BREVITY

Assignment Introduction

"2,035 to 2,041 characters is your range," the editor told me. Every week I wrote articles that were about 3,500 characters and cut back to between 2,035 and 2,041 before turning in my weekly travel article. Train yourself to write "tight" articles, and you will be glad you did. So will your editors.

The chances are good that, like many others who travel, you have sent postcards to friends and relatives back home. Ideally on a postcard in a few words you are able to tell the recipient enough about the wonderful trip you are having to catch his or her interest. Many travel articles are so short that they allow only two to three times the number of words that you can put on a postcard. Therefore, train yourself to write short, but sharp, eye-opening, yet key travel writing pieces.

Assignment Activity

Purchase a postcard at a local store or the post office. In pencil (so that you can erase and rewrite, if necessary) and using only a few words, convince a relative that might be visiting (see exercise number two) to want to visit the site about which you wrote for exercise number one. You might want to do several drafts of your postcard until you feel that you have done as good a job as possible within the tight constraints of the few words that you can handwrite on the back of a postcard.

Final Step: Add your name to the Instructor Comment Sheet for Writing Assignment Five in appendix 5 and staple it to your postcard brevity writing. Then turn in both sheets to your professor.

SECTION II

STARTING OUT—FIVE APPROACHES

There are many ways in which a travel writer may initiate work on a travel writing assignment or a travel writing project. This section introduces several common approaches.

Developing story ideas is the focus of chapter 6. Rumbaugh suggests two tracks to take in getting story ideas. Castleman offers a more direct approach. Poynter suggests researching the news and the trade press. Each details why and how their approach works.

Papay takes a different approach in chapter 7. She suggests keeping a travel journal to help travel writers hone their ideas into stories. She offers examples of travel journals that led to published travel writing and offers helpful hints on how to keep travel journals.

Like Papay, Lemmon maintains, in chapter 8, that press trips will produce not only story ideas, but story content. She explains how travel writers are able to get story ideas while on a press trip and how they can prepare a draft copy even before returning home.

There certainly are good approaches that are not presented in this section. However, all are encouraged to find an approach that works for them and then to hone that approach.

 **SUE RUMBAUGH** is a member of the faculty at Carlow University in Pittsburgh, Pennyslvania, where she serves as coordinator of the Professional Writing Program and teaches writing courses including travel writing, which focuses on both the travel experience and spiritual journeying. A former newspaper reporter, she is also a freelance writer and an independent resource development consultant, writing and producing materials for schools, healthcare institutions, and social service agencies. Rumbaugh completed her master's in public management from the H. John Heinz III School of Public Policy and Management at Carnegie Mellon University in Pittsburgh in 2000 and received her bachelor of science degree from the Perley Isaac Reed School of Journalism at West Virginia University in Morgantown. Currently pursuing a master's degree in creative writing at Carlow, she has written several travel stories and is working on completing her first book, a creative nonfiction memoir.

CHAPTER 6

Selecting and Narrowing Travel Article Ideas

Sue Rumbaugh
Amanda Castleman
James Poynter

THE IMPORTANCE OF STORY IDEAS— SUE RUMBAUGH

Storytelling is an ancient art. As communal people, we like to gather and tell stories—to communicate, to understand ourselves and our world, and to entertain. Cities and nations—from Rome and Greece to

Paris and New York—have been built on storytelling, both verbal and written. Inventions of the alphabet, pen, paper and ink, the automated press, printers, and now the computer have all influenced our methods of as well as our access to storytelling. With each new invention, stories were carried further.

So modern days here we are. Our access to audiences has never been greater. It no longer matters on what continent you live; with a computer and Internet access, you can gather people together and tell them a story—your story—at any time. Millions of people are writing online. And, at the same time, magazines and newspapers, as well as specialty publications and books, continue to be bought and sold. So, who is reading all of these stories and why? What do they—what do we—want?

We want to tell and hear our stories. It is human nature, and these are great times in which to live for those of us who enjoy storytelling.

As a travel writer, you must first understand your own interests in writing. It does not all have to be a narrow focus. Most writers write in a number of genres—fiction, poetry, creative nonfiction—and many of them are professional writers making their living or a portion of their living by the writing pieces they sell.

Sometimes travel writers begin writing a piece and realize it is not what they had set out to write, but the story has taken them down a path to become something of its own. This practice by writers, of crossing over into different venues, makes for some of the most interesting and best writing.

The writer, however, before attempting to sell or publish a piece, must be clear on the purpose for and focus of the finished product. Otherwise, a writer's work will never be successful. To identify your markets is to discover what the public wants, what they are willing to purchase, download, or borrow from a library. Their purpose may be for information, education, or pleasure—or a combination of all three.

Travel writers can pursue any number of writing outlets, and the opportunities for writers in the subject area of travel writing are plentiful. One writing critic observed that all writing is, in fact, travel writing. This may indeed be true because life itself is a travel adventure. The style, format, length, and other specifications set by a publishing source create predetermined limitations. However, these parameters may serve

Selecting and Narrowing Travel Article Ideas

to bring out the best writing ideas. It comes down to the fact that, if you want to be a travel writer, you must develop the ability to find and develop good story ideas by living your life, experiencing new things and places, and then writing about them. If you are interested in writing for newspapers and magazines, you should think about, work toward, and explore travel writing on two tracks.

Track one includes journaling, poetry, observation, sensory experiences, and the art of storytelling. Each of these will prompt story ideas.

Track two includes the marketplace, political and social issues, religion and spirituality, cultural and artistic trends, technology and media issues, and business and retail trends. These too are prompters of story ideas. In fact, together, these two halves will create the tension in which the travel writer lives, writes, and works to market stories.

TRACK ONE

Track one concerns issues involving the travel writer. By delving into issues of concern to all people, the travel writer is able to create a common ground to connect to the reader and to provide a bridge to understanding. This bridge will provide story ideas, and it will make the travel writer's stories more intriguing and attractive to the reader.

Journaling

Chapter 7 in this book goes into detail about keeping a journal, so the concept will only be touched upon here. Journals provide a place to record observations and impressions. It is easy to forget what happens along the way. A journal is an excellent place to jot down a story idea when suddenly an idea hits you and you say to yourself, "Aha—that would be a great article idea." Keeping a journal helps the travel writer to recall situations, places, conversations, and reactions. Reading your journal will invigorate your memories and help you to come up with story ideas. In addition, you will be able to relive your fun, funny, moving, frightening, enjoyable, and beautiful travel experiences—the heart of any good travel piece.

Poetry

Even if you are not Emily Dickinson, you can write poetry. It can help you to tap your inner thoughts and to weave together words that capture a particular moment that holds special meaning. Just as every story must have a theme, point, or purpose for being written and being read, so too must your travel writing story have a theme or purpose. Your attempt at poetry can help you to find and articulate the essential kernel of deep, human truth in your story. It can become for you the story idea within the travel story that captures your audience. It can build a connection that takes the reader through to the end.

Observation

Good ideas flow from the attention to the senses, interaction with people, movement in and out of places, and recording experiences. This skill of observation comes from the ability to be an observer while also being a participant in the journey. In travel writing, while the writer must be mindful to write descriptions that capture a place, the story idea is rarely complete unless the travel writer also conveys the ambiance and special features that make the place worth visiting and the story worth reading.

Sensory Experiences

An important part of many travel articles is making the reader feel like he or she is "there." This involves the senses. Thus, your observations (hopefully recorded in your travel journal) should include your experiences of sight, sound, smell, taste, and feel. Each is a part of the story idea and travel writing often includes accounts of what one sees and, if it involves restaurants, the taste and smell of the food. Engaging all of the senses in your story makes for a more experiential and memorable reading.

The Art of Storytelling

Even if your story idea is the destination, your travel writing story is also a story. You will have one or more of the storytelling components—i.e., subjects, characters, dialogue, setting characterization, plot, tone, and theme. However, you are a writer of truth, and, thus, you cannot make up any of these. You must be a keen observer and an accurate recorder of the truth. A big part of being a successful travel writer is the challenge of and opportunity for writing truth and fact as a creative nonfiction travel writer.

TRACK TWO

Story ideas come from many sources. This track is concerned with developing story ideas from issues that originate outside of the writer. These areas provide keys to the information, insights, and clues for important issues of concern for potential readers and travelers. If one is to be a successful travel writer, one must read and learn about issues facing the world, the particular location of the travel story, and the traveler himself or herself. In this way, the writer can position the story to capture the attention of the reader as well as of the editor.

The Marketplace

To sell a piece of travel writing, a writer must research the possible outlets for selling a piece before, during, or after the trip. Chapter 11 on selling travel articles discusses travel article buyers and how to reach them. However, working within travel buyer parameters will flesh out the story idea based on what the editor wants or requires. If, however, the travel writer finds the editor's requirements too cumbersome and stifling of creativity, the writer may take an alternative approach. This is to write the piece first using one's own judgment regarding story idea parameters. Then search for publications that might consider what you have written.

Political and Social Issues

Being knowledgeable of trends is important in developing story ideas. This is especially true if you are considering writing about international travel. Politics of countries can create tension and cause interactions overseas to be strained. They also can suggest story ideas. For example, when the United States government started requiring more stringent documentation to award visas to foreign visitors due to terrorist concerns, other governments adopted more stringent documentation requirements for Americans traveling to their countries in retaliation. In this case, documentation requirement changes became a travel story idea.

It is not often that people of another country hold individual travelers responsible for their home countries' negative politics. However, it is good to be aware and to keep one's strong opinions contained. At the same time, political upheaval can be a good opportunity to develop travel story ideas.

Religion and Spirituality

Human beings connect at a deep level through religion and spirituality. Thus, knowing the main spiritual and religious issues of a country, region, or community is a good way to develop story ideas based on the hopes, fears, and dreams of the people who live there. There are many religious and spirituality related publications interested in buying travel story ideas that they believe relate to their readership. Capturing interesting insights into the local people and documenting their religious and spiritual customs and habits can help to build a dimension to your story that helps make it more appealing.

Cultural and Artistic Trends

Knowing a city, state, region, or country's celebrated artists is a good foundation on which to base travel article ideas relating to art. Reading the local newspapers and magazines about the current successes as well as events and festivals may provide clues or angles for your story.

Technology and Media Issues

Keeping updated on issues of technology can help in relating to the growing technologically savvy public, as well as suggest travel article ideas relating to technology. For example, when the new Denver airport opened a little more than a decade ago, it introduced vertical ski delivery pods for the first time. This innovation resulted in several travel articles that appeared in outdoor- and ski-oriented publications. To read about and study technology and media changes and to understand their impact upon the public—particularly the public interested in travel—will help to keep you ahead of the curve and to keep your writing relevant and interesting.

Business and Retail Trends

Consumerism is a common thread within countries as well as across the globe. Are people traveling? If so, where? When? How? Why? Travel trends, in terms of purchases made, affect not only the travel industry but also the peripheral businesses of clothing, luggage, cars, and so forth. Read and learn about economic trends (an article on what destinations are a good buy with the current trend in currency conversion rates, for example) to help in story ideas and story angles.

THE DIRECT APPROACH—AMANDA CASTLEMAN

Amanda Castleman suggests taking a much more honed concept approach. She suggests working the angles, writing about what you know, sourcing ideas, and undertaking research.

HONED CONCEPTS

Travel concepts continually surface—a tub of hummus in the supermarket might spark visions of Lebanon—but writers learn to groom only the likeliest ones, before pitching to a publication or submitting a finished article.

Editors weigh many factors. They consider the pace of the magazine: the mix of briefs, columns, news reports, and in-depth features. (See appendix 3 to get a "feel" for the mixes of selected magazines.) Seasonal items must counterbalance "evergreen" content—stories of enduring interest. They monitor the ratio of trendy must-have topics to off-the-beaten track exclusives. Careful not to recycle subjects too often, they keep one eye on the archives. Then they mete out assignments first to staffers and stringers (regular contributors), before diving into the "slush pile" of unsolicited story ideas.

Thus the formula is tricky to predict. Bad timing can ruin the prospects of even the most suitable author and article. A pitch might founder because the destination is overexposed or because the publication covered it two years ago. Or perhaps an editor had a bad spring-break hangover in Cabo and nurses a grudge. The most critical lesson to learn is this: rejection is not always personal.

However, honed concepts can increase your hit-rate. As Roy Peter Clark, senior scholar at the distinguished Poynter Institute of Journalism Studies, wrote, "Only two kinds of writers exist in the world: the ones with ideas and the ones with assignments."[1]

ANGLES

You must persuade an editor that *this* story by *you* is noteworthy *now*. Journalists call these characteristics an "angle." This broad term ranges

---

1. Roy Peter Clark, *Writing Tool #50: The Writing Process*, Poynter Online (2005), www.poynter.org/content/content_view.asp?id=79244.

from recounting an extraordinary experience to exploring a current controversy or revisiting a historical landmark.

Capitalize on current headlines. Athens, for example, was a hot topic before the Olympic Summer Games of 2004. Gay publications targeted Vermont, Massachusetts, and San Francisco: areas that supported homosexual marriage in the United States. Indonesia remained on the radar long after the tsunami wreckage was cleared. As architects haggled over the World Trade Center site redesign, articles abounded on New York City.

A blockbuster—or bestseller—highlights an area; people fall in love with the scenery, as well as the story (remember how tourists flocked to New Zealand, as the *Fellowship of the Ring* trilogy unfolded?). Anthony Minghella filmed *Cold Mountain*, starring Jude Law, Nicole Kidman, and Renée Zellweger, in Transylvania. Eleven other Hollywood directors then shot in Romania: travel writers and tourists followed this star-studded path.

New landmarks, attractions, museums, hotels, and high-profile restaurant launches can all inspire fresh investigation of a place. Seek out exhibitions and festivals for a timely twist (pitch three-to-twelve months in advance for seasonal stories). Travel writers also mark the anniversaries of events: Numerous journalists retraced the route of Lewis and Clark a century after their epic trek across North America. How's Hong Kong following the changeover? Was Bruce Chatwin right about the Outback? Does the Himalayan region of Dolpo still resemble Peter Matthiessen's description in his travel literature classic, *The Snow Leopard*? Give readers a reason to revisit a location—in print or in person.

WRITE WHAT YOU KNOW

Writers bring much of themselves to any text, especially in the travel genre. An advertising executive in Taiwan has quite a different perspective from a Seattle mountaineer or a French housewife. Even if all three wrote about the same destination, their articles would be unique.

Dig deep into your memories and dreams. Where have you always wanted to go? Where are the best places you've been? Would your hobbies interest other travelers? Does your lifestyle—perhaps being a parent, minority, or disabled—influence your trips? What can you harvest from your experience to share with others?

"Beautiful Venice" isn't nearly as gripping as "An Amateur Artist at the Biennale." In the latter case, an insider's perspective—as well as the forthcoming international exhibition—makes the piece special, more timely, and more illuminating.

"Write what you know" is the oldest advice in the trade—for a reason. Try to pick topics that exploit your expertise. For this reason, many authors choose to chronicle their hometowns for visitors or armchair dreamers half a world away.

The advantages are numerous. Background knowledge frees a travel writer to concentrate on structure and style, rather than suffering a steep learning curve. It allows more time for other chores, such as self-promotion and market research. Also, local reporting confers instant authority, increasing the odds of a commission and good reception of the published work. Herb Miller explained in a 2000 *St. Petersburg Times* article: "Even the most skilled guidebook practitioner cannot fathom a place and credibly guide others there without immersion. Outsiders rarely get perspective right. Extent of coverage and detail become equally suspect."[2]

Talent can make even a vacant lot come to life, argued Pico Iyer in the introduction to *The Best of American Travel Writing 2004*: "I'd rather read Philip Roth on Newark than most of the rest of us on North Korea. As Thoreau put it, 'It matters not where or how far you travel—the further commonly worse—but how much alive you are.'"[3]

SOURCING IDEAS

Spotting Trends

Stop, look, and listen. Are your friends all planning trips to Eastern Africa? Is your hairdresser buzzing about an unspoiled Caribbean island? Is your father going on a yoga retreat he booked online? Has your neighbor swapped houses with an Austrian? Are the local kids suddenly choosing academic summer programs over traditional outdoor

---

2. Herbert Miller, *Who's Guiding the Guidebooks?* St. Petersburg, FL: St. Petersburg Times Online (2000),www.sptimes.com/News/051400/Travel/Who_s_guiding_the_gui.shtml.

3. Pico Iyer and Jason Wilson, eds., *The Best American Travel Writing 2004* (Boston: Houghton Mifflin, 2004), xxiii.

camps? Look for patterns, trends, unusual activities, or destinations. All could be the kernel of a travel article.

Ask people about their trips. Most are excited to discuss their life-changing journeys but reluctant to bore acquaintances with the Dread Vacation Snaps or Horrible Home Movies. Talk to people on planes. Talk to your meter reader. Talk to people at the supermarket checkout with a copy of *National Geographic* in their basket. Talk to anyone and everyone.

"All good writers express a form of curiosity, a sense that something is going on out there, something in the air," Roy Peter Clark wrote on Poynter's Web site. The best, he explained, "are explorers, traveling through their communities with a special alertness, connecting seemingly unrelated details into story patterns."[4]

Press Releases

Large companies keep lists of journalists, who then receive press releases (and sometimes even free samples, such as herbal remedies for jet lag or moisturizer designed for convertible drivers). Some PR sheets offer vital tips; others are just hyped-up junk mail. But these lists can be helpful, when casting a wide net for story ideas.

That said, getting onto press lists can be tedious and time-consuming. You need to track down the publicity office, then ring, write, or e-mail, supplying your contact information. Eventually, experienced travel writers land on master lists sold or given to public relations firms, but the process can be slow at the start. Limit efforts to companies that especially intrigue you. Say, if you've always dreamt of an Atlantic crossing, then approach Cunard. Perhaps the cruise line is launching a new luxury ship—the perfect excuse for a travel piece.

Harried staffers sometimes draft short items ("filler") from press releases alone. Avoid unbalanced pieces that echo the corporate party line. At the very least, call for comments (both pro and con, should the topic touch upon any controversy). Wherever possible, seek concrete statistics or experts to verify claims of "increasing numbers" or "a hot new trend." Search the Internet for more candid perspectives. The site

---

4. Roy Peter Clark, *Writing Tool #50: The Writing Process*, Poynter Online (2005), www.poynter.org/content/content_view.asp?id=79244.

TripAdvisor.com compiles guidebook and periodical reviews, alongside user rants and raves. Even fifteen minutes of research can save a story from becoming a puff piece.

Media Kits
Tourism offices, chambers of commerce, and visitor bureaus usually offer media or press kits, containing publicity material, recent articles on the region, leaflets, fact sheets, and sometimes slides or images. Many are happy to provide information via e-mail—or have extensive Web sites that include story ideas. Always identify yourself as a travel writer, and then ask to receive updates.

Countries also have travel promotion bureaus, which aggressively promote their charms. Louise Purwin Zobel, author of *The Travel Writer's Handbook*, advocates crossing out all the adjectives in a brochure, then reading the last page for the facts.[5] Don't let these superlatives infiltrate your text. Scan for generics like "beautiful" and "stunning." Then explain *why*: stretch for more precise, evocative terminology. "Show, don't tell" is the maxim to remember.

Easy to use and glossy, media kits are alluring. However, only one side emerges: the shiny, happy face of officialdom. Promotional material is useful for orientation but should be taken with a grain of salt, like press releases. Never rely on either solely. Apply the same skepticism to brochures gathered beforehand and en route, as well as information from publicity specialists, in-flight publications, and in-house hotel magazines. Glean the key information, then leave the jargon and hyperbole behind.

Press Trip and Tour Traps
Press trips provide many writers with article ideas. Chapter 8 in this book covers press trips in detail. Therefore, the subject will only be touched on here.

Don't copy the itinerary. Such travel articles are a characterless blur of name-dropped locations and activities. Travel writers are not obligated to mention every hotel, restaurant, and service they experienced,

---

5. Louise Purwin Zobel, *The Travel Writer's Handbook 5th Ed.: How to Write and Sell Your Own Travel Experiences* (Chicago: Surrey Books, 2002), 29.

even if they were subsidized. Their first duty is storytelling for the edification and amusement of the readers. Highlight the most compelling material, then banish the rest to sidebars—or from the piece entirely.

The audience enjoys a selective, vibrant tale far more. The publication retains its credibility, the writer his or her reputation. Ultimately, such an article may inspire more tourists, benefiting the local economy as a whole. Should guilt prompt a recap, stop and consider: some PR specialists admit a 50 percent success rate. Only half the writers on any given press trip publish *anything* as a result. So feel free to pick and choose, editing the experience.

Some British papers solve this dilemma—and that of accountability—with a small fact box stating, "The writer was hosted by this airline and these companies." The article might not even discuss its patrons—or could even criticize them. These editors prefer the work of veteran travel journalists—trusted to judge fairly a complimentary trip—over that of wealthy (but novice) moonlighters. Neither system is ideal, but the U.K. trend at least recognizes that writers earning $500–$1,000 per piece, without expenses, cannot spend $5,000–$10,000 on research. It errs on the side of polished prose by specialists, which many believe benefits the reader more.

Online Options

The array of resources online can grow bewildering. The average tourist spends ten hours surfing through these vast Web portals and online guides; imagine how much time a research-conscientious writer could waste. The Web is a powerful tool, used correctly, but don't get lost in cyberspace.

Sites like Mediakitty, TravMedia, and Travelwriters.com offer news and bulletin boards, though other writers are tapping these same sources, so the scoops are far from exclusive. Most services require registration and clutter your inbox, which can be distracting. List serves often provide better peer contacts and leads, as well as blogs such as Jen Leo's www.writtenroad.com and Carl Parkes' www.travelwriters.blogspot.com.

"Travelers are going online to get the real skinny from those who have gone before them," announced the *Wall Street Journal* in March 2005.[6] "Who says it's a lonely planet?" asked the next month's issue of

National Geographic Traveler, which devoted several pages to "burgeoning online communities."[7] Indeed, user-written sites—such as VirtualTourist.com, TripAdvisor.com, WikiTravel.org, and BootsnAll.com—contain a wealth of tips. They also contain trash: page after page of amateur observations, inaccurate facts, and bungled-holiday horror stories. Dip into these storehouses by all means, but focus more energy on credible sources. Good, free archives include MSNBC; Thisistravel.co.uk, affiliated with England's *Daily Mail*; and Concierge.com, which recycles material from Fodors and various glossy American magazines.

Internet bulletin boards may be most useful for networking. "A sure way to gain a true picture of a place is to meet a family and share a meal with them," instructed L. Peat O'Neil in *Travel Writing: A Guide to Research, Writing and Selling*.[8] Clubs, hobbies, religious groups, schools, and professional associations are also worth approaching, along with sister-city organizations.

Read Widely

Business and trade publications prove useful by highlighting projects in development. Monitor local newspapers, as many publish free online editions now. For example, the headline "Oliver Stone's Alexander Film Brings Jobs to Malta" could prompt an article like *Condé Nast Traveler*'s "Alexander's Cradle: An epic movie about Alexander the Great is on the way. G.Y. Dryansky goes to Alexander's homeland, Greek Macedonia, and finds an uncrowded idyll."[9] The trick is to stay ahead of the trend.

Study your target publications. What sort of articles do they favor and what tone? Observe the advertisements, carefully designed for that newspaper or magazine. What do they tell you about the readers? What stories have been covered recently? What departments might be on the lookout for short items? Don't forget to examine the masthead—the

---

6. Vauhini Vara, "Notes From Nowhere," *Wall Street Journal*, Technology, March 21, 2005, www.wsj.com.

7. Margaret Loftus, "Insider Connections," *National Geographic Traveler*, Smart Traveler, vol. 22, no. 2 (May 2005): 14.

8. L. Peat O'Neil, *Travel Writing* (Cincinnati: Writer's Digest Books, 2000), 33.

9. G.Y. Dryansky, "Alexander's Cradle," *Condé Nast Traveler*, vol. 39, no. 9 (September 2004): 182.

list of editors and staff members, along with contact details—typically found in the front pages. You may wish to transfer these details to a special notebook, contact file, or searchable database.

Read outside your tastes. Don't limit yourself to publications you would necessarily select for pleasure. Be voracious. Haunt the reading room of the local library. Scrutinize magazines in the waiting rooms of doctors and dentists. Ask friends and family to save old issues. Scrounge through thrift stores and flea markets. Trawl through Internet archives. Any publication could provide a superb story idea—or a potential market.

Some publications send free sample copies on request—or for a small fee. *The Writer's Market* and *Writer's Handbook* often indicate which companies are agreeable about this. And, if all else fails, whip out your wallet at the newsstand. Research expenses could be tax-deductible.

RESEARCH

Samuel Johnson once said, "Man must bring knowledge with him, if he would bring home knowledge." So too, the best travel writers research exhaustively before leaving on assignment. They already know the top three ice cream shops in Rome, temple etiquette in Thailand, and the best camping spot in Big Sur. Their discovery starts where the guidebooks leave off, taking readers that much farther into an area's heart.

Immerse yourself in the destination. Pore over maps. Ransack through not one—but many—guides. Search the Web. Read travel writing and fiction set there. Watch films. Dissect the local paper. Request media kits from the tourist office, chamber of commerce, or visitor's bureau. Set up interviews with key figures. Talk to your friends and acquaintances. In short, be an expert before departure.

Some travel writers compile their own "guidebooks," snippets culled from different sources, then photocopied or printed with large margins. They then scrawl notes onto the preliminary research. While composing, it's easier to locate material this way, rather then constantly flipping through a scribbled notebook.

Travel writers write not just with their hands, but with their legs, according to popular wisdom. "Reporters, like wolves, live by their paws," is another version of the maxim. Ian Frazier used the latter to remind colleagues that "reporting is a collaboration between mind and motion," in *The Best of American Travel Writing 2003*. "When the mind is dull and out of ideas, extra legwork can provide inspiring discoveries, and when the legwork is lazy, the mind can disguise that with embellishments added later."[10]

Indeed, post-trip data mining can illuminate a weak piece but never compares with going prepared. Research is essential, so knuckle down before traveling, when it's of use to you, as well as to readers.

Travel Writing and Literature

Digest the "classic" writers on a region, before setting out or, better yet, bring along a volume, if your luggage isn't too weighty. (Reading on site is fantastically evocative.) Often story ideas will lurk here, such as "Cannery Row: Seventy Years Later" or "Rediscovering Norman Douglas' Old Calabria."

Travelogues of a bygone era can add magnificent color. Keep an eye out for collections of travel writing, which eliminate a lot of library work. Quote the authors' observations, opinions, and bon mots. Other times, just digest the material and reuse it, especially quirky little historical facts. Here are a few examples:

> *1. Kirkudbright, Scotland: Even the town's downsides—like the sprawling mud flats left by intense tides—were turned to good advantage by these bohemians. Lord Cockburn didn't find it quite so appealing, however, during his 1844 visit. "The painters don't dislike this substance, which they aren't required to touch. It is not unpicturesque, of a leaden grey colour, very shiny in the sun even silvery in appearance; utterly solitary, except to flocks of long-billed and long red-legged sea birds."*
>
> *Cockburn, less enchanted with the muck, considered it "a world of sleech . . . a town surrounded by a lake of bird-lime." Yet that didn't stop him from coining the "Venice of Scotland" tag and admiring its charms. "I doubt if there is a more picturesque country town in Scotland. Small, clean, silent, and respectable, it seems*

---

10. Ian Frazier and Jason Wilson, eds., *The Best American Travel Writing 2003* (Boston: Houghton Mifflin, 2003), xix.

the type of place to which decent characters and moderate purses would retire for quiet comfort," he wrote in Circuit Journeys.[11]

2. Paphos, Cyprus: Fertility cults have a way of blossoming again, though. Lawrence Durrell hinted at pagan practices in his classic 1957 travelogue, Bitter Lemons of Cyprus. *"The youths of Paphos still anoint the stones of the temple with oil and almond-water on a certain night of the year, while women leave their rings and fragments of their petticoats as ex votos against barrenness." Today, no offerings brighten the shattered ruins. The site and its two-room museum are intriguing, but mainly for hard-core archaeology buffs (£0.75; Tel: 26.432.180; open daily 09:00–17:00).*[12]

3. Lefkada, Greece: The area has other nebulous claims to Homeric fame. Travel writer Tim Severin placed Scylla's lair on a steep eastern slope and the sucking whirlpool Charybdis in the narrow straight below. Italians would dispute this, preferring to imagine the monsters in the Strait of Messina. Lefkada did play a role in the epic, however. Laertes, Odysseus' father, gave the island to Penelope's family to seal the marriage.[13]

Seek out "postcard facts," snippets of history outstanding for their vividness or oddity. Which of the following would you rather send (or receive)?

"Wish you were here. The bay is really blue and the water's clean, nice for swimming. But a fisherman unloaded his nets near our restaurant on the dock last night. Stinky!"

---

11. Amanda Castleman, "Venice of Scotland," *Road and Travel*, July 2003, www.roadandtravel.com/travel%20directory/Scotland/kirkcudbright.htm.

12. Amanda Castleman, "Venus in a Half Shell," *Road and Travel*, February 2003, www.roadandtravel.com/travel%20directory/Cyprus/rr/aphrodite.htm.

13. Amanda Castleman, "Lefkada's alchemy: Turning scrap metal into gold," *Athens News*, May 25, 2003: A24.

> *"Kefalonia's wild, full of intense 'island characters,' as the Greeks say. During WWII, the Orthodox bishop told the Nazis they couldn't deport a single Jew, unless they took him first. His ultimatum worked—amazing! Today we swam off Scorpio, the Onassis family's private island (where Jackie was snapped topless). We didn't see any paparazzi in boats though."*

Susan Spano summed it up best: "Aspiring travel writers are only as good as what they read, which is why they need to do so widely and well," she wrote in "So You Want to Be a Travel Writer," a 2005 *Los Angeles Times* article.[14] "Foraging through literature and history provides themes and details beyond those rehearsed by every guidebook on the shelf. It suggests uncommon subjects for stories and magically makes your writing better."

Guidebooks

Skim three or four guidebooks before a major trip. Each writer or team had a different target audience, tone, and take on the region. Reading several volumes helps patch together a fuller picture of the area. This also eliminates the risk of following too closely in one author's footsteps.

Keep costs down by scrounging old copies at rummage sales, thrift stores, and library clear-outs. Don't feel compelled to stick to the big names though. Some of the best information can be gleaned from quirky local books bought on the road. Try to set aside money—and luggage space—to acquire a volume or two. Some writers even pre-order museum and archaeology site guides, as well as airline magazines, to reduce baggage and hassle.

Guidebooks sometimes lift material from each other: the same tired restaurants with barely rephrased reviews or identical inaccurate descriptions of a small town. Remember these books are not the font of all knowledge. In some cases, a stressed-out, inexperienced author may have covered too much unfamiliar ground too quickly. So double-check information wherever possible.

---

14. Susan Spano, "So You Want to Be a Travel Writer?" *Los Angeles Times*, May 22, 2005: L.7.

SOURCING FROM THE NEWS AND THE TRADE PRESS— JAMES POYNTER

Using your eyes and ears, you can get excellent ideas for travel writing stories. Your television and newspaper are unending sources of good articles. And, even better is a subscription to *Travel Weekly*.

HOME-BASED MEDIA

Getting story ideas is as easy as watching television or reading the daily newspaper. Upcoming events in sports, politics, the arts, and other areas of interest provide story ideas. The next Olympics is always a good travel story. A special event in the arts often offers a good travel writing opportunity. For example, the formal dances in Vienna at New Years or the opening of the opera season in any of several European countries provide travel writing opportunities many newspaper and magazine travel editors love. And don't forget the travel opportunities that open up when a new country is established from the merging of two or more countries or when there is a major change of government in a country. These news events make people interested in learning more, and they present an opening for a travel article.

THE TRADE PRESS

The trade press also provides a constant flow of travel article ideas. There are many trade publications in the travel industry, and each one of them offers story ideas that can be developed for travel publications read by members of the general public. However, *Travel Weekly* is the publication read by almost everybody who works in the travel industry. Originally, it was meant for travel agents, but increasingly it is read by people working for airlines, cruise lines, hotels, resorts, car rental companies, business travel managers, and, yes, travel writers. A glance at the headlines of just about any issue of *Travel Weekly* will give a travel writer story ideas that will sell—and often sell well. Has a cruise line announced that it is building what will be the largest cruise ship afloat? You can be sure that you will see the announcement in *Travel Weekly* well before the cruise magazines sold in the local grocery store carry an article about it. And why shouldn't you be the travel writer who wrote the article that will ultimately appear in the magazine on your grocer's shelf? Is there a new resort golf course being built that everyone will want to play? *Travel Weekly* will tell you about it well enough in advance that you can contact the travel editor of any one of the golf-oriented magazines and convince them to let you write an article about it for their publication. Join the many travel writers who subscribe to *Travel Weekly*, and you, too, will have an unending supply of good travel article ideas. To subscribe, contact the magazine's customer service office at (800) 446-6551 (phone) or (303) 470-4280 (fax).

ON-SITE—ONE OF THE BEST IDEA SOURCES

All of the story-idea generating suggestions in this chapter are good ones, but one of the best travel writing story-idea sources is the destination itself. As you journey through the city or country about which you are writing, you will be pleasantly surprised to find one good story idea after another coming to you. It will be important to have a way of recording these ideas, and a travel journal is one of the best places in which to write them down. In the next chapter, Twila Papay discusses travel journals in detail. And, of course, you will need to get to the travel writing story-idea generating destination—and either get there at no cost or at a low cost. In chapter 8, Katherine Lemmon details how to get a press trip and how to take maximum advantage of it once you are invited to participate.

End-of-Chapter Questions

1. According to Rumbaugh, as a travel writer, what must you first understand in writing?

2. Rumbaugh identifies two tracks for travel writers. Track one includes journaling, poetry, observation, sensory experiences, and the art of storytelling. What is included in the other track?

3. Does Rumbaugh maintain that if your travel article idea is the destination, your travel writing article is not a story?

4. If a travel writer finds an editor's requirements too cumbersome and stifling of creativity as a writer, what alternative approach can be taken?

5. Why might a travel writer want to keep updated on issues of technology?

6. According to Castleman, what broad term ranges from recounting an extraordinary experience to exploring a current controversy or revisiting a historical landmark?

7. What is the oldest advice in the trade?

8. Is it easy and fast for a travel writer to get on master press lists?

9. What does the small fact box in some British papers state regarding writers of travel articles?

10. What publication is read by almost everybody who works in the travel industry?

WRITING ASSIGNMENT SIX
SELECTING ARTICLE IDEAS

Assignment Introduction

   One of the biggest concerns for those new to travel writing is how to come up with article ideas that will sell. Many experienced travel writers find that they have so many good ideas, they cannot pump out the articles fast enough. Training yourself to always be on the lookout for good travel article ideas takes some effort. However, this assignment will get you started.

Assignment Activity

Purchase two small spiral notepads from an office supply store or a drugstore. They should be small enough to fit in your pocket or purse. Consider one of these pads to be your travel article idea book. The other pad will be your first travel journal which you will use in completing writing assignment seven. Carry your travel article idea book with you. For a week each time you watch the news on television or listen to it on the radio, listen for a travel article idea. Visit your library sometime during the week. Review some of the national newspapers, and ask if your library subscribes to *Travel Weekly* or one of the other travel industry publications. If so, go through some of the more recent issues, and ask yourself if there is something that you could write about for the

Selecting and Narrowing Travel Article Ideas

consumer press, i.e., local newspapers or a regional or national consumer-oriented magazine.

Try to come up with ten article ideas. If you have more than ten, that is even better. At the end of the week, identify your ten best ideas, and write down a working article title on each of the following lines. Try to keep your working title to not more than seven words. If you can narrow it down to three to five words, that will be even better.

Ten Travel Article Ideas

1. _____
2. _____
3. _____
4. _____
5. _____
6. _____
7. _____
8. _____
9. _____
10. _____

Final Step: Add your name to the Instructor Comment Sheet for Writing Assignment Six in appendix 5 and staple it to this sheet on which you have listed ten travel article ideas. Then turn in these two sheets to your professor.

TWILA PAPAY, professor of English and writing, has taught travel writing to a range of Rollins College students since 1993. An avid traveler, she spent 1992 exploring South America and Asia. Her 1999 sabbatical took her around much of Africa, where she participated in writing center development at the University of the Western Cape and photographed more animals up close than she had envisioned in her wildest safari dreams. In spring 2006, she returned to Australia for sabbatical travel and research. Among her more recent publications and presentations on writing, teaching, writing centers, and creative nonfiction are a chapter on the pedagogy of travel writing, a major article on South African writing centers, a keynote address on African peer-tutoring models, six public readings on her African journeys, and a number of smaller articles and conference presentations on her travels. Among her awards are several travel grants and a National Conference on Peer Tutoring in Writing Award (1998) in recognition of outstanding service to writing centers and collaborative learning.

CHAPTER 7

Your Travel Journal— The Tool for En Route and Destination Pieces

Twila Papay

Surreal
It was all too surreal. So there I sat, recalling once again those men who stood the ground where I rested, and their circumstances during the war. Shot by shot, I envisioned another figure, another man down, another life lost.

When student Dana Leddy wrote in her journal this reaction to having crawled through the tunnels of Cu Chi used by Vietnamese fighting against Americans, she was practicing a fresh level of sensibility, reading the place and the circumstance with a new and broader sense of conflict, taking into consideration both Vietnamese and American perspectives. This was not, of course, what she recorded at the time—hasty field notes jotted in a tattered notebook or e-mails sent back home days later. No, this more troubled comprehension of her journey emerged from thoughtful reflection over three months in a travel writing course the term after she returned from her Semester at Sea program. You can follow Dana's progress in her musings through several passages quoted in this chapter. And you will meet five other journal writers confronting the complexities of their journeys.

THE TRAVEL WRITER'S FIRST RECOURSE

What is the nature of travel journals? How can they serve us? This chapter will help you figure out how to use the journal not only to capture the details but also to explore the multiple dimensions of your experience, to figure out the deeper meanings of your journeys, and perhaps to give you ideas for travel articles.

A journal is the travel writer's first recourse for recording facts and exploring impressions. It is also a testing ground for ideas in process. But a journal only works if you are willing to press into dangerous territory, challenging your own initial impressions, seeking bolder and deeper perspectives. It demands a level of honesty that might raise a sense of your own vulnerability as traveler and narrator of the journey. Try the journal approaches introduced in this chapter to push your thinking deeper and to force yourself to raise tough questions.

GATHERING YOUR RESOURCES

Before the published article, before the drafts, before the proposal, before the very idea, lies a journey that surely began with a journal. Some travel writers develop a journal for the pure pleasure of it . . . to consider new ideas, to remember special people, to explore the mystery and majesty of place. Others conscientiously keep a journal to capture the vitality of the journey in vivid images and remembered conversations that will serve as the primary resource for articles to come. The more vibrant your depictions, the deeper your reflections will be. Your journal can serve not only as a memento but also as the center of ideas

> **The Physical Journal**
>
> Choosing the form of your journal in advance is important. If you can take your computer along, it will make writing (and storing what you write) much easier, though you must be certain your equipment is compatible with your destination. And you can mail home a backup disk or e-mail a copy of your journal entries from time to time. Still, you will want a pocket-sized notepad for jottings along the way and a notebook to write in when the computer is inaccessible. (At TigerTops in Nepal, I wrote until the battery was exhausted each evening, then went into the cooking tent where power was available each afternoon to complete my entry while the battery recharged.)
>
> If you opt to do all your writing by hand, choose lightweight but sturdy notebooks and good pens to be certain you can decipher what you wrote in haste. Hold on to itineraries and notes made along the way, by storing them in either a secured section of your notebook or a closed pocket of your luggage.
>
> Some writers like to find a physical way of layering writing, interweaving reflection with recorded details in different fonts, or dividing each page vertically to accommodate both. (Think about this carefully in advance. Separating logs of events from journals of commentary sometimes forces you to spend hours integrating the two in the end. You may find that a printed itinerary with space for jottings will allow you to preserve surface details without compromising the focus of your journal.)

for writing proposals and as the source of details that will bring your final published article to life on the page.

For travel writers, the journal frequently begins before the journey. If you are taking your computer along, it's easy to record details from reading and research, to note the questions you'd like to answer as well as the sights you'd like to see along the way. On Komodo Island I wished

I had recorded in advance the enormous size of Komodo dragons, their astounding speed, and the numbers one is likely to encounter. All of this information would have woven itself more naturally into my journal had I not had to wait several months to reassemble it. And I would have agonized far less over whether a reader would be likely to believe what I wrote.

Recording Preparations

Reading and recording is a natural entrée into travel. And documenting your sources can save hours of irritating rereading as you try to develop your piece back home. As a good reporter, you will be able to compare expectation and reality and advise your reader of where the research falls short or the promises of grandeur are overstated. Of course, if you are not taking your computer along, then the problem of carrying the record with you becomes more difficult. If you are taking a guidebook, you might annotate it with some key information you'll want to remember, knowing the full text has already been indexed back home. (And don't forget to record some of the commonplaces of the journey, such as a list of what you packed to take along; this could be useful for your readers when they are preparing for similar travel, especially if you review it later and note what you should have left behind.)

Some travelers prefer a more relaxed approach, learning little before the journey and trusting a blank slate of the mind to absorb the nuances of experience. If you choose this approach, be aware that you may miss sites and, more importantly, people who could enrich your journey and challenge your first impressions. You may be limited to standard tourist fare rather than sampling the rich diversity of the lived life of a place you may not know how to explore. Should you find yourself in this situation, though, you can at least improve your chances for discovery by expecting the unexpected, turning to local people as frequently as possible, and recording in your journal the questions you have not been able to answer, the kinds of information you will want to gather when you return. One warning: this after-the-fact research may leave you yearning for another journey to visit the undiscovered land.

Finally, you can greatly enrich your journal by recording expectations on the eve of the journey, capturing your feelings about the planning and the complexity of what you may encounter. Such thoughts may be grandiose or melancholy, but even the most pedestrian recounting will help you examine the truths of the journey in the face of your original vision. Here, for example, is a journal passage written as I awoke on a plane headed for five months of travel in Africa:

> *The truth is, Africa scares me. I know the travel will be hard, the days grueling, my arthritic knee seriously stressed. My work at the University of the Western Cape is troubling, too. So much to learn, to exchange—and I so inept at communication. Actually, I am most myself at home in my head, in conversation with my dear husband, or in quiet reflection on earthly wonders and the hope that we humans can learn at least to leave each other alone, if not to stop the hatred. And here I am—lone reporter streaking toward the dawn of all we are, trying to be honest with myself and true to all those who have brought me here—to this moment—poised on the cusp of all that went before—the preparation for the mystery and wonder of the moment.*
>
> *And all those personal issues—how they fade in the face of Africa! Dawn of consciousness, cradle of life, home of lost cultures and arrogant atrocities, a continent of stereotypes nestled in a sea of uncertainty, a vast expanse of veldt and savannah, desert and jungle, poverty and greed, sorrow and wonder. Yes, I've headed toward putting some faces on Africa. But what face, I wonder, will Africa put on me? Who will the woman be who returns from this curious adventure? Oh, Africa scares me all right. Tantalizes too. Five months from now, how will the globe be changed? And my perceptions of it?*

This entry was quite different from the one I tried to piece together the day after my return, weary but already missing a continent I'd come so quickly to love. Afterthoughts being as important as initial expectations, it is useful to capture both before they fade. If you are fortunate, you may find a series of themes to echo through the pieces you create upon your return.

Field Notes and Logs

Sometimes the moment overwhelms the writing, or circumstances prevent it, or we have to make a choice. ("Shall I write or watch? Participate or snap another photo?") At a performance or in a pub, hiking up Mount Kenya, or studying sand paintings in Australia's Kakadu, real writing is trumped by the adventure. But such moments are fraught with detail and emotion, color and scent, and sometimes whirlwind action. Before the journal, we capture what we can in field notes. A supply of pocket notepads can preserve the essence, and a pile of details will help to recreate the journey.

Here, for example, are some field notes I jotted in a tiny hotel notepad as we rode off just after dawn on safari from Savuti Elephant Camp in Botswana:

> *Rosy sunrise glow melting into soft yellow. Lion paw prints in soft sand. Smell of wood fires. Impala, zebra droppings, Senegal coucal. 2 lilac-breasted rollers. Oh, another, 7 pastel shades caught in the sun. Lion prints, then elephant's. Looking for the lion. There! Beside the road lying close in the grass. 10 yards away at most. He pops up out of the cool grass, walks a bit and roars! Sniffing—and there's the female, strolling past, turning to look back at him. He sniffs her from behind, confirms her readiness. She turns, but he's on her. Rolling in grass too tall for us to see. He mounts. Minutes passing. And a roar as he leaps away. Her purr, so LOUD! She's lying down again, he standing by her. Then marks his territory. Gazes down at her, lies down facing her. (Lions can mate every 45 minutes, 3-4 days, we're told.) They walk further through grass along the road. Mate again, and again, then roar and purr! And low deep growls. They lie down in the grass and disappear! 7:20 am.*

"With a Purr and a Roar" I called the journal entry I later wrote, which emerged from further musings on this extraordinary morning. But the moment arises for me from those field notes, kept by chance, as I generally dispose of the rough notes after transposing them into a log, making space in my luggage for writing yet to come.

Field notes are meant to capture the details, but they are jagged, full of holes, lacking the shaping into meaning the traveler offers through repeated reflection on the journey's experience. Too often they are hard to interpret in retrospect, offering up moments later lost in the totality of the adventure. When we are lucky, though, they hold flashes of insight that suggest a theme, like my focus on the astounding sounds of two lions mating ten feet away from our safari vehicle.

To preserve as much as you can from your travel experience, record the field notes, but do not rely on them over time. It is best to transpose them as quickly as possible into a log where you try to capture the nuance underlying the notes you tossed off in haste. Again, this will take less time than a full journal entry and can usually be accomplished later the same day, while the memories are fresh.

Here's a moment with a leopard, transposed into a log in the gray hours of dawn the morning after, while we waited for our safari driver to pick us up at camp in the Masaai Mara:

> *"The music of Swahili,"* Stephen had spoken of, the love of Kenyans for their land and their language. Certainly he was as excited as we were over the lions—and the leopard.
>
> The end of night sounds we hear as we drive into rocky terrain. With effort we see Stephen's leopard, muted against the steep slopes of black volcanic rock. Quiet she stands, alert, tail tip waving slightly. As she sees zebra moving on the hillside just above, she strolls across loose rocks and drops into a small crevice of cool mossiness between gray-black rocks. She yawns, stretches, washes her paws, lies quiet. Walks a bit, washes her face, lies down. She prefers this rocky slope, where there are fewer flies than in the open.
>
> *"Isn't she beautiful,"* murmurs Stephen. *"She looks like the rocks."* As she settles in, he adds, *"Now we say to her, 'Lala salama, sleep well.'"*
>
> She ripples her muscles; flies pass; zebras wake her for us, but she sleeps again. For forty-five minutes we watch her, a golden-black cat from the top, all white and black underneath, spots getting larger the further back from her face. Such long footpads. Gradual movements keep us watchful. She turns her soft golden eyes in our direction, white whiskers thick as quills. Getting up, she stretches, moves a few yards. As she strolls down toward us, we move the vehicle,

watching her pose on rocks until . . . she walks right up to us! Joe starts to close the window, but Stephen stops him with a gesture. Regally she strolls past us and down to a new rocky post. Smells a hollow within it, then stretches out again. In time she heads on down.

"It was worth waiting, no?" smiles Stephen to our companions, who had objected to not moving on after the first photos. "We call her Zawadi. (*This means* present, *or* gift.) *Her mother was also rather tame and hunted here."*

Fuller than rough field notes, the log suggests a wider picture, as when I recorded Stephen's musings about his people's love of the land, then illustrated that with his own tenderness over the leopard. Later we saw a cheetah carrying off a newly killed baby reedbuck to feed her cubs. "The reedbuck will miss her baby tonight," Stephen sighed, his empathy extending both directions. Nature's acceptance, but with no hardness of heart, was a theme for consideration in the journal later on.

Logs are also more valuable than field notes if you must delay your journal writing for more than a few days. Just a few hours' remove from the events will offer a perspective and give you the chance to draw connections that will be useful as you begin to mull over the focus of the

■ The Leopard Zawadi (The Gift), *Twila Yates Papay, Masaai Mara, Kenya, February 1999.*

journal entry you intend to write. And logs are occasionally more useful than journal entries as you seek out particular details to include in your more formal writing for an audience. Raw details still emerge from the page, to be combined in new ways as you consider larger segments of your journey. If I were writing a piece on the big cats of the Masaai Mara, for example, I could draw on the details with Stephen and contrast them to what we observed later with other drivers, whose perspectives were rather different. Unlike field notes, then, logs can both begin the process of reflection and retain an immediacy sometimes lost in the journal that follows.

Local Materials

While you are traveling, it will be worth your while as a writer to gather as much local material as you can. Sometimes the local information can be conveniently woven into your field notes or log each day, then incorporated into the pages of the journal you are shaping as you go.

This is certainly the case with information you pick up from escorts and guides, curators and cab drivers, lecturers and gurus. Record everything you hear along the way, particularly as it shades your interpretation of events and places. (And record it *quickly*, before you lose the details!)

Just as important are your conversations with local people, who provide not only your sense of the place but also your means of interpreting political and sociological events. Even local television and radio are useful in this regard, perhaps offering both official governmental views and alternatives from newscasters and comedians. (Imagine trying to understand the complexity of American politics without listening to the wide range of cultural and political commentators. Some travel writers even insist that playing local radio as we drive across the United States is the most efficient way to understand how opinions shift and cultural values vary.) You will want to record whatever affects your thinking.

Books and documents picked up at information centers and cultural locales also help shape our understanding. Select those with detailed information you may need for developing your travel piece, like the titles of artworks you will want to recall or descriptions of monuments, fishing piers, and geological wonders. And, of course, select those that are light enough for your luggage. Similarly, you may learn a great deal from local newspapers, even if your translations are rudimentary. While you will not have the space to save newspapers, don't forget to clip out key articles and photographs to enclose in your log. (When Dana read a draft of this chapter, she advised: "Hold on to tickets, pamphlets, anything you receive; just holding them in front of you as you write can evoke deep emotions. Even my plane ticket to India called to mind complex reflections.")

Another local source of information is postcards, particularly where photos are hard to take or not permitted. Look carefully at locally designed postcards, as they offer clues to how people of a given region may perceive their surroundings. Japanese postcards of Mount Fuji, for example, are more likely to show the famous mountain shrouded in mist, while American photographers prefer the clearness of a blue sky. Investigating the philosophy behind this choice will offer you a snapshot of Japanese thinking. Looking at locally designed postcards may help you see Hindu shrines from a new perspective as well. Or look at local renditions of the Great Wall of China ("the dragon") before you frame photographs of your own. Some travelers even arrange in advance to send postcards to friends who will save them to inform the later writing.

All of this local information should find its way into your journal, first as rich details and compelling facts, later as the source of new perspectives and the means of looking beneath the surface. Some of your material may well be scrawled on napkins or bus schedules as you collect it, but you will need to get it in coherent form so that you'll be able to use it later on. You may want to dedicate part of your log to conversations and scraps of overheard dialogues, news accounts, and trivia. Decide in advance how you want to gather and use your local materials, so that you can select only the most essential to bring back home.

Gathering resources and recording a wide range of materials is essential for the serious travel writer. But as you do so, you will want to be thinking of the more complex and reflective journal entries to come. It is best to write on the road, letting experiences soak together in your unconscious, then teasing out the threads as you make meaning out of the journey. What you write in late evening sessions or over a pot of tea the next morning may well need to be refined and tightened on your return. Or you may find yourself constructing the actual journal entries back home. Either way, following are some methods of journaling to help you focus and enrich your understanding of the journey.

> **Titling Your Entries**
>
> Now that you are ready to move beyond the gathering of details and into the making of complex meanings, you will need to focus your thinking. One way to do this is to choose a tentative title for each journal entry. (Remember that a *title* is not a *topic* but rather an evocative phrase intended to capture your reader's attention and hint at what is to come.) Give some thought to the journal entry for a day or two before you write it. Think about what you want to capture and how experiences you are assembling speak to each other. If you are writing en route, consider the piece while you are on the train or bus, over a meal, or at the airport. If you are writing the next level of journal entry back home, consider the idea while you exercise or walk about campus or head off to work. Sleep on it if you have a chance. When a title suggests itself, jot it down. You may not even understand its significance until you finish the piece. (And you can always change it later.)

Perhaps the hardest part of travel writing is rendering another place and time in the crystal clarity with which you first saw it and later comprehended the meaning of that moment. Try the journal types below to recapture the details and begin to build connections among your observations.

Recollections and Memory Wells

A simple form of journaling is a trip into the past, dipping into the well of memory to recover traveling you've done. You may decide to remake old travel logs, to retrieve vanishing memories, or to recall and recreate places you've been and people you've seen. Record the *stories* of a real journey, using some of the strategies you've enjoyed in your own reading. Try to dig deep into the material, reliving and revitalizing. In short, use the details of the story to comprehend in some new way the journeys fast slipping out of reach. To gather the story together, try using vivid sensual images, snatches of dialogue, descriptions of objects and treasured artifacts as well as anecdotes to render your travel days real to the reader. Consider whether you are conveying your own rich and intuitive comprehension of the place. By reflecting and examining the meanings behind the experiences, you will be able to deepen your own comprehension.

Vanessa Sain sought just such comprehension when she wrote the details of her visit to New York City in November of 2001. "I couldn't understand why the view [at Ground Zero] was blocked. When I tiptoed onto something for a better look, a policeman yelled at me. I remember thinking, 'This is *my* country; I should be able to look if I want to.' But afterwards I read about the blocked view and awful stench. All the bodies had not been discovered, and body parts still had to be picked up. Riding away in the cab, I still couldn't grasp the enormity. How many deaths? I couldn't remember. But it was such a small space in reality for so many deaths." In recreating the details of that horrific journey, Vanessa sought to understand both why her younger self had felt offended by the police officer, and why she was left with such a jolting sense of personal loss. As the details rose to a more mature consciousness, she was able to see herself actually processing the realization of death on a scale she had not previously comprehended.

Like Vanessa, you might like to try some question pieces. Why do you travel? How? What feelings did a particular experience evoke? Experiment with local journeys as well, traveling to nearby locales previously unknown to you. What discoveries can you make by traveling alone? What ideas or people have you not previously encountered? As Vanessa notes in a later piece, "If travel is really intended to overcome ignorance, then anywhere should work. It is important to become the conscious 24-7 traveler, always investigating differences, abandoning preconceived notions."

Character Commentaries

Recreate some fascinating or typical or bewildering people you've met in your travels. Focus on a few visual images; sounds and voices; inexplicable, strangely familiar, or delightfully surprising actions. Recreate a character you knew well or one you only observed for a few minutes. Samantha Lopez recalled Fannie Casale, "a small, fragile, eighty-nine-year-young woman with the largest toothless smile I have ever seen," not the denizen of a Third World country, but a "Meals on Wheels" recipient living with dignity in a shabby trailer in Florida. "I wanted to be shocked by the primitive plumbing or the sight of cockroaches on the wall, but it didn't happen that way. Having been misled all my life by exteriors," she reflected, "I was astounded when my initial fears over safety were overwhelmed by the discovery of humility and love."

Let the reader see your struggle for acceptance. Show Korean children surrounding you, a busload of tourists in Paris, bicycling business people in Shanghai, the train station waiting room in Madrid, the overcrowded Austrian hostel. Bring the characters of an alien culture to life. See if the choices you make and the language you use can reflect the commentary as you shape an attitude as well as a vision. Figure out your reaction . . . and its cause.

This was Christie Jones's motivation for writing of a homeless man in Oviedo, Spain. "When do we realize that we aren't the only ones in the room?" she mused, reflecting on how focused she was on herself, a fact she believed her travels evinced. For weeks she had passed Manuelo on a stoop, looking away nervously when he smiled. When her friends spoke with him in her presence, he asked why she had never said hello. And he told her of the new baby down the street, an elderly couple's romance, the lives of people he cherished. "What's the use of language," she wondered, "if I never inquire what the rest of the world is thinking about? Why do I pretend I have the room to myself?"

Reader Responses

No one writes in a vacuum, least of all the travel writer. In these entries, respond to the writing of others. What do you like? What bothers you? What can you learn from a given writer? Read a range of travel writing to find how your work will fit the frames of the genre. Try reading the fiction of your destination. Another way of understanding the culture, reading will immerse you in local ways of thinking. It may also suggest new topics of conversation, particularly if you ask your local contacts to recommend some reading for you. What do *they* enjoy reading? What represents their country, their culture, their values? Then write about their perspectives—and yours. How do your readings broaden your understanding of the *place*?

Dialogues, Descriptions, Recreations
Good travel writing demands the effective recreation of people and place. Use your journal to render the dialogues, descriptions, and memories of your journey. You may want to try some meditative reflection exercises to call forth the necessary details. Sit in a quiet, comfortable place. Try to relax your body and then your mind. Slip slowly back into the moment you wish to render. Relive it for as long as you can retain your focus. (If you are familiar with guided meditation exercises, try one.) Now you are ready to write.

Use all your senses to situate the reader in the scene. Let us know the time, the place, the reason for the journey. Call upon our sensibilities to experience your lived moments in another time and place. Let us perceive what is distinctive, what startled and delighted you. But don't spend a lot of words *explaining* it. Give us the details of the moment, scents and sounds, snatches of conversation, what you absorbed and how it elicited your response. Notice how readily in just a single sentence Dana calls us to the moment as she walks hesitantly through Fung Tao: "Between kids grabbing onto my arms for money and walking barefoot in pure urine, and the Vietnamese bathing themselves on the streets in brown water, I now see I was sick with shock, not the food I blamed for my queasy feelings." Try, then, to bring the place and the people to life as they slowly arose or burst quickly upon your own consciousness.

EXPLORING THE ETHICS OF YOUR JOURNEY
Every journey engages us in choices and assumptions that may challenge our values. Your reader will want to experience how the practice of travel enlarged your frame of reference, deepened your understanding, or offered a new perspective. Try to explore this new thinking in reflective journal entries.

Values, Quests, and Explorations
In these entries, look deep into the meaning beneath your travels. Why did you go? What did you seek? What surprises awaited you? Was your

quest successful? Consider Vanessa Sain's musing on the purpose of the journey: "Does my family really travel at all? Our idea of a vacation is lying by a pool and thinking of nothing. My own favorite trip is to the mall about four hours away. Why do we do this? [I want] to become a more thoughtful traveler, to turn hatred into understanding. However, this definitely doesn't happen at Bloomingdale's checkout where I've just bought my new perfume." Note how readily she moves from the facts of her family vacation to the deeper question of the values she is trying to shape.

Other questions may follow from such musing. Is adventure external . . . or internal? Did you get something different from what you bargained for? Try to discover your internal journeys. As Dana concluded in one entry, "India allowed me to clarify my thoughts and emotions, my real values, all I had taken for granted in the rich life with which I am blessed. It offered me a purity of mind and spirit: because of India I am fulfilled; I am full."

Decisions Revisited

Inevitably, travel engages us in questions and contrasts, alternatives and decisions. When and where shall I go? With whom? What are the extended implications of this journey? How might it change me? Each choice you make is a reflection of values. Revisit several problems you've faced as a traveler and reflect upon reaching a decision. What was your process? The outcome? In hindsight, do you see the problem more clearly? Would further analysis or more information have led you to a better choice? Looking back, consider what you learned and how it may have helped you grow (up) a bit. That is, how does the troublesome process of decision making, especially when we make mistakes, shape our values at least as much as it defines them?

Austin Tellam mused over the "seasonal massacre" of illegal lobsters in which he had been invited to participate. "I was not raised to treat the ocean like a bowl of candy with which to stuff my pockets," he reflected. "But our decisions define us as people; as a defining moment, this was not what I wanted to be." In an entry aptly titled "Worldwide Sportsman," he illustrated how the examined journey can expand our ability to behave justly in a global arena:

> *Wherever we go, the atmosphere of fishing provides a perfect environment to test values, a place for the cheaters to cheat and the strong-valued to play by the rules even if no one is looking. It tests the purpose of the game. And new responsibilities arise in international waters, like my favorite haunts off Bimini: following local laws, observing more stringent rules of conservation, showing appreciation . . . behaving with respect and generosity. If being a worldwide sportsman is something I strive for, I need to contribute more than a few dock fees and bar tabs to the community. And if I were to declare my new philosophy for traveling, it would be to change my behavior, to strive to become a worldwide sportsman, in fishing, in traveling, and in life.*

Beyond the personal wish to be the sort of global citizen we hope others will be, consider how the process of decision making may affect a larger audience. If our decisions reflect our values, what messages are we offering our hosts wherever we travel? And might our own reflections on those decisions help us reshape our practices? Vanessa Sain considered her excitement over learning to bargain in Caribbean markets. Do we have an obligation to buy, to support the crafts of the poor, or are we using poverty and desperation for cheap entertainment? "Looking back," she concluded, "I feel I was bargaining down [the Bahamian women's] self-worth, stripping away shreds of dignity. . . . I remember faces longing for something, and me continuing to bargain. Every tourist was doing this. But that doesn't mean it was right." As you develop these thoughtful journal entries, consider as well how your writing might shape the understanding of an audience of readers who have not yet confronted your issues.

Ethical Reflections

Travel often invites us to redefine our ethics in the light of wider global comprehension. Reflecting on the diversity of our destination may show us our own values more clearly. For these journal entries, try to identify experiences that challenged your beliefs or left you uncertain about what to do. Look for ethical dilemmas in your journeys, those moments when you had to choose among admittedly undesirable alternatives.

How did the options you finally chose reflect—or challenge—your values?

Brad Deutsch approached the dilemma of being seen as a commodity through a simple question: "What is our obligation in response to the privilege of travel?" No easy answers emerged as he described being surrounded by desperate sellers of *faux* merchandise in Bali:

> *The ethical issues are manifold and complicated. Tourists are the main source of Balinese income. If vendors do not sell their products, their families might starve. But what right have they to sell copyrighted goods? Am I stealing money from some factory worker in Iowa when I buy a fake Puma cap? Was it made by six-year-old girls on a neighboring island? But I don't have time to answer these questions, since no fewer than fifteen people at once are trying to sell me t-shirts, necklaces, and shells on the beach. I bought four hats; I don't even wear a hat. It was hard to remember I was dealing with actual people. They probably saw me as prey. In Southeast Asia, white people are assumed to have money, treated better than people with dark skin, and targeted. When I chose not to buy, the merchants were offended, finding their hard work insulted. In fact, it was an American reaching his material limit for the first time. Never before had I had more money than I knew what to do with. My family was not rich, but we could have retired in Bali. I just didn't want any more.*

Such dilemmas, of course, are generally understood more clearly in hindsight, when the press of people and expectations is lifted. Hence, your journal can serve not only to record experience but also to ponder its significance. In this way we move from sharing the journey with an audience to the deeper possibility of *making meaning* out of the shards of memory.

Other questions may help you examine the ethical dimensions of your journey. What is the difference between a tourist and a traveler? Consider the impressions you are making on local people as well as the ones you are taking away. Did your expectations change as you came to know your destination? Were you comfortable with cultural alternatives? Or did you feel squeamish over some of what you saw? (On a bus in Kusadasi I once endured a lecture on Turkish carpets, with the merchant's repeated refrain that the best were made by little girls who went blind by the close work over fine silk. As they get older, we were told, their hands roughen so they can only work with wool. My thirst for local culture did not overcome my feminist indignation or my humanist horror over this means of valuing a life.) What ethical obligations do we have as visitors in another country? Your reader will want to know how you handled conflicts and what exchanges might have arisen.

Dana repeatedly questioned her own comfortable lifestyle as she traveled in India. Here she captures the effects of her journey on her value system:

> *Children swarmed around me, blotting out the sea of wrappers, bottles, and discarded rags, puddles and urine, and the stench of rotting food. Women squatted, their legs feebly holding them just inches above the ground, abrasively scrubbing clothes in buckets of rusty-brown water. Yet the children laughed and struck poses, pointing to my camera. After snapping their photos, I passed the camera off to a little boy and posed with his siblings. Bending my knees to their level, I felt the lips of a little boy touch my cheek. In that moment I realized something had happened to me. Given my disposition prior to India, it is inconceivable to think I would have allowed that little boy to get so close—so unkempt, so unshowered, so unlike me.*

Like Dana, you'll probably be drawing connections, critiquing concepts, discovering truths about your home, too. Other questions may follow. Can you select a place you'd choose not to visit and explain why not? What about traveling with a group versus traveling alone? (Do you have pet peeves about fellow travelers?)

But you'll also want to think about your role as a travel writer. Perhaps you'd like to include interviews with other travelers on the issues you've encountered or to explore the concept of the "ugly American." What do guidebooks fail to tell you? How might a guidebook differ from the travel journal or article? While you're at it, what are the ethical obligations of the travel writer? As you turn to your journal, think

Your Travel Journal

about how your role as a writer might have transformed the journey itself.

Last Thoughts

Of course, the more time and effort you put into your journal, the more committed you will be to the language and details of its pages. It's easy to get caught up in the journal, as it captures so vividly the essence of your travel. Sometimes, then, we have to step back and remember that the journal is really just another step in the journey. Much revision is

> **Workshopping the Travel Journal**
>
> While your journal is not polished writing, it has gone through several stages of recording and reflecting. You will want to test your images and explorations on friendly fellow writers. Tell them any special questions or needs you'd like to have addressed.
>
> Ask for an "echo reading," in which workshop partners can summarize your ideas, paragraph by paragraph. Where does the account differ from your intention? Try a memory well analysis of imagery, asking readers to note telling details and vivid moments, then to show you where questions arise or more details are needed. Seek out analysis by type, asking readers to describe your characters or summarize your recreations, to tease out the decisions you believe you've analyzed and explain your ethical issues in their own words. Invite discussion of structure and advice on the immediacy of sensual appeal.
>
> Be sure not to argue or explain while your readers critique your journal entry. Just take careful notes on everything they say. Workshop advice often sounds much better in retrospect, after you are alone again before the computer. And you will want all the suggestions you can garner to revise your journal into more polished public prose.
>
> Finally, remember to offer as much feedback as you can to others in your group, moving beyond simple praise of the piece to real advice for the revision.

still needed to produce a professional piece, and it may be difficult to omit good writing or a special moment that does not fit with the shape or intention of writing for a given audience. Some of the best help you can get for this process is the careful response of fellow writers in a workshop. If you are not workshopping in a classroom setting, find some like-minded travel writers and meet regularly to discuss everyone's work in process. Remember to tell your colleagues how far you have come with a given piece, what sort of input you need, and how ready you are for the rough and tumble experience of serious critique.

At length you will learn to refine your journal entries into richer depictions of the traveler's life and the lure of your destinations. But as a seasoned traveler, you will keep every journal entry you have written, knowing that the source of many articles may stem from that initial reflective writing.

Here is Dana moving from her journal to a travel article on India, capturing the complicated and fascinating interaction among the people she encountered, the haunting and often troubled visions of the place, and her own very human transformation:

> *Leaving the Orphanage, we're leaving India. Just a few hours remain. Peering out the window of the bus, I notice a gathering of small boys extending their arms up for something, anything I might have to give them. Their faces, all so dark, capture my attention and my heart. So thin, that pane of glass separating us, though the differences between them and me are thick and deep. Searching my bag, I want to toss them anything I have . . . lotion, shampoo, peppermints, my Bic pen, a box of cereal. I know we're not supposed to, but they are so eager, and I so needy. I want to throw the world to those boys, toss them all my experiences and opportunities. I want them to have it all.*

End-of-Chapter Questions

1. Can a journal help to give you ideas for travel articles?
2. For travel writers does the journal frequently begin before or at the start of the journey?
3. What can you record on the eve of the journey to enrich your journey?
4. What kind of writing is meant to capture the details but is jagged and full of holes?
5. What do some travel writers insist is the most efficient way to understand how opinions shift and cultural values vary throughout the United States?
6. For whom is it essential to gather resources and record a wide range of materials?
7. According to Papay, what is perhaps the hardest part of travel writing?
8. Can a travel journal render the dialogues, descriptions, and memories of a journey?
9. According to Papay, in light of wider global comprehension that may come about from travel, what is it about us that might be redefined?
10. Is it normal for a professional piece of travel writing to come directly from a travel journal?

WRITING ASSIGNMENT SEVEN
YOUR TRAVEL JOURNAL

Assignment Introduction

Keeping a travel journal is one of the best ways of getting ideas for a travel article and for providing much of the manuscript draft content. This assignment allows you to get started in learning how to keep a journal.

Assignment Activity

The second small spiral notepad that you purchased should be your Travel Journal for writing assignment seven. Contact your chamber of commerce. Tell the person who is assisting you that you have a relative coming to visit and you want to know what the five top sightseeing destinations are within a twenty-mile radius of downtown. Then select one of those destinations as the subject of a travel article. Plan a half-day visit. When you go, take copious notes in your journal.

Even before you leave home, make notes about how you feel about the visit. Write down what you expect to find, how you think the visit will affect you, and what you expect to sense, learn, and understand.

During your visit, pay attention to all of your senses. Sit and watch for a few minutes, and describe the kind of people who are visiting, what they are wearing, the age of the average visitor, and whether or not there are a lot of or only a few children. How good are the handicap facilities? Then walk around and take notes. Remember, you are not there to be a tourist. You are there to write for would-be tourists. Decide what kind of tourists you would recommend visit this place. Is it a "must-see" for some tourists, but a place to avoid for others? How expensive is it? Are food and beverages available, and what are the costs? Is there an abundance of restrooms, or do you see long lines waiting to get into restrooms? What are the hours of operation? Is there a courtesy desk, a concierge, or someone available who will answer questions? Think of writing a sidebar that is titled "If you go." Then make sure you get all the information for the sidebar.

After you leave, write down your final thoughts. Look back at what you wrote before you left home and verify your initial thoughts or note that you were wrong in some cases. If you thought it would be different

Your Travel Journal 123

than it actually was, what about your reader? Is it likely he or she will think differently also?

After you finish your journal, put it away, and don't think about it or reread it for at least a week. However, if you have additional thoughts you want to add to your journal, open it to the last page on which you have notes, and add your new thoughts.

You will go back to your journal shortly to be able to use your journal notes for a travel article draft. But you need a few days between writing the journal and writing the first article draft that is based on your journal.

Complete the following information:

1. When did you visit the sightseeing place for which you kept your journal? (day, date, and time of day) _____

2. How long did you visit? _____

3. How many pages of journal notes did you take? _____

4. How do you feel about the experience of keeping a travel journal? Please write one short paragraph.

   _____
   _____
   _____
   _____
   _____
   _____
   _____
   _____

Final Step: Add your name to the Instructor Comment Sheet for Writing Assignment Seven in appendix 5 and staple it to your answers to the above four questions about your travel journal. Then turn in both sheets to your professor.

KATHRYN LEMMON has been a freelance writer since 1990 and has 570 published credits, primarily covering travel-related topics. She was accepted as a member of the American Society of Journalists & Authors (ASJA). Some of her media visits have included: Costa Rica, Egypt, Germany, Spain, Holland, St. Kitts, Toronto, St. Barts, Yellowstone National Park in Wyoming, Texas, Florida, Maine, California, and more.

CHAPTER 8

Press Trips

Katherine Lemmon

THE SECOND BEST JOB

The television channel A&E once presented a program on the top ten best jobs in the world. The number two occupation on its list was travel journalist, right behind rock star! Those who write travel might tell you it's not quite as glamorous as that and certainly not as lucrative. However, having the opportunity to travel the world, usually at the expense of others, is appealing.

One way travel journalists, both on staff and freelance, accomplish their work is by participating in press trips. Some find it feasible to travel monthly, or even more frequently. Others may take only one or two press trips per year, preferring to write about destinations in their own backyard or where job assignments take them. For freelancers at least, it's a personal choice—where you gather material and whether you wish to travel forty miles or four thousand miles.

WHAT IS A PRESS TRIP?

It's an organized method for a resort, city, state, country, or other entity to get positive publicity from travel journalists. A press trip is entirely a business arrangement between host and writer. The host invests their time and money bringing travel writers and/or travel photographers to their destination.

Once back home, the participants are expected to sell their stories and/or images about the destination, enticing consumers to visit. In essence, it's an important public relations tool in the competitive world of travel marketing. The hosts are seeking favorable media coverage, and the travel writers, with their ability to get stories in print, can make that happen.

Press trips go by other names such as junkets, media visits, or "fam" trips (short for familiarization). The term "fam" is also commonly used when travel agents visit. Whatever the name, the travel opportunity remains the same.

TRAVEL ARTICLE IDEAS

Finding travel article ideas is a big benefit of press trips. Even with advance research, you may not see a certain story angle until you arrive. A good freelancer can use one trip to generate multiple stories, with a variety of slants. Press trip sponsors want as many travel articles about their destination as possible. They are constantly presenting travel writers with information that can be the nucleus of a travel article or something that might fit into an article. Feel free to bounce ideas off of them. An especially good technique is to ask each on-site expert what he or she would write about if they were a travel writer. You will be pleasantly surprised at the responses you get.

WHY THE NEED FOR PRESS TRIPS

One major reason is the expense of travel, as compared to the typical paychecks travel writers can expect to receive. This might be best illustrated with an example. Let's say as a travel writer you take a ten-day walking tour to explore Costa Rica. The cost would probably range from $4,500 to $6,000 or more. Upon your return, after writing articles about Costa Rica and walking tours, you stand to make somewhere between zero dollars and $3,000 realistically—even with multiple sales. You can do the math and see this represents a financial loss. Travel writers need to make money, or they can't continue in the business.

Payment for travel writing hasn't changed significantly in thirty years. In the seventies, one dollar per word was a decent rate of pay, and even now one dollar per word is considered good. That's not to say the larger, glossy magazines don't pay more, because they do, perhaps up to three dollars per word. However, those particular writing jobs go to a small group of veteran freelancers with thirty years experience and who have a long track record working with those publications. Middle-of-the-pack writers can expect to make money, but not always three dollars per word.

There's a need for press trips because they provide a cost-effective and efficient means for travel writers to do editorial research on a destination. Travel bureau experts can prepare the itinerary and lay all the ground work. Travel writers can do their part in advance by reading material about the location and finding slants for the stories. Once on-site, writers see the highlights as shown to them by their tour directors. While you won't see everything in-depth, you also won't waste time getting from point A to point B. It comes down to fewer worries and more experiences.

Press trips are necessary (along with the ongoing publicity they generate) because many destinations depend heavily on tourism. Consider Florida or the islands of the Caribbean—these places live or die by tourism numbers. From top government officials to the smallest mom-and-pop restaurant, when tourism is down, they all suffer the consequences.

There's a need for press trips because, for the host entity, they provide a less expensive alternative to paid advertising. A single full-page ad in a major travel glossy magazine can be out of reach for many tour companies or other small operators. These ads range from $20,000 to perhaps $40,000. Destinations realize a high value for their dollar when they invest a fraction of that amount per writer, per day. Bringing down the overall press trip costs even further, hotels, restaurants, and airlines will sometimes join with the host to provide free services or agree to a lower "press rate."

For the hosts, a productive travel writer will become a long-term investment, whereas an advertisement may run once. A writer could easily be selling stories about the islands of Turks & Caicos two years after a press trip, with some updates to the material, of course. It's a win-win situation for everyone: the client, the trip sponsors, and your bank account.

PUBLIC RELATIONS IN TRAVEL

No discussion of press trips is possible without first understanding the significant connection between public relations firms and travel writers. Think of it this way, like Tide detergent or Crest toothpaste, the island of Jamaica needs promotion, as does London, England, or Halifax, Nova Scotia. Tourism is a highly competitive business. Consumers must pick and choose where they will spend their vacation dollars. For their part, each location wants to get its fair share of visitors and their cash.

In an ongoing effort to entice more tourists, resorts, cities, states, and even countries will often hire a public relations firm for representation. These PR (public relations) agencies perform a wide variety of functions to promote their client. They might prepare TV commercials, arrange for publicity photos, write and distribute press releases, and arrange and escort press trips. The bottom line is attracting tourists who spend money.

Thus PR firms work hand-in-hand with travel writers, not only for press trips but also to provide images and press materials. The PR representative and the travel writer share the same goal, so it only makes sense.

Let's say a travel writer visits a Sandals resort in Jamaica on a press trip, arranged by a PR firm. The writer goes home and two months later sells a front-page feature about Sandals in Jamaica to the *St. Louis Post-Dispatch*, for instance. The PR people who represent Sandals will be especially pleased at this nice bit of publicity, and they can show concrete evidence of the good job they're doing for their client.

PR people can figure the actual value of that article with something called an advertising equivalency. Without going into specifics, it's a way of calculating the dollar value of the article, in comparison to the purchase of an advertisement.

As you might expect, a positive, well-written article about Sandals has a great deal more impact on consumers than a print ad, no matter how large or colorful. As a general rule, editorial is considered more trustworthy by the reading public than advertising, and it's valuable because it comes from an unbiased source.

The calculations for ad equivalencies use numbers which take this into account. Because of the cost of advertising, a travel writer can be a "million-dollar producer," if the publication circulation and ad costs are high enough.

MAJOR ORGANIZATIONS SPONSORING PRESS TRIPS

Besides public relations firms, press trips can be organized by other groups. Here's a list of the most common:

- **Convention and Visitors Bureaus**—This group acts much like an outside PR firm, usually representing a city, region, or state. However, their focus is wider, and they would also deal directly with individual tourists and meeting planners. Travel writers can approach the CVB (convention and visitors bureau) for assistance when needing hotel rooms, admission to attractions, and press materials. If their budget allows, CVBs may offer organized group press trips.

- **State and National Tourism Offices**—This group is larger in scope and purpose but can overlap somewhat with the CVBs. The Netherlands Board of Tourism is one example. A state example would be the Wyoming Office of Travel and Tourism.

- **In-house Sales and Marketing for Individual Resorts**—Larger resorts or hotel chains may choose to handle their public relations tasks within their organization. The resort itself or the chain of resorts may sponsor a press trip, which is resort-based, rather than destination-based.

- **Miscellaneous Others Banding Together**—Any group can join together in an effort to increase their media coverage. An example might be when thirteen German cities pool their resources and hire either a PR firm or an individual to act as a representative for them. Working together as a consortium, they might offer press trips as part of their promotional campaign. Even small businesses within a single city (which stand to gain from larger tourist numbers) will sometimes join together in this fashion.

Along these lines, new travel writers should beware of ads or teasers such as "get paid to travel the world" or "join the glamorous world of travel writing." This is usually just ad copy written by individuals trying to sell writing courses or books, not a group hosting a legitimate press trip.

HOW ARE PRESS TRIPS ORGANIZED?

Press trips generally fall into two categories: either individual or group trips. Organized group trips could consist of anywhere from two to 150 travel writers, but on average most are five to fifteen people. The itinerary, including meals, accommodations, and schedules, are pre-scheduled—probably well before you ever agree to the trip.

Although they are arranged in advance by those operating the trip, you should ask to see the daily itinerary before agreeing to anything. Not every trip is general in scope or focus. For example, if the trip is primarily a whale watching expedition off the coast of Mexico, and you get seasick, there's a problem. Or if the trip is all about the best shopping on the island of St. Barts and you write for all outdoor, adventure travel outlets, then you might want to skip that particular trip to St. Barts. If you don't see the itinerary in advance, be prepared for anything!

Travel writers are flown to the destination unless they live close enough to drive. Then the participants are escorted around to the attractions by bus, van, or car.

Sometimes you will have input into the sightseeing plans. Some organizers send the participants options in advance. So, for instance, while the entire group may stay together to do a walking tour of downtown Nashville in the morning, the afternoon time is split between three different attractions. Before arriving at the destination, you can preselect which of the three afternoon choices best meet your editorial needs. Then each van load of travel writers goes off to their designated location, probably meeting up again at dinner time.

There are travel writers who argue against group trips and rarely participant in them. In their opinion, the overall experience is too contrived and prepackaged. They feel the sanitized travel experience provided on a group trip is so perfectly planned that the average traveler would never be able to recreate the experience.

Individual trips can be handled in a similar fashion, or not. The rules can be wide open, depending upon how much "escorting" you prefer, the type of location you're visiting, and what is offered by those in charge. Every aspect of an individual trip is open for negotiation between the host and writer.

If the press trip consists of four days and nights at a beach resort on St. Kitts, the PR firm or CVB may not see the need to send a tour director or tour manager. Arrangements will be made for airfare and transfers and perhaps a meeting with the on-site sales office, but otherwise you could be primarily on your own.

If the trip is not to a resort but to a specific city or even moving around one area, then typically the daily time will be split between escorted time and free time. You may be "assigned" a local driver/guide and given a media pass, which allows free entry into museums and other attractions. You and the guide may be free to work out meeting times and stops.

For individual trips, travel companions may or may not be included. Airfare may or may not be offered. If you get to the destination on your own, then most CVB or PR firms will at least assist with media passes to attractions, some meals, press kits, etc.

For the travel writer, an individual trip can mean a great deal of time spent in advance preparation, in terms of contacting individuals with requests, copying and sending writing samples, etc. But on the other hand, the trip itinerary will be your choices, not the choices of someone else.

In yet another variation, travel writers are sometimes "attached" to group tours, consisting of regular folks, just taking their vacation. This might be true of a walking tour of the Lake District in the U.K. or a ten-day organized tour of Costa Rica.

THE CHOSEN FEW

It's a common misconception that only staff writers and editors get invited on press trips, but that certainly isn't the case. Freelancers often make up a large percentage of the participants.

For the trip sponsors, there's a disadvantage to staff or editors. Chances are a staff writer or editor will only produce one story from a press trip, for their own publication. Ambitious freelancers, on the other hand, can produce multiple sales. In addition, staff and editors can be too busy with office commitments—producing their publication—to be away very often. In some cases, the "higher-ups" at the publication may insist staff members use vacation time for press trips, so these staff members may not wish to use their precious vacation time for work.

Press trip sponsors always prefer firm assignment letters signed by an editor. These are letters travel writers receive from editors specifying that they will buy an article or book, how much they will pay, and the parameters within which the travel writer is expected to work (number of words, first or third person, how many photos the editor wants with the article, etc.). However, there are advantages and disadvantages to obtaining these letters in advance of a trip.

As a writer, having a letter (or at least an e-mail commitment) is an advantage, since you've accomplished one of the tougher tasks, even before leaving home.

What are the possible disadvantages you might wonder? Here's one scenario. All starts out well, as you learn of a trip to Aruba and you begin pitching editors about the specific attractions listed on the itinerary. Fortune smiles in your direction, and you find an interested editor. With letter in hand, you sign up for the trip and await the departure. Since time allows, you continue pitching stories and round up one or two additional sales.

However, what if the trip gets cancelled, or you can't attend for some reason? Then you have a dilemma. The editor is expecting a story, most likely by a deadline, and you can't produce it. Keeping editors happy is extremely important in this business. Backing out on a story will definitely not please an editor, and there's a chance you won't be trusted in the future.

What will you do about this situation? You can attempt to arrange an individual trip. It could be pieced together by contacting airlines and resorts individually. You could bite the bullet, use your frequent flyer miles, and do the trip as cheaply as possible. You still might lose money, but at least you won't jeopardize your relationship with the editor. With enough persistence you could make more sales later and recoup some of your expenses.

Assignment letters are one criterion of who makes the cut for a press trip. If you have a letter for a publication with a decent size circulation, chances are good you'll be on the roster.

However, these days assignment letters are not as easy to obtain as they once were. Press trip sponsors are aware of this situation. Although they might request them in the formal invitation, actual requirements for a firm letter can be labeled "soft" or "flexible" criteria.

Transportation costs are often the sticky issue with press trips. Some of the trips offered will not cover airfare. Thus, you may find yourself invited, but there will be relatively high expenses, putting the final decision on your shoulders.

If the destination is within a reasonable driving distance, travel writers might opt to drive. Airfare is often negotiable. Tourist board executives can, and sometimes they do, contact airlines serving their destination and request free or reduced cost air travel for travel writers. If you have a firm assignment with a high circulation publication, you should consider asking the publication to negotiate with air carriers on your behalf. Alternatively, you may contact airline public relations directors yourself and request free or reduced cost air.

Others who get invited on press trips are known in the business as "good producers." If you continue to show a consistent record of placements from past trips, this will be noted, and you have the clips to prove it. In other words, if you traveled to Stockholm on a press trip and a year later you've sold three stories about the trip and have two more slated for publication, the sponsors will feel you were a valuable investment. Your clips are tangible evidence you've done your part. By the same token, if you only sold one story but the outlet had a circulation of one million readers, then again, you've met your obligations.

If you have never sold a travel article, the sponsors will hesitate before asking you to any of their destinations. Tourist boards subscribe to clipping services, and those who run familiarization trips maintain contact with one another. While you may get invited on an initial trip before you have written and sold a travel article, the word may get passed around that you are a nonproducer.

WHEN DO PRESS TRIPS OCCUR?

Press trips occur year round, but many are planned at the beginning of the year and span the remaining months. A country such as Spain or Mexico might arrange and offer five or six trips over the course of the year, with each one focusing on a different region or different subject matter. These trips would probably be spaced out every other month or similar.

Other hosts may only plan their trips four to six weeks in advance. But if a trip is tied to a specific event, then certainly the dates must coincide. An example would be a major art exhibition or the opening of a new museum.

The more a destination relies on tourism, the more press trips it will offer over a year's time. Florida is one such place; Indiana is not.

To save money and not conflict with fully booked hotels and full airplanes, destinations may opt to offer their trips in their off-seasons, such as Alaska in snowy March or the island of Puerto Rico in the heat of summer.

WHERE DO TRAVEL WRITERS LEARN ABOUT PRESS TRIPS?

Many invitations go out as mass mailings to members of writer's organizations such as the American Society of Journalists & Authors or the Society of American Travel Writers. If and when you qualify, it's a wise idea to join the group that best matches your writing interests and work history. Organization membership looks good on your résumé, and press trip invitations will follow. Such membership also enhances your reputation and lends instant credibility.

In some cases, public relations firms will actually post their up coming trips online, either on their own Web sites or on freelance writing Web sites. Snail mail, faxes, and phone calls are all means of getting the word out. It can work both ways; you can find them, or they can find you. Travel writers also share the information among themselves.

HOW A PRESS TRIP DIFFERS FROM A VACATION

When you prepare to depart on your first press trip, all your friends will repeat over and over, "Have a great vacation!" It might be a good idea to remind them (and yourself) that you're not going on vacation. While it is true that a travel writer does as *work* what an average person does while on *vacation*, journalists researching stories are not on vacation. Some unfortunate travel writers learn this the hard way.

On vacation you're in complete control of your time. You can sleep until noon, shop for hours, and have a cocktail at 3 P.M. On a press trip, you're giving up control of your time and agreeing to a daily schedule prepared by others. By agreeing to go in the first place, you're basically saying, "I will, within reason, do what you request of me." So, even if 8 A.M. bird-watching on a chilly morning isn't your idea of fun, the hosts expect you to participate.

There are some exceptions to this rule. If a late-night pub visit is on the agenda and you won't be writing about pubs, you can request to return to the hotel. If the group is offered the opportunity to go skydiving, you can decline and not feel undue pressure.

Of course, it's easy for the line between fun and work to get blurred. When lying by the pool at an upscale resort in Cozumel, you might need to remind yourself, you're at work. If you're allotted free time on the itinerary, then pool sitting is fine. On the other hand, if a hotel or resort tour is scheduled for that time, you'd better attend.

Timing is different on press trips. While vacationers would spend an entire day at Busch Gardens, for example, you may be there for two hours and then in the bus or van again. You'll be taking notes, interviewing experts, and seeing the highlights only. The hosts want to include as much as possible on every press trip, yet without completely exhausting the participants.

Daily schedules can run from 8 A.M. in the morning to midnight, with only a thirty-minute afternoon break to change for dinner. Two-hour lunches and three-hour dinners are often the norm. Most vacations don't run to such extremes.

In the worst case scenario, you might be staying in a different hotel each evening for seven to ten nights in a row, thus unpacking is not practical. Never getting the chance to unpack can leave some people feeling miserable and unsettled. In terms of editorial research, it's tough to recall and write about a specific hotel when you arrived after dark, took a fast tour, slept, and left again by 9 A.M.

Finally, unlike your vacation, your journey is with strangers, not with your loved ones. These other participants can be loud, demanding, or difficult. They may smoke, get drunk, and miss appointed meeting times. Whether it's just their personality or they're jaded from too many press trips, these folks make the trip uncomfortable for everyone. Some bring along significant others who might also be less than congenial traveling companions.

UNDERSTANDING PRESS TRIP ETIQUETTE

First and foremost, remember a press trip is a business trip. Hosts or sponsors expect you to behave as you would on any other business trip—even if you're not wearing a suit and sitting in meetings all day. You should, however, dress to suit the activity. Never be late for designated meeting times, or you'll make the other writers and tour director angry. You definitely don't want the tour director pounding on your hotel room door at 9 A.M., when all the others are already in the bus or van waiting to leave—bad feelings could result.

Organized trips, by necessity, run on rigid time schedules, so don't be the one to foul up the plans. Always tip drivers, chambermaids, and others as appropriate, unless the tour directors tell you otherwise. Offer to pay for small purchases like cups of coffee and don't just assume the tour directors are paying, until they make the offer.

Monitor your words carefully, and don't complain about every little problem. Be patient if things go wrong, as they will. The tour directors and/or resort hosts are striving to make the best possible impression and are hypersensitive to complaints by travel writers.

If you have a chilled bottle of wine in your villa, think twice before complaining that it's not hard liquor. Or, if the champagne cruise is serving hard liquor, don't make an issue about not having champagne. Politely drink what's offered and appreciate it. Your fussing will cause the tour directors to fret, and you'll be remembered as the "problem" writer.

Be friendly and congenial with your fellow writers. Group dynamics can make a trip really fun or unbearable.

Once the trip is over, send thank-you notes (via snail mail) to your sponsors. When your stories are published, even years later, send copies to the hosts or sponsors immediately.

OBJECTIVITY AND MARKETS

While press trips may seem a perfect avenue for journalists seeking material on travel, there is one snag. There are newspapers and magazines that will not accept stories from writers who have done their research on a "sponsored" trip. Their argument against the practice comes down to a question of objectivity and ethics. Will writers on sponsored trips be honest, since they "owe" their hosts positive publicity?

Some outlets go so far as to request travel receipts from their writers. Others favor the "press rate" or "editorial rate" plan. That means the writer must pay at least a nominal fee, from as low as the cost of one breakfast, on up to perhaps half the true cost of the trip.

As you might expect, this topic is a sensitive issue, much debated by travel writers. Do theater critics pay for their own show tickets? Probably not. Do sports writers attend games and get in free? You bet. Whether we like it or not, a double standard of long duration seems to have developed for travel writers.

In addition, as mentioned above, if a newspaper is only willing to pay $250 for a travel feature on a safari in Botswana, can it really expect professional travel writers to first purchase and participate in a tour at the cost of $7,000? Apparently they do.

Some markets favor using the writing of doctors, lawyers, and other nontravel writers who take expensive vacations and write up their experiences afterward. Of course, this means less work for those who are legitimately attempting to make their living from travel writing and is also the cause of much discussion. Are they more objective because they used their own money? There's no easy answer to that question.

Another thought-provoking issue raised by both editors and writers concerns the tone of travel writing and the idea of objectivity. Does the audience, many of whom are armchair travelers, really want to read negative things in a travel article? Or do they want to fantasize about an exciting trip they might take someday? Will they stop reading if the story turns unpleasant?

Compounding that issue, publications must always attempt to please their advertisers. Understandably, a tour company operating in Peru won't be particularly happy if the article about their country, printed immediately next to their advertisement, is full of reasons not to travel to Peru. Depending on the editor, this could present a balancing act.

There are further ethical questions for consideration—are travel writers first and foremost critics or just storytellers? Some write their experiences as simple narratives, so who paid for the journey is of less consequence. Does a travel writer need to have a personal preference for a place to write a well-received article?

For better or worse, other publications have adopted a "don't ask, don't tell" policy on using sponsored material. In other words, the writer proposes a story without mentioning the press trip. The editor doesn't ask, and the writer doesn't volunteer the information.

In yet another variation, some publications have chosen to clear the air and make a brief disclosure at the end or beginning of the article, indicating to the readers the trip was sponsored. It might read: "Our frequent contributor John Smith flew to Key West as a guest of the Florida Keys Tourism Association and the Hyatt Regency."

OTHER PRESS TRIP BENEFITS

Press trips can offer other benefits besides the obvious. For example, it's not unusual to meet editors while on a press trip. This provides a wonderful networking opportunity. You should exchange business cards and get to know them, without being too aggressive. Once home, you can propose stories, and your odds of acceptance will be vastly improved, since the editor has met you personally.

Comparing notes with other travel writers while at dinner or chatting at a cocktail reception can prove valuable. Although we're all doing the same thing, everyone has developed his or her own techniques and different ways to accomplish the same goal—selling travel stories. You're bound to start "talking shop," so take advantage and share ideas, swap editor contact information or names of new markets, for example. You can learn a great deal from these exchanges. Other writers can and often will share upcoming press trip information, so keep an ear open.

Author's Note: The examples and incidents sited in this chapter are true. They've been taken from personal experience during my own press trip travels.

WHEN THE TRIP IS OVER

After the trip, keep the lines of communications open. Chances are good you'll be contacting your hosts and/or tour managers for images, to confirm quotes, or to verify other details. But if not, remember hosts and public relations people want to hear from you, especially when you make sales. Drop a quick e-mail to let them know when you have news.

Your real obligations begin once you get home. Hopefully, you pinned down at least one sale before the trip. Even so, everyone involved benefits if you make additional sales. Strive to be a million-dollar producer and not only will your e-mail inbox overflow with invitations, the paychecks will soon follow. You'll be able to pick and chose your trips, plus make money.

Use a database or have some other way of keeping track of your sales related to each trip. That way, if the hosts come back a year later and ask what you've accomplished, you have a complete record.

A FINAL WORD

It's been said all travel is a series of peaks and valleys. When you take an hour-long camel ride next to the Pyramids in Egypt, you've definitely reached a peak—an experience of a lifetime. When you're stuck overnight at O'Hare airport in Chicago because of ice storms, with no hotel rooms to be had, you've hit a valley. Yet in the bigger world of navigating the globe, you can't have one without the other. Maybe it's human nature, but, after the fact, the peaks stand out in your mind, while the valleys tend to dim in comparison.

Press trips provide working travel writers with opportunities they might never have in any other occupation. You can get up close and personal with manatees in Florida, visit medieval castles in Wales, or wake to howler monkeys in the jungles of Costa Rica. It's your choice. If travel is your passion, not only can you experience these things, but you can share it with your readers. Travel writing is a career like none other.

Tourism Offices Worldwide Directory

This helpful Web site will link you to any tourism office in the U.S. or abroad, with more than 1,400 listings: www.towd.com.

End-of-Chapter Questions

1. What is the number two occupation on the A&E list of the top ten best jobs in the world?
2. According Lemmon, what are press trip hosts seeking?
3. The term "fam" trip is short for what kind of trip?
4. Is finding travel article ideas a big benefit of press trips, according Lemmon, the author?
5. What might you ask each on-site expert in order to get ideas for travel articles?
6. What dollar amount producer should you strive to be to get your e-mail inbox overflowing with invitations?
7. What might you want to keep track of in case your hosts come back a year after the press trip and ask what you've accomplished?
8. Can middle-of-the-pack writers expect to always make three dollars per word or more?
9. Are press trips more expensive for host entities than paid advertising?
10. When you have met an editor on a press trip, can you expect that your odds of that editor accepting a future story proposal from you will be better?

WRITING ASSIGNMENT EIGHT
WRITING WITH YOUR FIVE SENSES

Assignment Introduction

Most North American travel writers write about what they see or, even better, what the reader might see. We rarely engage the other four senses. This assignment will help you engage your other four senses and help you to be able to write more about smells, sounds, things that you touch, and foods that you taste.

Assignment Activity

Without rereading your travel journal, write a paragraph about what you felt, heard, tasted, and smelled during your time at the local sightseeing point about which your journal notes were taken in writing assignment seven. Do a rough draft of the article rapidly off the top of your head with little or no pre-thought.

Next, go back and think of each sense at a time. What did you feel when you touched things while you were at the tourist site? Was it the smooth touch of a polished bannister or the roughness of walking over courtyard stones—or perhaps both? Go back through your paragraph, and make modifications so that you describe what you felt with your hands, feet, or even with other body parts.

Now turn your concentration to what you heard. Was it the wind blowing in the trees? Perhaps it was the noise of children as they scampered through the place. Perhaps you best remember the cries of a hot dog vendor as he called out his menu to all passing by. Again, go back through your paragraph, and make modifications so that you describe what you heard.

Taste can be as simple as describing the tepid gurgle from the only water fountain when your turn came after five other tourists ahead of you. Or perhaps the multi-course gourmet meal was the highlight of your visit, and you will be able to describe the unique tastes of many exotic foods and a most unusual wine. Go back to your paragraph, and make sure the sense of taste is well represented in your travel writing.

Some people have especially strong senses of smell. Others do not. But think about the smells you experienced. It is possible that some of the smells were so powerful that they seemed to assault you. Others, most likely, were subtle and might well have been missed by a casual observer. Document the smells in your paragraph. Go back through it, and make sure that the interesting aromas are discussed.

Remember the importance of brevity. Keep your paragraph to no more than two hundred words. Draft it right away. Then every day go back and count words. Don't leave out anything that is important, but write more and more tightly until you have whittled your paragraph down to two hundred words.

Final Step: Add your name to the Instructor Comment Sheet for Writing Assignment Eight in appendix 5 and staple it to the two hundred-word paragraph you have written for this assignment. Then turn in both sheets to your professor.

SECTION III

AIMING FOR THE BEST

Quality sells. In almost every field, those who produce and market top-quality items are able to sell their wares—unless they are priced too high. The same is true of travel writing. Editors expect good writing, are pleased when they get it, and usually will compensate writers well for excellent travel writing. Although most editors are on a predetermined budget and, therefore, are unable to pay the travel writer more for an excellent article than for one that is just passable, excellence is remembered. Future assignments go to the producer of consistently excellent work. Whether the travel writer is trying to sell a new article idea or the editor wants an article or book that will round out the publisher's offerings, one can be sure that the editor will remember the travel writer who has provided top-quality articles and books in the past. It is a nice feeling to pick up a ringing phone and hear an editor asking you to write something for his or her publication. Therefore, it is suggested that you make excellence a byword in your travel writing. It will pay big dividends.

In chapter 9, Sue Rumbaugh explains why good writing is important and what top-quality travel writing is as it relates to newspapers, magazines, and guidebooks. She discusses, in general, what editors look for in the different media. The chapter closes with a discussion of other things to consider in delivering a total quality package.

Tom Swick is known for railing against less than excellent travel writing. In chapter 10, he discusses the division between poor travel writing and excellent travel writing and provides an evolution of the travel book and of travel journalism. Swick then reviews the three phases of writing a "good" travel narrative. The bulk of his chapter, however, is devoted to a discussion of the seven missing elements and the ten sins of traditional travel writing.

By studying these two chapters, the novice travel writer can make notes and then set up written guidelines to follow in making sure that everything submitted to an editor measures up and that every submission is excellent travel writing.

CHAPTER 9

Quality Travel Writing

Sue Rumbaugh

GOOD WRITING WILL SELL MORE RAPIDLY

No one likes to do someone else's work; we feel used or neglected. Editors are no different. They expect us, as serious writers, to know and to follow correct grammar and word usage. If we do not supply editors with well-written pieces, they may not be inclined to accept and publish our work.

One reason newspapers and magazines are more eager to accept work that is considered clean copy—free of grammar and punctuation errors—is that they have limited staff and cannot spare the time of one of their employees to rewrite your work. Since newspapers and magazines seek to print error-free stories, they prefer to receive writing that is well-written and uses correct style and format over those stories that require a lot of attention. Therefore, you gain a competitive edge for selling your work by learning and using correct style.

This is why one of the first things a writer should do is to purchase and read a copy of a stylebook. There are several good ones, including Strunk and White's *The Elements of Style*. Pick one up, and keep a copy at your desk; refer to it often. You'll be glad you did.

WHAT IS TOP-QUALITY WRITING?

Top-quality travel writing contains several elements. For a travel writer hoping to sell his or her work to a newspaper or magazine, each of these elements is important and will play some role in each story. However, depending upon what type of travel article you are writing, the emphasis of each of these elements will differ.

Six Hallmarks of Quality Narrative Travel Writing

Many travel articles are written as narrative pieces. There are some special touches or marks of quality that apply to narrative travel writing. Some of these apply to other forms of travel writing, as well, but some are unique to narrative travel writing.

1. Tell a Story

Narrative travel writing must tell a story. It must have a theme, thesis, or point to it. Each story must have an opening, a middle, and an end. Usually, the better the storytelling ability of the author, the better the narrative travel article. Quality, therefore, often equates to being a good storyteller.

2. Narrative Openings Capture Attention

The opening or *lead* must capture the attention of the reader. Travel articles in newspapers and magazines help to sell the publication and are in competition for readership, up against all of the other stories in that specific publication as well as in other publications one may consider purchasing. So, a travel writer needs to develop an inviting opening and catch the reader's attention quickly.

3. Quality Means Good Theme Development

The body of the quality narrative travel article should develop the main theme using the careful preparation of scenes and presentation of information. Each paragraph should be written in such a way that the reader moves through the story effortlessly. A reader should not have to search the dictionary for meanings of words or work to understand the meaning intended within each paragraph. The substance of the travel article should be clear.

4. Quality Requires Smooth Transitions

Smooth transitions constitute a mark of quality. The paragraphs should flow easily into and out of one another. Transition words and sentences should be used to connect varying thoughts and advance the story line.

5. Quality Provides a Sense of Completion

Quality narrative travel writing provides the reader with a sense of completion at the end of the article. It should affirm what the reader has figured out by reading your interesting opening and well-developed paragraphs. It should give the reader a sense of resolution. The end should provide some link back to the opening or the *theme* of the piece. The exact wording or approach depends upon the writer's style and the type of piece being written.

6. Excellent Narrative Travel Writing Often Contains a Plot

Borrowing from fiction and poetry, a good narrative travel piece that is written as creative nonfiction, in addition to developing a theme, will contain a plot or a series of events or occurrences. This is important in story development because no story can exist without a series of events or activities to give it shape.

FACTUAL VERIFICATION IS A SIGN OF QUALITY

One sign of quality in travel writing is factual verification. Each travel article should contain factual information that has been verified through research. Do not trust your memory or guess at details. Look up facts, or contact someone knowledgeable and credible to confirm them. Getting the details correct will help to build your credibility as a writer.

PROVIDE EXPECTED INFORMATION TO MAINTAIN A QUALITY LEVEL

Quality means providing expected information. A good travel article will answer the journalist's guide to story writing: *who, what, where, when, how,* and *why*. Again, depending upon the type of travel article and its focus, each of these elements will be given a different amount of emphasis, provide a varying amount of detail, and be allotted the amount of space necessary to develop the story while providing factual information.

Include People

People can make a travel article memorable. Whether it is a narrative, a destination article, an essay, or even some roundup articles, authors should consider the inclusion of people or "characters" in their travel piece. Characters and their descriptions add a human element to travel articles and bring them to life. Without human beings, a place is nothing more than images and shapes.

Raise the Quality Level with Texture

Writing with texture—providing descriptions of the sights, sounds, tastes, tactile elements, and smells—engages the reader by tapping his or her senses. This makes for a much more interesting travel article.

Humor Adds to Article Quality

The use of humor, particularly directed at the writer, is acceptable and often makes for a fun and funny travel writing piece that most readers will enjoy. But, be careful if writing with humor. People's senses of humor vary. Be sure to be clear that you are writing with the attempt at humor, and do not make someone else's misfortune the object of your joke. Your readers will turn on you.

QUALITY MEANS ADD-ONS

Because newspapers print many pictures and graphics, travel articles sell much better when they are accompanied by pictures and sidebar roundups. Travel writers seeking a reputation for top-quality work should always consider adding sidebars and photos to the packages they send to newspapers.

QUALITY MEANS HELPING EDITORS EDIT

Travel articles, if not printed in their entirety, may be printed in a series, over several issues, or cut in the middle. And they usually include a lot of details and descriptions to create scenes, explain transportation details, make the characters come alive, or fully develop the article's theme. Like hard news, paragraphs need to be short and words are usually kept to one or two syllables—to make efficient use of limited space. While inverted pyramid style articles are not required, most editors still prefer them. When laying out a travel page for the next day's newspaper and the article is too long, editors usually like to be able to take a travel article and chop off the last paragraph or the last several lines. Giving the editor the ability to cut from the bottom or the middle can, and sometimes does, result in articles being run rather than discarded.

QUALITY MEANS HELPING TO SELL MAGAZINES

Travel articles that are written for magazines also are expected to provide information and to entertain readers. Since magazines invest resources to identify the demographics of their readership, the travel writer should also have an understanding of each publication's target audience and write in a style and about a travel subject of particular interest to this group. Otherwise, the choice of details for scene and story development will not resonate with the magazine's audience. It will not help the magazine sell its publication. Therefore, a competent travel writer will spend time researching the publication and understanding the issues and trends of importance to this particular magazine and its readership.

QUALITY WRITING FOR GUIDEBOOKS

Quality guidebook writing requires writers to be detail-oriented and highly organized. They also have to be able to spend a lot of time and money, confirming addresses, phone numbers, hours of operation, etc. so that the finished book is as accurate as possible at the time of printing.

Guidebooks that also include descriptions of places, hotels, restaurants, etc. require writing that is interesting, creative, thorough, objective, and inclusive in its description. People who purchase guidebooks are seeking information that will be helpful in supporting decisions they will make before and during a trip. Readers rely upon the accuracy of the information as well as on the description provided by travel guidebook writers. Therefore, writers must research, check, and double-check their information before including it in their chapters or books.

Quality travel guidebook writing means understanding the culture of the average buyer of the guidebook as well as the culture of the country or area about which you are writing. That Viennese pub crawl described in detail for the twenty-something readers may go over well with British young people, but it might be a disaster for a group of Dallas, Texas, mid-level professionals. There is a reason why U.S.-based guidebook publishers seek Americans to write their guidebooks. But it is not enough to just be an American. The guidebook to Israel that will appeal to those wanting to bar hop in Tel Aviv will be different than the guidebook sought by those wanting to follow via dolorosa (the Way of the Cross). The key, then, is to know your guidebook buyer (customer) and to know him or her well.

FROM GOOD TO EXCELLENT

Excellence is a goal to strive for. While this chapter has presented a good starting point for developing good travel writing, the next chapter addresses the concept of travel writing excellence. According to author Tom Swick, few writers have consistently delivered excellent travel writing. This, perhaps, is the most compelling reason to strive toward excellence in all of your travel writing.

End-of-Chapter Questions

1. According to the chapter author, what might give you a competitive edge?
2. What stylebook does the author recommend?
3. Must narrative travel writing tell a story?
4. Should a reader need to search a dictionary when reading a travel article?
5. What should the end of a travel article do?
6. Should factual information be verified?

Quality Travel Writing

7. What questions are asked in the journalist's guide to story writing?
8. What often makes for a fun and funny travel writing piece?
9. What two add-ons add quality to a travel piece?
10. In addition to understanding the culture of the country or area about which the guidebook author is writing, what additional culture must the guidebook writer understand?

WRITING ASSIGNMENT NINE
WRITING SIDEBARS

Assignment Introduction

Many travel articles have sidebars. Most of them relate to a hotel or a restaurant featured in the article. The sidebar is frequently titled "If You Go." You may already have prepared the notes that you may need for a sidebar for an article based on your travel journal. Now you will do one that ultimately will accompany an article you write based on your travel journal notes.

Assignment Activity

Reread your travel journal. In this assignment, you will write a sidebar for a restaurant that you feel comfortable recommending to the reader of an article you will write based on your travel journal. If the sightseeing place that you visited has a restaurant and you feel comfortable recommending that restaurant, then write your sidebar about that restaurant. However, frequently there are better and much less expensive restaurants within a few blocks of sightseeing points of interest. You might decide to make a second visit and drive the neighborhood in which the sightseeing point is located looking for restaurants. Based on your drive-by, select one or two restaurants that you feel might be good to feature. Walk in during lunch or at dinner time. Tell the host or hostess that you would like to see a menu before deciding to dine at the restaurant. Don't hesitate to make notes in your journal. Note the ambiance, the aromas, the sounds, and the feel of the place. If you tell the host or hostess that you are a travel writer, you might be allowed to keep the menu. If not, jot down the more interesting menu items and the prices.

After visiting two or three restaurants, decide which one you think you want to feature. Go back and order a meal. As you are seated, look at what other diners are eating. If something looks especially good, stop and ask the patron what they are eating. Don't be shy. Your job is to get information. Order something different than standard fare. Take copious notes.

When you get back home, draft your sidebar. Head it with the important facts, i.e., the name of the restaurant, the address, the phone number, and the Web address if it has one. Include the hours of operation, and, if you think it might be difficult for the reader to find the restaurant, put in driving directions from the sightseeing point. List four or five main entrées with prices and any special notes. (Example: The portions are huge. Ask for a large take-home box. Their regular boxes are much too small.) In your sidebar, add a short paragraph that describes the ambiance and any unusual or signature menu items or restaurant details.

Remember, sidebars are short. They are an add-on to an article. Your sidebar should not run more than about 100 to 300 words.

Final Step: Add your name to the Instructor Comment Sheet for Writing Assignment Nine in appendix 5 and staple it to the sidebar that you wrote for this assignment. Then turn in both sheets to your professor.

THOMAS SWICK has been the travel editor of the *South Florida Sun-Sentinel* since 1989. He has written for numerous publications, including a critique of travel journalism for the *Columbia Journalism Review* and an overview of travel literature for *The American Scholar*. His stories have appeared in *The Best American Travel Writing 2001, 2002,* and *2004*. He is the author of two books: a travel memoir, *Unquiet Days: At Home in Poland*, and a collection of travel stories, *A Way to See the World: From Texas to Transylvania with a Maverick Traveler*.

CHAPTER 10

Toward Excellence in Travel Writing

Thomas Swick

As recent times have clearly demonstrated, there is a great divide in this country: the vast chasm that lies between travel books and travel journalism. Travel books, despite a declining popularity, still tend to be of high quality—thoughtful, stylish, illuminating—while travel journalism, with some exceptions, does not. To put down a book by Pico Iyer, Jan Morris, or even Paul Theroux and to replace it with a travel magazine, or most Sunday newspaper travel sections, is to journey from Mount Parnassus to the Vegas Strip.

The division is difficult to explain. Newspapers are not literature, but newsrooms are traditional spawning grounds for writers, who come from all ranks: beat reporter, film critic, sports writer, op-ed columnist, but rarely travel editor. This is odd when you consider that travel is the one section of the paper that doesn't insist on timeliness, brevity, or objectivity but allows for, or at least could if it wanted, a leisurely, nuanced, passionate approach (i.e., the kind of writing one finds in books).

Of course, newspapers have always seen their job as that of providing information, and readers—people who are still transported by the written word—have pretty much had to depend on magazines. Unfortunately in travel, the magazines have not been of much help. The two biggest focus primarily on the material aspects of travel—the "how to" as opposed to the "why?"—and cater to a decidedly upscale audience. Their sumptuous photographs of idyllic retreats have something about them of an airbrushed centerfold.

All of the travel magazines are obsessed with lists—The Twenty-two Best This, The Nine Secret That—which often squeeze out good writing, be it in the form of humorous columns, reflective essays, or evocative narratives. Each year *The Best American Travel Writing* anthology contains numerous stories from publications not devoted to travel.

Both the travel book and travel journalism have evolved as the public's travel habits have changed. The first travel writers followed in the footsteps of the explorers or were part-explorer themselves. Their objective was clear: to describe to the people back home an unimagined physicality, to satisfy a concrete curiosity about the other. Travel writing was a necessary adjunct to discovery, bringing a place into existence through the creative power of words.

In the nineteenth century, as movement increased, travel writing became more personal. Alexander Kinglake, in his book *Eothen*, described not just how the world looked but how it felt. He was not alone in his pursuit of quiddity; George Borrow befriended the Gypsies in Spain (theirs being one of the dozen languages he spoke), and Richard Burton—possessing not only guile but the wherewithal—entered Mecca disguised as an Afghan pilgrim. They were joined by novelists—Dickens, Trollope, and Twain—who by comparison were frightful dilettantes but who brought the imaginative skills and intuitive instincts of their trade.

The focus on the human increased in the twentieth century, as did specialization. Freya Stark staked out the Arab world, while Norman

Douglas laid claims to Italy. Gerald Brenan exiled himself to Andalusia where he promoted the "sedentary" school of travel writing, in which a writer, instead of moving through a place, settles down in it. Followers included Lawrence Durrell (in Greece), M.F.K. Fisher (in France), and Elliot Paul (in Paris and Ibiza). Their books took travel writing out of its itinerant sphere and created with it a kind of novelistic anthropology.

As more people started traveling, the travel book changed. It was no longer necessary to describe what had already been seen by most potential readers (if not in person, then at least in pictures). Travel writers were put in the position of interpreting, trying to understand not just what was there but what was invisible to the eye. They moved from pure aesthetic appreciation to intellectual analysis. The best of this group—Pico Iyer, Jonathan Raban, Colin Thubron—are, not surprisingly, travel writers first and novelists second.

Nevertheless, some of them are loath to admit it. While travel writing workshops overflow, the people who practice it most brilliantly chafe under the title. Their reaction is understandable when you realize that the travel writing most people see is that which appears in their Sunday newspaper or sits next to *People* in their dentist's waiting room.

Going to the dentist in the '50s and '60s was a lot different than it is today. The pain of the drill was mollified, somewhat, by the pleasure of finding (if you chose the right healthcare professional) a copy of *Holiday* on the disheveled coffee table. For the magazine paired famous writers with famous places—Irwin Shaw on Brooklyn, John Steinbeck on Paris, Nikos Kazantzakis on Crete, Paul Bowles on "The Incredible Arab." Today, when we should be reading about the incredible Arab, we get "Eleven Gorgeous Getaways."

There was a moment in the '80s, the modern golden age of travel writing, when a magazine took up where *Holiday* had left off. *Granta*, under the editorship of the American Bill Buford, gave space to established stars (Bruce Chatwin and Paul Theroux), new voices (like Isabel Hilton and Bill Bryson), and old globetrotters (like Martha Gellhorn and Norman Lewis). Though it was not the sort of thing you'd find at the dentist, *Granta* did all it could to make travel writing respectable again.

The road newspapers have traveled to their current how-to station is less heroic. Basically, they have gone from flowery accounts—the inevitable result, in the old days, of free trips—to service articles and consumer tips. The growing tendency in travel sections is toward quick information (to help the growing legions of travelers) as opposed to leisurely stories (In an age when people are too busy to read). Which begs the question: if people are so much under the gun, how is it that they have all this time to travel?

People have more time for reading than they let on (how else to explain the popularity of TiVo?) and not as many of them travel as the staffs of travel publications think. The elderly often lack the health and/or the money to travel, and young couples with small children are not great vagabonds. Even when we do travel, American do it on less annual vacation time than almost any other people in the industrialized world. In an age of widespread Americanization, we as a nation don't spread very widely; only 22 percent of Americans possess passports. What good, for the other 78 percent, are lists of the ten best spas in Sweden?

Of course, travel magazines and sections need to provide people with helpful, up-to-date information. But if that's all they do, they unnecessarily limit their readership. There is certainly room, in the glossies as well as in newspapers, for both service articles and evocative travel narratives. The latter, when done well, can entertain and amuse (recent studies have shown that laughter strengthens the heart) and instruct and enlighten (Americans' ignorance of the world has become a global joke) and, thus, be of far greater value—indeed, helpfulness—than any number of practical tips.

Surely one of the reasons that consumer articles are more common than armchair stories is that they are so much easier to do. A good service piece can be researched over the phone; a good travel narrative entails three heavy-laden phases.

PHASE 1: PREPARATION BEFORE THE TRIP

Only amateurs think that writing begins when you sit down at the computer. The professionals remember Sir Joshua Reynolds who, on being asked how long it took him to do a painting, answered: "All my life." Travel is a genre of writing that encompasses, not surprisingly, the world: flora and fauna, architecture, language, history, food, music, religion, politics, art. All of a writer's experience goes into his or her writing; it's just that travel writers, because of their chosen form, need to experience more than most.

The first thing travel writers do is decide where to go. This decision is more important than it sounds. If you choose an obvious place—Paris, Hawaii, Sydney, Tuscany—you automatically increase the competition, not just against your fellow freelancers but against all the writers who have gone before you. Writing is about novelty, freshness, originality—"Make it new!" Ezra Pound exhorted young poets—and one of the most difficult things in travel writing is saying something new about a place that has been written to death.

Unsung places often provide the best subjects for travel writers. Not only is there less pressure to come up with something different, but the story is often better because the experience was often richer. People in less-visited places tend to be more curious, sympathetic, and grateful than those who live in heavily touristed regions. They appreciate that you took the time to come to their overlooked part of the world, and they are happy, usually, to share their stories.

As soon as you've decided where to go, you start your research. You read the guidebooks, just like a tourist. But you also read history books and novels set in the place. (If it's a foreign country, read both those by English-language authors—you will not be at this long before you run into Graham Greene—and those in translation). Travel books are, of course, also important, but stick with the older ones; anything written within the last few years will be too close to your own visit, and you don't want another person's impressions coloring your own.

If it's a trip in the United States, get a hold of a local Sunday paper before you go. Online publications will be no help, because you will not be interested in the news—news is the same everywhere. You want the arts section (what are people there seeing?), the book section (what are they reading?), and the advertisements (what are they buying?). A New Mexico paper will carry lists of New Age meetings; a South Florida paper will include names of establishments specializing in liposuction and breast enlargement—each tells you something specific about the place.

If you've chosen a country whose people don't speak English, learn some of the language. A few basic words help immeasurably in everyday transactions, and, as you'll find if you go deeper into your study, both vocabulary and grammar reveal a lot about the culture.

It is also important to pore over maps; they give you a sense of the layout, a feel for your subject before you've seen it. Films can be as transporting and illuminating as literature—especially foreign ones—and CDs can fill your home with the music that will soon be your daily soundtrack. The idea is to immerse yourself as completely as possible in the place before you leave home.

There are some travel writers who tell everyone they meet where they're headed next—for two reasons (three if they're braggarts). One, it's interesting to hear other people's perceptions. (For those taking the unsung route, a "Huh? Why you going there?" is the sweetest sound imaginable.)

Two, you'd be surprised how often someone says he has a cousin or an old sparring partner in your new favorite place. And, like that, you have your first contact. Get names, numbers, and e-mail addresses. The more contacts you collect the better (and the more you travel the wider your web of contacts becomes). Some will not pan out: the address has changed; the phone's been disconnected; they're on vacation; they can only see you for an hour, and they're as dull, it turns out, as your Sunday travel section. But others will be eloquent experts, tour guides manqué, kindred spirits. The travel writer's best friend is, often, a friend of a friend.

PHASE 2: ON-SITE ACTIVITY

Travel writers, when thought of at all, are seen as charmed figures, always moving, never stymied in front of an immigration officer (or computer screen). Travel writers, if we reflect at all, see ourselves as aimless, inconsequential, and nevertheless under-appreciated beings.

Once in the place, we are at sea. Business people have their meetings, aid workers their clinics, tourists their monuments. Even reporters have a specific story to cover: a crash, a kidnapping, a coup d'etat. Travel writers have no itineraries or obligations—mummies bore us, nobody's expecting us (if we haven't gotten our contacts)—and we have no leads, since we don't know what our story is. We have to look for it, and, frequently, it is whatever happens to us.

So we mosey, wander, poke around. Walking is the first thing you should do when you arrive in a new place—not planning to see anything but hoping to see everything. It is in those initial hours that everything appears in sharp focus; after a few days, the world will return to its customary blur. So you walk and take in the facades, the doorways, the shop windows, the mannequins, the cars, the streetlamps. All the things that make this place different from home.

Walking is tiring, so after a while you take a rest (there's a sidewalk café right over there). Sitting, too, is important: it takes you out of the passing parade, so you can observe its individual features better. What are the people wearing? How do they walk? (Slowly? Sleekly? Slouchily?) Do they greet by kissing or shaking hands? How many kisses?

Since you're no longer navigating, you can concentrate more on all your senses. You've ordered a little snack, a local specialty, soaked in butter, that would be even more delicious if the smoke from your neighbor's cigarette weren't floating in a direct line to your nostrils while the strange wail of an ambulance sounds in the distance.

You pull out your notebook and describe, perhaps even sketch, the scene; you will never see it as clearly again. Be sure to jot down the name of the café and the street that it's on—names can be as evocative as descriptions, part of the detail that will give your story not only authenticity but life.

Having walked and sat you want something a little richer. You've observed the surface, and now you want to venture beneath it; you want to participate in the life of the place.

You call your contacts. You search for a character or an incident or even a calamity that can become your subject. The worst trips, it is famously said, make the best stories, and, in a kind of proof of that, Vintage published in 1991 an excellent anthology of travel writing titled *Bad Trips*.

This philosophy is behind the trend in adventure travel. Risk, its heated buildup and colorful consequences, is an irresistible subject. The problem with much of the writing that results is that it's heavy on personal rather than worldly insight, portraying not the place but the author's mettle. You could call these journeys "ego trips."

But at least the adventurers have a quest, a reason to be in the place they have come to. You struggle with definition. (And not only you; the great travel writer Bruce Chatwin titled his last book *What Am I Doing*

Here.) You are not one of the tourists, though you share their transport, their hotels, their intoxication with the new. You snap pictures and send postcards, but you are not on vacation. You shun tour groups—traipsing through neighborhoods, sitting in dives—and thereby make yourself even more out-of-place.

You are engaged in work that looks a lot like play but without play's essential carefree quality. There is a story, you know, that has to result. And it weighs on you, this thought, along with the idea of your impertinent existence.

So you go to the places where you'll find locals: a game, a bar, a church (even if you're agnostic), and you stay for the coffee hour. (The Anglicans in Porto, Portugal, serve port wine, and in Bangkok, if you're lucky, you'll eat shrimp curry.)

It helps if you pursue a passion or a hobby: a love of bridge will find you partners around the globe who speak your language, and an interest in genealogy leads you into government buildings that are not surrounded by tour buses and forces you to ask questions. Being in need of assistance is a great boon to conversation.

In the evening, you head off to a concert you've read about in the paper or to an art exhibition in a neighborhood far from the center. (Neighborhoods are to you what museums are to tourists.) You're interested in art—you're interested in everything—but you're especially interested in people. And not just anyone—those warm, quotable souls who will be your entry into the place.

It can sometimes be difficult meeting people—depending on the place (holiday resorts where you don't speak the language are especially tough) and on your own degree of comfort in approaching strangers. But once you do, it's easy to talk to them because you're so well-informed; you've read their hometown paper, you've watched the films of their great director, you're curious about the Nobel prospects of their feminist novelist.

If you travel with a spouse, especially a wife, you may find it easier to strike up a conversation. While women traveling alone are sometimes vulnerable, men traveling alone are often suspect. People feel less threatened by a couple.

But most travel writers go it alone. So much of what you do as a travel writer is unexplainable wandering and inexplicable dawdling.

Because, after years of doing it, you get a sense—or think you do—that perhaps, if you head down this street instead of that one or hang out on this square for awhile (there's something indefinable in the air), you're going to find gold. And most sane companions will have had enough of this by the end of the first day.

You have so little time in each place you visit that, even if you split up during the day and get together only for dinner, that meal is valuable minutes lost. You are in your own little bubble, talking about home. You are not noticing the rows of river bass hanging on the far wall, the couple at the next table gossiping about the mayor, the way the waiter wears his apron.

A companion provides you with a comfort level that is inappropriate to your task. It is not that you have to suffer to write well, but the loneliness—a true travel writer spends a great deal of time watching other people have fun—will push you, eventually, into action.

So much of travel is serendipity, but you can help it along through knowledgeable positioning and careful observation. You get an idea by picking up the free weeklies, by studying human behavior, where to go and whom to approach.

Through the inhabitants of a place, you learn and, often, connect. A wonderful trip is when you meet good people, discover new things, and participate in the everyday life. You get invited into someone's home, for instance, the travel writers' Holy Grail. And there are those amazing times, not frequent but occasional enough to keep you coming back, when you get on such a roll that the people become friends, the information becomes insight, the participation becomes engagement. You find yourself emotionally attached to the place. The best trips, you suddenly suspect, make the best stories, and you almost can't wait to get home to your computer to prove it.

PHASE 3: THE WRITING

Your head is as full of unrelated impressions as your notebook is of illegible scribblings. Your task: to consolidate them into an accurate evocation of the place (as you experienced it), tell a story while doing so (the best travel stories read like short stories), and in the process throw in a few keen observations and fresh insights on the place or, if you want the story to transcend the narrow confines of a travelogue, on life.

If that sounds daunting, remember Flannery O'Connor: "All writing is painful," she once wrote to a friend, "and if it's not painful, then it's not worth doing." If you have a low threshold for pain, there are many editors who will be happy to see you write a consumer piece. But that means leaving out the people, the jokes, the confidences, the emotion—in other words, all of the things that made the trip meaningful.

A number of years ago, Paul Theroux wrote a piece for *Granta* about his feelings before he took the train trip that he turned into one of the best-selling travel books of modern times, *The Great Railway Bazaar*. He complained that most travel writing then (this was in the early '70s), was focused on the sights and hopelessly boring. He quoted a passage from a travel book by Anthony Trollope, *The West Indies and the Spanish Main*, and after it wrote: "Something human had happened, and Trollope recorded it: that, it seemed to me, was the essence of good travel writing."

And you think: Oh, that's Theroux, being eccentric again. A travel story is about description, atmosphere, capturing a sense of place. But then you recall favorite scenes from travel books—Patrick Leigh Fermor disappearing in a haystack with a Transylvanian peasant girl, Colin Thubron flying to Beijing and asking his seatmate if the Chinese think Westerners smell—and you know he's right.

But many travel articles patently avoid the human. In fact, they often appear inhuman, so formulaic that they seem to have been churned out by a computer somewhere. They commit the first sin of the genre: *All travel stories sound the same.*

To stand out, your story must have a personal voice—one of the seven elements missing from the traditional travel article. Almost any place you write about has

> **Ten Sins of Travel Stories**
>
> 1. They sound the same.
> 2. They are riddled with clichés.
> 3. They tell instead of show.
> 4. They cover too much.
> 5. They gush.
> 6. They avoid people.
> 7. They are humorless.
> 8. They lack continuity.
> 9. They are superficial.
> 10. They fail to inspire.

been written about before; your challenge is to find something new to say about it, preferably in an interesting way. And, since every person is unique, the best way to do this is to examine your own individual reactions: What surprised you, amused you, depressed you, intrigued you? Theroux wrote in his book about the Mediterranean, *The Pillars of Hercules*: "No one has ever described the place where I've just arrived." It is some-

> **Seven Missing Elements in Traditional Travel Writing**
>
> 1. A personal voice
> 2. Imagination
> 3. Point of view
> 4. People
> 5. The present—what's going on now
> 6. Dialogue
> 7. Humor

thing all travelers have felt, but no travel writers had ever said. We all see things in our own way.

Keep in mind, however, that you are not the subject. (You're writing a travel story, not a memoir.) The best travel stories are written in first person, as are, editors love to say, the worst. These latter come with an embarrassment of I's. The trick is to write in first person but to make sure that each time you put yourself in the story it tells us more about the place than it does about you. A good idea is to read over your sentences—constantly, often aloud, to get a sense of the rhythm—and excise any excess I's. (For example: "I saw a man carrying a mannequin" works just well, better in fact, as "A man carried a mannequin.")

It's possible to write a fine travel story without using first person, usually from a trip when not much happened or, conversely, when you talked to so many people that you can't introduce them all and instead use their comments to shape your own conclusions. And if you succeed you feel like a small, high-flying Georges Perec, who wrote a 304-page novel, *La Disparition*, without using the letter "e."

Another feature that will make your piece unique is imagination (the second element missing from the traditional travel story). This is not to be confused with invention. Travel writing is nonfiction, especially if it's being done for a newspaper or magazine. In books, writers sometimes take liberties, most notably Robert Byron who is said to have made up large chunks of conversation in his classic *The Road to Oxiana*.

But your concern is with depicting what's actually there, what's truly happening, and comparisons, similes, metaphors, and allusions will help you do this in a more interesting fashion.

The third aspect that will make your story unique—and the third element missing from the traditional travel article—is a point of view. Traditionally, travel articles have been characterized by a bland rosiness, a leftover from the days when writers took free trips and felt obliged to say nice things.

A critical eye makes your story more believable, to say nothing of accurate. (No place, as you'll see shortly, is paradise.) And it serves your readers better by preparing them for the realities. How many travelers, fed a steady diet of travel publications, go to the Caribbean expecting only palm-fringed beaches and colorful gingerbread? The advantage that writers have over photographers is that, while it is extremely difficult to take a beautiful picture of blight, it is quite possible to pen a pleasing paragraph about ugliness. As long as you avoid the second sin of travel stories: *They are riddled with clichés.*

Clichés are the jetlag of composition: moments of tired thinking. Travel writing has managed to make single words into clichés from massive overuse. We no longer take a weekend trip or a short excursion; today it is a "getaway" or—continuing the criminal motif—"escape." Most any experience outside of an urban area is an "adventure" ("new adventure," "great adventure," "wild adventure"); if it happens to occur beyond the borders of North America and Europe, it automatically becomes an "exotic adventure." Backward lands are "unspoiled"; places that have yet to build an international airport are "best-kept secrets." Cities with a proven track record for tourism are "gems."

Virtually any place with palm trees is "paradise." (In 2002, *National Geographic Traveler* magazine discovered the hazard of using this particular cliché when its October cover—"Bali—Still Paradise?"—stared out from newsstands for weeks after the Kuta beach bombing.) "Places" are "destinations," and they, like people, are unable simply to change— journalism's lemmings instead insist that they "reinvent themselves."

Clichés were inventive, clever turns of phrase when first coined. Good writers ignore them (or read over their writing and, finding them lurking, flush them out); gifted writers give birth to future ones.

In fiction writing workshops, students are always instructed: "Show, don't tell," and the same advice applies to travel writers, whose writing too often commits the third sin of travel stories: *They tell instead of show.* It is easy to say "the people are friendly," but the observation has little effect. For one thing, readers have to take your word for it. For another, friendliness is subjective—one person's friendliness (for instance, a New Englander's) may not be another's (say, a Southerner's). Much more effective is to write a little scene in which you were the recipient, or witness, of a kindness. It will convince the reader subtly, without force.

The same rule applies to the physical world: Don't say that "the harbor was beautiful"; describe it with individual details—the colors of the houses, the types of boats, the kinds of trees—that make the reader see its beauty.

Some writers, true, employ a more didactic, essay style, but they are people, like Jan Morris, who write with such long-term authority and imaginative exuberance that they can get away with it. In other words, wait till you're in your 50s with a couple of books under your belt. In the meantime, be like Evelyn Waugh who, on visiting the Spanish-American Exposition in Seville in 1929—not a good year for travel—described "silent rifle ranges with heaps of ammunition lying undischarged and mountains of bottles unbroken."

Showing takes more time and space than telling, which is fine because that could keep you from committing the fourth sin of travel stories: *They cover too much.* Travel writers go to a city, sometimes a country, and for some reason feel that they have to squeeze it all, in its entirety, into one story.

They don't. Rarely does a newspaper travel story exceed three thousand words, and there are few hamlets, let alone metropolises, that can be done justice in a medium-sized story. Instead, focus on a single aspect—one day of your trip, a neighborhood of the city, your hotel—which can serve as a microcosm of the whole.

The all-inclusive travel story may well be the result of the high price people pay to travel, which makes them reluctant to leave anything out. The expense may also be behind travel writing's habit of *gushing* (the fifth sin).

Bad writers pick up on all the predictable things and, in hopes of elevating them to a grander status, write noisily about them. Good writers notice the unexpected things and present them calmly, without fuss. Evelyn Waugh is a perfect example of the latter. As is the man who went to the Smoky Mountains in winter and wrote that the locals "carried their skis on their gun racks." There are few things as pleasing as the telling detail delivered on tiptoe.

The sixth sin of travel stories—*they avoid the people*—is something of a cardinal sin, for it encompasses three of the elements missing from the traditional travel story.

People themselves are missing element number four. For years they were conspicuous by their absence. There was a formula, which everyone seemed to follow (probably because it appeared front and center every Sunday in the *New York Times* Travel section), that allowed no humans, other than the author and, usually, his or her spouse, to darken the pages of a travel story. Writers would go to Sao Paulo, Brazil, and tell their readers (tell) that it was a city of eighteen million people, and they wouldn't introduce them to (show) a single one.

The preference was for sights over inhabitants or, in other words, the past over the present (missing element number five). Writers were constantly going off—visiting museums, climbing ruins, admiring monuments—and coming back with stories of what had happened years before. Their well-educated readers thought: I knew that.

The past, of course, is essential to our understanding of the present, which is why you read up on the history of a place before you visit it. But it's been covered already, by everything from guidebooks to middle-school teachers. Your challenge, and thrill, is finding out what's going on now. And if neighborhoods are your museums, then people are the artifacts that talk (missing element number six)

Most of the places we visit resound with voices, yet the traditional travel story is mysteriously hushed. It is like traveling with the deaf through the land of the mute. Vladimir Nabokov used to flip through novels and, if they contained too much dialogue, put them down. You should flip through your travel story and, if it has no dialogue, start again.

The absence of dialogue often suggests the presence of the seventh sin of travel stories: *They are humorless.* (Humor being missing element number seven). This is remarkable when you think about it, since travel is one of the funniest things we do. We leave home, where we know the score, and go someplace where we haven't got a clue. If it's another country, we're stymied by a pay phone; if it's another language, we can't even ask for ice. The possibilities, on the comedic scale, range from broad slapstick to droll misunderstandings.

Everybody comes back from vacation with funny stories—they're usually the ones told first—but few writers put them into their articles. Because, like people and dialogue, they've not been a part of the traditional travel story. The perception is they don't belong.

Humor has a hard time of it generally (nobody, the old saying goes, takes it seriously). This is in part because it's not easy to pull off. This is why high school productions of *Hamlet* are more successful than those of *Measure for Measure*. Writing a humorous story demands a strong command of language, a refined comedic sensibility, and a well-developed sense of timing.

Also, humor can be overdone (like the first-person pronoun). Just as too many I's in a travel story will make it a memoir, too many yucks will produce a predictable piece (and a possibly not very funny one at that, since humor depends on the element of surprise). The best travel humor not only amuses but reveals something interesting about the place.

S.J. Perelman was a great humorous travel writer (though a great humorist first) and—following in his two-first-initial footsteps—P.J. O'Rourke is the current king (though too infrequently on the road). Many other travel writers find humor useful from time to time: Thubron clinically discussed how Westerners smell with his Chinese seatmate until discovering that she had understood him to say "smile." And in relating this miscommunication, he gave his readers the dual thrill of a cultural insight and an unexpected ending.

The eighth sin of travel stories—*they lack continuity*—is more understandable (if not forgivable) than its predecessor. As mentioned earlier, travel writers usually go off without a story in mind and come back with an ill-shapen bag of random impressions. The solution is to find a theme. Sometimes you will have one to start with—you're visiting the hometown of a favorite writer or a region recovering from a natural disaster. Other times, you'll find one in the course of your journey; a particular cultural trait—a love of hiking, a religious devotion, an underdog aspect—keeps repeating itself as you move from place to place. It will happen, too, that you'll come home and still won't know what your central impression is until you start to write your story.

Once you get a theme, it will allow you to sift through all your notes and impressions and decide which ones to use (the ones related to it, of course) and which ones to discard. And, when the story's published, readers will have a thread to follow, which, along with the narrative, will carry them along.

The ninth is a related sin of travel stories: *They are superficial.* In the 1970s, Paul Fussell wrote an excellent book about British travel writing between the two World Wars, *Abroad,* which concluded, much too melodramatically, that the age of tourism had brought about the death of travel and, subsequently, of travel writing. It didn't, anymore than televised baseball brought an end to a day at the ballpark. There is still the true, authentic experience but, like being a spectator at a game, it is now affected by the other.

Travel writers, as discussed earlier, now depend on their minds as much as their eyes (because of the mass appeal of travel and video). Just as travel journalism has become more practical, travel literature has become more analytical.

Jonathan Raban, writing years ago in *Granta* about the Mississippi River floods, opened with this jaw-dropping sentence: "Flying to Minneapolis from the West, you see it as a theological problem." He went on to describe, from his window seat, the straight lines of "this right-angled, right-thinking Lutheran country" and the affront on it made by the Mississippi, "a broad serpentine shadow that sprawls unconformably across the checkerboard." The river, he wrote, "looks as if it had been put here to teach the godfearing Midwest a lesson about stubborn and unregenerate nature."

It would be unrealistic to expect all travel stories to reach these heights, but it is sad that, for the most part: *They fail to inspire* (the tenth and final sin). A journey is often a passage into an epiphany—or at least a new understanding. And the story describing it can be equally revelatory, possessing the narrative flow of a short story, the substance of a history lesson, the discursiveness of an essay, and the elegance of poetry. It embraces multiple genres just as it accommodates numerous subjects. It is, or can be, a house with many mansions.

End-of-Chapter Questions

1. The great divide to which the author of this chapter refers is the vast chasm that lies between what publications and travel journalism?

2. Fill in the blanks. "The first travel writers followed in the footsteps of the _____ or were part- _____ themselves."

3. Did travel writing become less personal as movement increased in the nineteenth century?

4. Are the best travel writers those who have moved from pure aesthetic appreciation to intellectual analysis? Are they travel writers first and novelists second?

5. According to the author of this chapter, "A good travel narrative entails three heavy-laden phases." These include: on-site activity and the writing. What is the third phase?

6. Are "unsung places" sometimes the best subjects for travel writers?

7. Are the best travel stories written in third person, according to the author of this chapter?

8. Is it true that the best travel humor not only amuses but reveals something interesting about the place?

9. What newspaper's policy was possibly the reason why so many travel stories avoid people?

10. Is it better for a travel writer to *tell* or to *show*?

WRITING ASSIGNMENT TEN
FIRST DRAFT OF YOUR SPEC ARTICLE

Assignment Introduction

Travel articles can be either written on contract or on speculation. A contract article is one that you have pre-sold to a magazine, and it must be written in accordance with the "writers guidelines" for that publication. A spec (speculation) article is written and then sent to many newspapers or one or more magazines hoping that they will run the article and pay you for it upon publication. Since it is easier to write, a spec article will be the first to be undertaken.

Assignment Activity

Go back to your travel journal. Draft an entire article based on your notes. Do not be too concerned with the length of the article, but remember that your final length will be 1,200 words. Most authors write their first rough draft twice as long as the final article they plan to submit. Therefore, your first draft should not be longer than 2,400 words.

Provide a logical flow to your article. You don't need to do this in your first rough draft, but it helps to keep it in mind as it will mean less work in preparing future drafts.

Write in third person. There are some first-person articles that sell, but most editors want third person. Therefore, train yourself from the beginning to write in third person.

Use simple words. Keep in mind that most newspaper readers read at about a tenth-grade level. Many read at a lower level.

After your first rough draft, go back and ask yourself questions, modifying your article accordingly. Do you have an attention-getting article title? Does your first sentence make readers feel as if they were at the destination? Is there a good flow from one paragraph to the next clear to the end of the article? Can the last paragraph and the last two paragraphs be chopped off and still the article will seem complete? You may decide to hold these sophistications for the second or the third draft, but remember they will be necessary in the final manuscript.

Final Step: Add your name to the Instructor Comment Sheet for Writing Assignment Ten in appendix 5 and staple it to the rough draft spec article you wrote for this assignment. Then turn in both sheets to your professor.

SECTION IV

DEVELOPING AND HONING THE ARTICLE

Probably the most important part of travel writing is developing and honing the article. This is the process whereby a travel writer creates a product. The outcome is the article itself.

One starts with the story idea or article concept, which was addressed in section 2. Next, an outline is prepared, then a rough draft. Finally, the draft is massaged (worked) until the final article is created.

In the next several chapters, we will learn how to cement an article sale through either query letters or phone calls. This will bring with it the article parameters required by the purchasing publisher. James Poynter will discuss writing for the editor, for the reader, or for both. Next, Karen Carmean and Sue Rumbaugh will provide an overview of the process from the generation of the story idea to the completion of the finished article, and James Poynter will take us through a more detailed discussion of the tasks required from the first draft to the final product. Then Amanda Castleman will discuss writing styles and types. The section will wind up with two chapters relating to providing photographs.

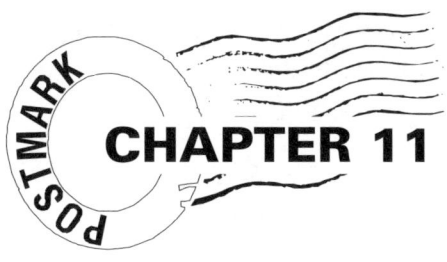

CHAPTER 11

Query Letter or Phone Call

James Poynter

SELLING IS IMPORTANT

There are many members in the local writers' association to which I belong. One woman would be the first to admit that the quality of her travel articles is not good. However, she writes and sells a lot of travel articles. She says the reason is that she finds markets nobody else finds. She spends hours at the library researching. She buys and studies publications that identify buyers. She communicates with travel-article buyers frequently so that she knows what they want. For her, the sales job is a substantially greater job than the writing job. A common complaint from especially new travel writers is that they want to spend their time writing, not selling. However, to be successful, the writing must sell.

TWO CHOICES

Travel writers have two choices. One option is to find a buyer first and write an article or a book that has been pre-sold to a magazine or a book publisher. This is called contract writing. The second option is to write an article and then find a buyer. This is called "spec" or writing on speculation. There are permutations in between.

Most writers prefer finding a buyer and then writing a pre-sold article or book, i.e., contract writing. Taking this approach, the writer knows exactly what to look for before going on a research trip. In addition, having a pre-sold article can help in obtaining free or reduced rate travel for a research trip.

Traditionally, a contract travel writer had a real contract prior to writing a finished article or book. In many cases today, it is not a formal contract but rather a letter of agreement. The editor basically agrees to buy the article or book that has been proposed by the author. Sometimes the editor will include a check with the letter of agreement or the contract. The check is an "advance" on the royalty or the full payment that has been agreed to.

In marketing, it is important to know that the market for "spec" (speculation) articles is different than that of contracted travel writing. Newspapers almost always buy spec articles. A few of the largest newspapers will buy contracted articles, but, even with the larger newspapers, almost all purchases are for spec articles. In other words, the editor reviews the final article and then decides whether or not to buy it.

The reverse is true for books. Almost all book publishers buy contracted travel writing. Typically they will contract for either the entire book or for chapters in a book.

Magazine editors buy both contracted articles and spec articles. Many will lean heavily one way or the other, but most magazines will purchase both types of articles.

SELLING SPEC ARTICLES TO NEWSPAPERS

Most travel writers who market spec articles to newspapers will send the article to a large number of non-competing newspapers. If the article is good, typically between 5 and 10 percent of the articles that are mailed will be picked up and run by newspapers and typically a check and a tear sheet (the article itself "torn" from the newspaper issue in which it appeared) will follow shortly thereafter. Because newspapers pay so little (many pay as low as $15 to $25 per article), most travel writers target magazines and book publishers instead. However, some articles are ideal for newspapers and an article that seems to be an excellent fit will sometimes be picked up by as many as 30 or 40 percent of the newspapers to which it is sent.

SELLING CONTRACT ARTICLES TO MAGAZINES

Matching the article to the magazine is one of the major keys to being able to sell articles to magazine editors. Appendix 2 contains contact information for a number of magazines that buy travel articles. They are listed in alphabetical order based on their titles. For a travel writer to maximize income, it is important that articles be marketed to magazines that are both likely to run the article and those that pay the best. Therefore, it is recommended that you start at the top of the list in the appendix and work your way down the list attempting to identify magazines that will match the type of article that you have written. For example, if you plan to write a cruise article targeted to retirees, you will find several publications that are cruise oriented and several that are retiree oriented. Most cruise-oriented magazines will be interested in articles that target retired seniors, and the editors of many magazines for seniors will be interested in cruise articles. One publication you might consider is *Travel & Leisure*. However, even though it pays better than most other magazines that might strongly consider cruise-oriented articles, its target is much wider than seniors, and it covers all aspects of travel and vacations, not just cruises. *Porthole* also might be a good choice. This is a magazine for those who want to take cruises, and while it also does not cater strictly to seniors, people who are fifty-five years old and older make up a substantial percentage of *Porthole's* readership. In addition, for most cruise-oriented articles *Porthole* pays better than *Travel & Leisure* and most other cruise-oriented and retiree-oriented magazines. It is recommended that you attempt to identify a minimum of five magazines but try to find as many as ten magazines that target the readers for which you plan to write. For a wider choice of publications, use a search engine on your computer. Enter key words such as *cruise* and *magazines*. List the publications you select in order of compensation.

CONFIRMING THE CONTACT

Phone the magazine and ask whoever answers the phone for the name of the person who makes the final decision on purchasing freelance travel articles. Editors change frequently, and, although the listing in this book is current as of the publication date, it could well be that there was a change the next day. Some magazines seem to go through travel editors rapidly, whereas other publications keep the same editor for years. It is important that you ask who the person is who is ultimately responsible for purchasing travel articles. If instead you simply ask if John Adams is still the person who purchases travel articles (because that is the person whose name is on your list), you may run into a problem. If the person with whom you are speaking does not know and is in a hurry, it will be tempting for that person to say, "Yes, he is still the person who is responsible for that." Then you have a confirmation for a person who is no longer with the magazine (or book publisher) or who has changed jobs with the publication.

BUY A CURRENT ISSUE

The next step is to get a copy of the current issue of each publication whose editor you plan to approach. It is important to review a current issue of the publication so that you can determine for yourself several critical factors. These factors include the average length of articles, whether or not articles are typically written in first or third person, the educational level of the average reader, and similar but important facts about the publication. When you talk with the editor or if you send a query letter, you will be in a better position to pitch your article if you know something about the publication and the types of articles it runs.

KNOW YOUR ANGLE BEFORE YOU PITCH

Before making contact with a magazine editor, clearly identify for yourself why that editor should be interested in running an article that you plan to write. If you are planning a vacation to Europe and you expect to be in London for four or five days, you might well want to write a travel article about London. However, London has been done many times. Editors will not be interested in buying a travel article titled "London." The chances are that they will be much more interested in running an article that is targeted. For example, you might write any of the following:

"Cheap Sleeps in Downtown London"

"Underground London"

"Unknown London Museums"

"Don't Forget the Umbrella—A Take-Home Purchase You Will Be Glad You Remembered"

Once you have an angle, find publications that match. For example, if you will be writing an article on unknown British museums, you will definitely want to eliminate publications that only feature domestic destinations in the U.S. or Canada. You will probably want to concentrate on publications that specialize in museums. Searching the Internet with the two words *museum magazines* will give you seventy-five listings. Many of the magazines will not be what you want, but by requesting sample copies, you should rapidly be able to narrow the list down to no more than five to ten publications. Generally speaking, the closer you can match your "angle" with a publication, the better.

STUDY WRITER'S GUIDELINES AND RECENT ISSUES

You have choices. You might study the entries for each targeted magazine in the current year's edition of *Writer's Guidelines* (ISBN 1-884956-40-8). It lists the writer's guidelines from more than 1,500 magazine editors and book publishers. However, it is surprising how many travel publications are missing. Keep in mind that some publications simply do not have guidelines for writers.

Frequently a better approach is to call the number on the masthead for each of the magazine editors to whom you plan to consider pitching your article. Ask if they have writer's guidelines for travel articles. If so, request a copy. If not, at the least confirm both the name of the person with the magazine who purchases travel articles and contact information, i.e., the phone number for that person and the address for the publication. Whether or not the magazine has writer's guidelines, go to your library and study three recent issues of each magazine. You will find that most magazines have two standard sizes of articles. Many times their writer's guidelines are wrong and say that their articles should be something different than what they really are. Keep in mind that some writer's guidelines were written ten or more editors ago. Therefore, do sample counts of one or two articles of what appear to be standard-length articles so that you will be sure of what they are actually running in recent months.

Get a good feel for the educational level for which the magazine is written. Is it a high level, such as *Condé Nast Traveler*, or is it a lower level similar to the reading level of your local newspaper? Once you have determined the reading level, jot it down on a page where you have talking notes. That page, for example, might indicate that the average reader is probably one who is interested in visiting museums throughout the world. You also might note there that the average short article is 450 words and the average longer article is 750 words and that the average educational level is one of the following: sub-high school, high school graduate, BA or BS degree, master's degree, or doctorate and above. You may be somewhat wrong, but remember this is for talking points; if you are even close, that is what is important.

You might want to consider other factors about the magazine as well. For example, how many photos normally accompany articles? Are articles written in first person or third person or a combination? Are articles primarily about destinations, or are they travelogues describing the travel experiences (trips) of the authors or a combination? Do they have a lot of roundup articles or few to none of these? Whenever you notice that there is something special or different about the magazine, i.e., something that sets it apart from others, write it down.

Ideally you will identify ten magazines that you feel match your angle. If you find more, try to narrow down to the ten best matches. If you find fewer, recognize that you may have to work with less than an ideal number of publication contacts.

QUERY LETTER OR PHONE CALL?

A large number of travel writers swear by query letters. Many have said that a well-written letter is the only way a travel writer should contact an editor. And there is no question that query letters do work. If they did not work, such a strong percentage of travel writers would not be using them. However, the reality is that many travel editors get so many query letters that they do not even open all of them. In fact, many travel editors will just take a brief glance at query letters and then throw them in the trash.

Telephone calls to travel-writing buyers (normally editors) are also effective. Again, if they were not effective, so many travel writers who make phone calls rather than writing letters would not do so. While a telephone call can easily miss an editor who may be out of the office at the time of the call or it might connect the travel writer with the editor at a time when the editor is busy and does not have time to talk, a phone call also can result in a conversation with an editor who, because of the phone call, will seriously consider the article concept. My personal preference is the telephone call. I have never made ten calls without getting the reaction I want from at least one travel-writing buyer. In other words, I have always gotten a sale. This is partly because of the parameters set up within which the phone call is made.

TELEPHONE PARAMETERS

Telemarketing is hard, and selling editors by phone on your travel article idea is telemarketing. Therefore, let the following suggestions guide you to successful travel writing telemarketing: 1) confirm contact information; 2) group your calls; 3) make your calls from an empty, quiet house; 4) call at a good time for the editor; 5) be prepared; 6) find a special angle for each magazine; and 7) put yourself in the mood.

Confirm Contact Information

Editors move and so do the headquarters of magazines. Before you plan to make your series of phone calls, turn to the masthead of each magazine whose editor you plan to contact. Write down the name of the person who buys travel articles (if it is on the masthead), and write down the contact information (phone number, address, etc.). Pick up the phone, and call the number for the magazine's editorial offices. Tell the person who answers the phone that you are a travel writer and that you want to confirm contact information for the person who buys travel articles. Then ask who is currently buying travel articles, what his or her phone number is, and what the best address would be to mail articles so that they will arrive at the travel buyer's desk. Again, a caution—it is best not to ask if Elaine Bedford is still the travel editor. The person who answers the phone may not know, and, instead of showing her ignorance, she may say yes and hang up, even if Elaine has not been with the magazine for several years.

Group Your Calls
Telemarketing is much easier when it is done one call after another without interruption or with minimal interruption. It is for that reason that professional telemarketers work with electronic systems that automatically dial the next number as soon as they hang up from a call. This does not allow the telemarketer to procrastinate, and, because telemarketing is not a comfortable thing to do, it is easy to procrastinate. Therefore, it is important to set aside a time and a day to make all ten calls and not leave the phone until all ten are completed or until a sale is made, i.e., an editor says, "Yes, I want the article."

Make Your Calls from an Empty, Quiet House
Make your phone calls at a time when there is no one else at home. To be interrupted by someone asking you a question or for the travel editor to hear television noises or other family sounds in the background is not good. In addition, you can easily be distracted from saying what you need to say to sell the article idea. So, it is just better to make sure that you operate in a quiet environment.

Call at a Good Time for the Editor
Although you cannot be certain when an editor will have an upcoming deadline or an office meeting to go to, you can schedule your call at a time that will probably be better than other times. As a general rule, it is wise to never call on Monday morning or Friday afternoon. It is also wise to avoid times when the editor may be out to lunch or has just arrived for work in the morning or just before the end of the business day. Keep in mind that we have multiple time zones in North America. The timing of your call in the editor's local time zone is far more important than the time that it is where you live.

Be Prepared

Before you make your phone calls, purchase and have at hand where you can easily reach it the most recent issue of each publication whose editor you plan to call. Either read or skim the current issue and two back copies of the publication before you call. Sometimes you will need to review even more than two back copies. For example, when I wanted to write an article on what would soon be the largest cruise ship afloat, I went back to the date the ship was announced. I looked at every issue since that date of the magazines whose editors I was calling. I wanted to determine whether or not they had already run something on the ship that soon would be the largest cruise ship afloat.

Another example relates to the follow-up after my press tour of the new Denver airport. I went back to the date of the announcement of the airport and skimmed every issue to determine whether or not the targeted publications had already done a full-length article on the topic. Only after this research did I call the travel writing buyers.

Find a Special Angle for Each Magazine

If you have done your homework well, you should be prepared to compliment the travel editor on something relating to his or her magazine and ideally relate that compliment to your article concept. For example, "More than any other cruise-related magazine, yours seems to target retired seniors far better. As a soon-to-be-retired senior myself, I notice those things. But I don't understand why you have not featured what will soon be the largest cruise ship afloat since the cruise line's public relations office clearly identifies retired seniors as being its primary market. I would like to consider writing the article for you, and these are the reasons why . . ." While you cannot always find a special hook or connection between the magazine and your article concept, if you look closely, you will be surprised at how often you can find something that will work.

Be in the Mood

As noted earlier, telemarketing is hard. Being able to handle rejection is a big part of successful telemarketing. Therefore, putting yourself in the right mood before you start your phone calls is important. There are many ways people do this, but for me the best way is to consume two strong alcoholic drinks before making the first call. Then, if an editor says no, I don't care.

QUERY LETTERS

Query letters are easier since you do not have to put up with verbal rejection. In sending out query letters, the research steps noted above are also important. This means that you will want to find out the standard sizes of articles, determine the educational level of readers, understand how many photos will be needed, know if articles should be in first or third person and if most articles are about destinations or are travelogues. You will probably want to group your letters (write all of them on the same day) and review back issues of each publication to see what, if anything, has already been published in the magazine about your subject.

Just as with phone calls, the query letter should be tailored to the publication. And a "special angle" that links your article idea with the specific magazine should be identified. While the query letter should not be a long letter, it is important to identify why your article concept will fit the publication.

Draft your letter as carefully as you write your travel articles. Review your draft letters, and make changes until you are satisfied that, in each case, your letter will sell the editor. Make certain that the editor can easily contact you if he or she has questions. Use professionally printed letterhead and make certain that your return address, contact phone number, fax number, and e-mail address are prominently displayed. Increasingly travel writers are including their cell phone numbers as well.

Envelopes should be professionally printed with your return address in the upper left corner. It is best to use a computer printer that will print the name and address of the editor and the publication on each envelope rather than printing names and addresses on labels that are affixed to the envelopes. Always use a real stamp rather than a postage imprint.

SAMPLE QUERY LETTER

Consider the query letter example in figure 12-1. Notice how it is both short and business-like, but also note that it clearly identifies why the editor should consider buying the article that you propose to write.

■ **Figure 12-1:** *Sample Query Letter*

> Mr. John H. Gelman
> Travel Editor
> Beautiful Beaches Magazine
> 1231 East Belleview
> Suite 94
> Santiago, Florida 91876
>
> Dear Mr. Gelman:
>
> Your coverage of beaches throughout the world is matched by no other magazine. Your readers are people who can afford to visit any beach in the world. Therefore, I am surprised that you have no more than mentioned (in the September 1998 issue) the beach that many consider to be the most beautiful in the world, Little Dix Cay, off the coast of Argentina.
>
> In February I will have an opportunity to visit Little Dix Cay, and I would like to explore with you the possibility of writing a feature article about the beach for your magazine. A listing of some of my travel-writing credits is attached.
>
> The article would be approximately 1,100 words long, the average length of the longer articles that have appeared in the last nine issues of Beautiful Beaches Magazine. The focus will be on why the "beautiful" (rich) people vacation at Little Dix Cay, the luxury accommodations available right on the beach, and the sophisticated night life in the beach community.
>
> Mr. Gelman, it would be a pleasure to discuss this article concept further. I look forward to the possibility of hearing from you soon.
>
> Sincerely,
>
> James Poynter
> Travel Writer
>
> Enc.: Listing of selected previously authored titles/publications

Although a query letter can have a standard format, it should not be a form letter, and it should not appear to be a form letter. Travel editors are most likely to throw away letters that are photocopies and that start with the words, "Dear editor." Always try to address the editor by name. Use the name of the editor and the name of the magazine often, and use the words "I" and "me" as rarely as possible. Keep in mind that the content of your letter and your article should meet the needs of the editor and the publication, not your personal needs.

WHICH IS BETTER?

Which is better, a phone call or a letter? Neither is better, and neither is worse. Both work, but there are pros and cons of each. Study the advantages and disadvantages of both methods of contact. Then try out the one that you feel will work best for you. If that way does not work satisfactorily for you, switch to the other way. But make sure you sell to editors. Selling is one of the most important components to making money as a travel writer.

A SCENARIO

Let's say you pre-sold your article concept for the "Unknown London Museums" article to one of the museum magazines. The editor wrote a letter of agreement specifying what she expects you to deliver to the magazine, and she agreed to pay you $500 for the article. With her letter she included a check for $250 as an advance for your article. The balance will be paid when the article is received and accepted.

You also pre-sold an article on "Cheap Sleeps in Downtown London." The editor for the publication that is buying the cheap sleeps article agreed to pay you $550 and sent you an advance check for $200.

You wrote to the British Tourist Board and told them about all of your article concepts—those that were pre-sold and those that will probably be spec articles. You included photocopies of the two advance checks and the two letters of agreement. You asked for their assistance in narrowing down the museums, and you requested a listing of lodging places to visit for the cheap sleeps article. You also asked their help in getting discounted air travel and inexpensive accommodations.

In response, the tourist board sent you a nice letter suggesting several museums and included brochures from many of them. It also sent you the names and contact information for a number of inexpensive lodging establishments in downtown London. The author of the letter invited you to stop by the board's office in London if you needed anything further and indicated that the board had a good library of photos of London museums. The author of the letter to you said he had arranged for a reduced cost ticket for you with a new British airline flying between JFK airport in New York City and London Gatwick airport. Your round trip price will be only $220, but you will need to reconfirm and purchase your tickets right away. After contacting them to set up scheduled interviews for you, two of the cheap sleep places agreed to provide free lodging for you for two nights. However, your contact noted that the quality of the places might not be up to your standards. Nevertheless, he provided contact information for you.

You want to make a profit from your travel writing. You now know that your income from the two articles that you pre-sold will more than cover what you will need to pay for your airfare and the balance of your lodging expenses. However, you will have more expenses (food, ground transportation, etc.). Since you want to end up with a reasonably good profit from your London trip writing project, you reason that writing additional articles on speculation may be your best answer.

SELLING SPEC ARTICLES TO MAGAZINES

While you are in London, you write an interesting article on the city's subway system (the tube) and explain how easy it is for North Americans to figure out how to use it. The tourist board will give you multiple copies of a good overview subway map to accompany your article.

You also write an article on buying umbrellas as souvenirs while in London, and the tourist board will give you two excellent photos of interesting London umbrella scenes. These two articles were not sold before you left for Europe, but you feel that they will sell well now that they are almost finished.

When you got home, you sent the subway articles (with appropriate cover letters) to eighteen magazines and encouraged them to buy the article. You sent the umbrella article to fifteen magazines and again you encouraged the editors to purchase the article. In each case, you cautioned the editors, however, that you were submitting the articles to other publications (multiple submitting) and urged the editors that, if they agreed to buy an article from you, they (the editor) will need to contact you right away so that you can send a letter to the other publications telling them that the article is being purchased and that they should no longer consider buying it. If you are lucky, both of your spec articles will sell and you will have a profit of between $200 and $400 (possibly more) for your additional spec article writing efforts.

ARTICLE PARAMETERS REQUIRED BY PURCHASING PUBLISHERS

When magazine editors agree to buy a travel article from you, it is normal for them to specify exactly what they expect. They will tell you how many words they want (usually within a fifty- to one hundred-word range), when (the deadline) they expect to receive the completed article, what they expect the article to cover (a brief description or outline of the expected content), and so forth. In developing and honing your article, it is usually wise to start with the contractual agreement or letter of agreement and make sure that all points covered by the editor are included.

FROM EDITOR'S REQUIREMENTS TO POLISHED ARTICLE

While the editor's requirements constitute a starting point for developing and honing the travel article, they are only a starting point. In the next two chapters, you will learn how to start with the editor's requirements and end up with an article the editor should love.

End-of-Chapter Questions

1. Travel writers have two choices in the writing that they sell. One choice is contract writing. What is the other choice?

2. Most travel writers who write newspaper articles sell their articles to only one newspaper.   A) True B) False

3. How do you determine the average length of articles from a current issue of a publication?

4. Can one find the writer's guidelines of all or almost all travel publications in *Writer's Guidelines*?

5. Why should you get a good feel for the educational level for which a magazine is written?

6. Considering how difficult selling article ideas to editors can be on the phone, should one take a break after every telemarketing call before making the next one?

7. When should a travel writer review multiple copies of a publication targeted for an article the travel writer wants to author?

8. Which is easier for most travel writers: query letters or calls to travel editors?

9. Should query letters be long and detailed?

10. When submitting a query letter together with a spec article to multiple publications, what caution should you provide to the editors?

WRITING ASSSIGNMENT ELEVEN
SELECTING TARGETED MAGAZINES FOR YOUR CONTRACT ARTICLE

Assignment Introduction

Well thought through targeting of a potential contract article almost guarantees selling your article concept. The challenge is making your article precisely fit the interests and readership of multiple (usually ten) magazines. This means knowing exactly what you will write, developing a list of target publications, and finding magazine editors that want your article.

Assignment Activity

Go back to the list of ten potential travel article titles that you developed as writing assignment number six, Selecting Article Ideas. After reviewing the ten titles, ask yourself which one would probably sell best. You should not be as much interested in how many people will read the article as how many editors will want to buy the article. For example, which of the following two potential article titles do you think will be easier to sell: 1) *The World's Largest Cruise Ship* or 2) *The Townsen City*

Paper Museum's Tenth Anniversary. Make your job easier. Select the title that will sell.

Next, prepare a brief outline of your article concept. The outline should be no longer than half a page.

Your next job is to find magazines that will match your article concept. Look at key words in your title and write them down. You will want to find magazines that have the same or similar key words in their title. For the cruise ship article, for example, you would find magazines that are oriented toward cruising. Be aware, however, that some will not have your key word(s) in the title. *Porthole*, for example, is a major cruise-oriented magazine.

Review the magazines in appendix two. Some, but probably not all, of the magazines whose editors you might want to approach will probably be in appendix two. However, you will probably want to search beyond the appendix. Do a key word search in several of the major search engines. For example, for an article on the world's largest cruise ship the key words *Cruise Magazines*, *Cruise Ship Magazines*, or just *Cruise* might be used. It would be a good idea to go to the largest library in your community. Look in *Writer's Market* to see if there are magazines you should consider which you did not come across in your previous searches. Strive to find ten magazines which you think would be a good match for your article idea.

Fill in the blanks on the next page by identifying each of the magazines and the reasons why you feel each publication will be a good match for your travel article concept.

Selected Targeted Magazines for My Contract Article

Working title for the contract article:
_____

	Magazine Title	**Reasons for Selection**
1.	_____	_____
2.	_____	_____
3.	_____	_____
4.	_____	_____
5.	_____	_____
6.	_____	_____
7.	_____	_____
8.	_____	_____
9.	_____	_____
10.	_____	_____

Final Step: Add your name to the Instructor Comment Sheet for Writing Assignment Eleven in appendix 5 and staple it to your list of ten targeted magazines. Then turn in both sheets to your professor.

CHAPTER 12

Travel Writing Styles and Types

Amanda Castleman

THREE CATCH-ALL CATEGORIES

Travel journalism splits into three broad groups: 1) the inverted pyramid format, 2) commentary, and 3) feature-style, also called narrative writing. The Readership Institute discovered that the latter increased satisfaction, as well as comprehension and retention of the material.

Its landmark Impact Study also revealed that the public craves more "go and do" information—the nitty-gritty details like phone numbers, times, dates, addresses, contact names, and Web sites. Women, especially, want more travel coverage.[1] Younger readers favored a weekend getaways section, while occasional readers requested less staff-generated, local articles. International issues are desirable in the food, science, technology, and environmental sections. Remember that the travel genre can stretch to include these topics—and others.

Inverted Pyramid

News stories traditionally begin with the most important details, tapering to less critical ones toward the end. This inverted pyramid format "organizes stories not around ideas or chronologies but around facts," explained New York University Journalism Professor Mitchell Stephens in *A History of News*. "It weighs and shuffles the various pieces of information, focusing with remarkable single-mindedness on their relative news value."[2]

Some historians link the style's birth to the expense of the telegraph. Flowery nineteenth-century language fell by the wayside, as Civil War stories clicked across the country at a penny a character. Wire services inspired brisk impartial news, bulletins useful to all papers, regardless of their political persuasion. As Columbia University Professor James Carey observed: "It eliminated the letter-writing correspondent, who announced an event and described it in rich detail as well as analyzing its substance, and replaced him with a stringer who supplied the bare facts."[3]

The inverted pyramid was crucial in the days before digital design. Typesetters laid down columns of text. When the space ran out, the article ended with a decisive swipe of the exacto knife. Yet newspapers still employ the technique, especially for hard news. It survives for good reason, according to Christopher "Chip" Scanlan, director of the National Writers Workshops. "Many readers are impatient and want stories to get to the point immediately. In fast-breaking news situations . . . the pyramid allows the news writer to rewrite the top of the story

---

1. Readership Institute, "Impact Study 2000," Northwestern University, 2000, www.readership.org/content/editorial/feature-style/main.htm.

2. Mitchell Stephens, *A History of News from the Drum to the Satellite* (New York: Viking, 1988), 254.

3. Christopher Scanlan, "Writing from the Top Down: Pros and Cons of the Inverted Pyramid," Poynter Online, 2003, www.poynter.org/column.asp?id=52&aid=38693.

continually, keeping it up-to-date," he observed on the Poynter Institute's Web site, where the senior faculty member is a columnist. "It's also an extremely useful tool for thinking and organizing because it forces the reporter to sum up the point of the story in a single paragraph."[4]

That chunk of text is traditionally called a "nut graf": this passage showcases an article's essence and traditionally follows the lead, the introductory hook. Ken Wells, a writer and editor at *The Wall Street Journal*, described it as "a paragraph that says what this whole story is about and why you should read it. It's a flag to the reader, high up in the story: you can decide to proceed or not, but, if you read no farther, you know what that story's about."[5]

Commentary

Authorial voice holds sway in the commentary, a category that includes signed columns, reviews, critiques, advice Q&A, op-ed pieces, and editorials. Essays, first-person pieces, and travel literature also fall under this remit: think Bryson, Morris, and that legendary grouch Theroux. Character and color catapult these writers to fame, not extraordinary journeys alone.

Guard against grandstanding, however. Avoid pompous pronouncements à la Wizard of Oz, advised John McCormick, deputy editorial page editor of the *Chicago Tribune*. Target your tone to the audience. Have clear goals for the piece (changing the status quo, official action, entertainment, etc.). Support well-reasoned arguments with scrupulously reported facts.[6]

The legwork is far and away the most difficult aspect—unfortunately one that some travel specialists avoid. "I'm a writer, not a reporter," they insist. Yet artistic license doesn't permit laziness. From books to blogs, every text should be anchored by accurate observations—your own and others.

"Writers collect words," stressed Poynter Institute Senior Scholar

---

4. Ibid.
5. Christopher Scanlan, "The Nut Graf, Part I: Giving Readers a Reason to Care," Poynter Online, 2003, www.poynter.org/dg.lts/id.52/aid.34457/column.htm.
6. John McCormick, "Deconstructing an Editorial," Poynter Online, 2003, www.poynter.org/content/content_view.asp?id=19724.

Roy Peter Clark, as well as "images, details, facts, quotes, dialogue, documents, scenes, expert testimony, eyewitness accounts, statistics, the brand of the beer, the color and make of the sports car, and, of course, the name of the dog."[7]

Like icebergs, only one-ninth of the writer's expertise shows above the waterline. The remainder molders in the notebook or files, but its strength supports the story and bestows authority. As Clark said: "A sharp focus is like a laser. It helps the writer slice material that might be tempting, but does not contribute to the central meaning of the story."[8]

Feature-Style

Vivid storytelling—a.k.a. as narrative writing and creative nonfiction—was once the norm. Mark Twain was a newspaperman and travel writer, as well as a novelist. The "yellow papers"—led by Joseph Pulitzer's *New York World* and William Randolph Hearst's *New York Journal*—teemed with color (much of it tawdry tabloidism, but color nonetheless). The practice continued until World War II, when Ernie Pyle's compassionate columns resembled "letters home."

Boston University Professor Mark Kramer observed in *Literary Journalism*: "James Agee, Ernest Hemingway, A.J. Liebling, Joseph Mitchell, Lillian Ross, and John Steinbeck tried out narrative essay forms," he wrote. "Norman Mailer, Truman Capote, Tom Wolfe, and Joan Didion followed, and somewhere in there, the genre came into its own—that is, its writers began to identify themselves as part of a movement, and the movement began to take on conventions and to attract writers."[9]

Authors like Hunter Thompson and John McPhee applied these techniques to travel writing—and won great renown. But newspapers on the whole fostered a drier, more factual style. "Storytelling went out the window," complained Jack Hart, managing editor of *The Oregonian*. "We had only the inverted pyramid and the standard news feature:

---

7. Roy Peter Clark, "Writing Tool #50: The Writing Process," Poynter Online, 2003, www.poynter.org/content/content_view.asp?id=79244.
8. Ibid.
9. Mark Kramer, "Breakable Rules for Literary Journalists," *Literary Journalism* (New York: Ballantine Books, 1995), 21.

Travel Writing Styles and Tips

quote, transition, quote, transition, quote, transition, kicker . . . you're outta there!"[10]

Then New Journalism blazed and helped banish "the pale beige tone of the inverted pyramid," Hart insisted.[11] Best of all, readers connect more with this personable style. They comprehend complex topics easier, retain information, and even buy more papers, according to Northwestern's "Impact Study."

So what is this miracle fix, exactly? Experts bicker on the finer points, but Lonely Planet's Don George nutshelled it well: "Essentially, a good travel story is like a good work of fiction, with a beginning, a middle, and an end; characters and conflict; dialogue; telling details; a narrative arc. The full range of literary techniques should be employed."[12]

Events unfold around a protagonist in narrative writing. Jon Franklin, author of the classic *Writing for Story*, declared that "a story consists of a sequence of actions that occur when a sympathetic character encounters a complicating situation that he confronts and solves." [13]

Hart broke down the plot arc thus:[14]

1. Exposition: introduce the protagonist, the person who makes things happen (if you're stuck, start with the protagonist's name and a transitive verb).

2. Inciting incident: something knocks the protagonist off the status quo. "Think of a movie . . . a Hollywood movie, not a Danish one," he joked.

3. Rising action: the protagonist struggles with confrontations.

4. Point of insight. The solution or outcome clarifies.

5. Climax: the confrontation resolves.

6. Denouement: Wrap it up.

---

10. Jack Hart, "Narrative Skill Class," Society of Professional Journalists Region 10 Conference, May 7, 2005, Seattle, WA.

11. Ibid.

12. Wayne Yang, "Interview with Lonely Planet's Don George,"*Eight Diagrams*, May 11, 2005.

13. Jon Franklin, *Writing for Story* (New York: Plume, 1986), 71.

14. Jack Hart, "Narrative Skill Class," Society of Professional Journalists Region 10 Conference, May 7, 2005, Seattle, WA.

Hart considers the "point of insight" most valuable. "Here's what people are looking for in stories. They want to learn from the experiences of others how to be a more successful human being. Find the universal theme."

Narrative writing is an advanced technique. Experiment, but don't panic if this new medium takes time to learn. Mimicry really is the best tool. Read stories—and watch films—with these techniques in mind. Then perhaps try a brief piece in the format. As the great writing coach Hart said, "Narrative articles needn't be one hundred-inch goat-chokers." The short length forces your concentration onto the plot—picking, choosing, and crystallizing the essential elements—rather than a glut of expression.

FINDING THE RIGHT FORMAT

The Readership Institute discovered that U.S. newspapers use inverted pyramid style for 69 percent of all stories, feature-style writing for 18 percent, and commentary for 12 percent. Magazines, books, and the Internet mix techniques a bit more. But a simple truth emerged from the "Impact Study": publications "that run more feature-style stories are seen as more honest, fun, neighborly, intelligent, 'in the know,' and more in touch with the values of readers."[15]

Not all articles merit the narrative treatment. A "front of the book" 250-word hotel review, for example, rarely manages rising action. Some pieces are bulletins; some are stories. However, even a fact-based brief can borrow powerful tools, such as the universal theme, from features-style. Likewise, a hint of inverted-pyramid prioritization or a nut graf can clarify a story with a looser structure. The important first step, especially for a novice travel writer, is to consciously choose a style (inverted pyramid, feature, or commentary), then refine the concept.

DESTINATION ARTICLES

This perennial standby offers a general introduction to a city or area, followed by brief descriptions of major attractions, transport options, hotels, restaurants, and activities. A destination piece is usually a commentary. This could be a simple peek at a major tourist hotspot—like

---

15. Readership Institute, "Impact Study 2000."

Miami, Nice, Bangkok—or it could include a theme: "Athens After the 2004 Olympics," "Touring the Vineyards Around San Francisco," "A Winter Weekend in Toronto."

The author need not strive for literary polish, just workmanlike prose. Information is the key—crisply presented, up-to-date, and fact-checked extensively. Think of a guidebook's tone: a dash of color, then lots of practical advice so travelers can follow in your footsteps. Always collect full contact details: address, phone, fax, Web site, and rates. Consider corralling the "go to" information in a box or sidebar (short stories that accompany the main article). These "help the reader get factual information so the story can concentrate on experiences and visual description," advised L. Peat O'Neil in *Travel Writing: A Guide to Research, Writing, and Selling*. "Keep the story moving."[16]

ESSAYS

These assignments are glamorous and highly prized, as are personal memoirs where a writer can truly shine. Essays are self-indulgent, both in subject and style. You can showcase verbal pyrotechnics, flights of fancy, opinions, and reminiscences. With all this freedom, it's easy to derail, so exercise tight control while writing. Essays can be feature style or inverted pyramid style.

Storytelling (narrative) tools include "moving both backward and forward in time, recreating believable dialogue, switching back and forth between scene and summary, and controlling the pace and tension of the story," stressed Judith Barrington in *Writing the Memoir from Truth to Art*.[17] Start with a clear vision of your theme. Why is this story important? What universal elements can readers identify with? Add vignettes, using evocative language.

Avoid a step-by-step recital of your itinerary. Ruthlessly cast aside good material that doesn't support your story line. The momentum should build up to a turning point, an insight into the area—and perhaps also into your own heart and mind. As Barrington pointed out:

---

16. L. Peat O'Neil, *Travel Writing: A Guide to Research, Writing, and Selling* (Cincinnati: Writer's Digest Books, 2000), 118.

17. Judith Barrington, *Writing the Memoir from Truth to Art* (Portland, Oregon: The Eighth Mountain Press, 1997), 22.

"Self-revelation without analysis or understanding becomes merely an embarrassment to both reader and writer."[18]

Look sideways for the "defining moment," advises Pico Iyer, one of the editors of *The Best American Travel Writing 2004*. Some of the best writing blooms from "the elaboration of an incident that would be humdrum at home into something that is revealing both of setting and of self."[19] Misadventures can provide great fodder for memoirs: a bizarre scenario almost always makes a better tale than seamless comfort. Martha Gellhorn—a pioneering female war correspondent, as well as Ernest Hemingway's third ex-wife—explained the "chaos commodity" in the preface to *Travels with Myself and Another*. "The only aspect of our travels that is guaranteed to hold an audience is disaster," she wrote in the memoir, which rattles wryly from China to Africa. "They can hardly wait for us to finish before they launch into stories of their own suffering in foreign lands."[20]

Be funny, but don't be bitter. Don't let emotion overwhelm the article, drive your pen across the page (or—more likely—your fingers across the keyboard). You're spicing a story with travel mishap, not venting your spleen at the Turkish ticket vendor who stole 20 million lire from your fumbling hand or the bellhop who sneered at your luggage. Remain in control of the anecdote—and yourself.

A travel journal is an invaluable source of material. How did you feel when your bag was snatched? Was the spa's mandatory bathing cap floppy or migraine-inducingly tight? What sort of flowers fringed the tea garden? Such details diminish over time, so jot them down on the trip, even if they're just sentence fragments to kick-start your memory.

FLAVOR ARTICLES

Evocative articles draw upon personal observations and reflections. They are often narratives, but frequently they have a wider scope than essays. The mood of the place is the focus, not the writer. Your job is to set the stage, so armchair travelers can slip into another

---

18. Ibid, 29.
19. Pico Iyer and Jason Wilson, eds., *The Best American Travel Writing 2004* (Boston: Houghton Mifflin, 2004), xviii.
20. Martha Gellhorn, *Travels with Myself and Another* (New York: Jeremy P. Tarcher/Putnam, 2001), xix.

world, full of curious shapes, scents, and shades of color. The style is almost literary with a strong structure and graceful transitions from paragraph to paragraph. Practical details—the nitty-gritty—are sparse and usually banished to a few italic sentences at the end or jammed into a fact box. The goal is to inspire, not to blaze a path, while still providing key information.

This format blends elements of sociology, philosophy, and poetry. Many consider it more difficult than a memoir or straightforward destination piece. The author must recognize the essence of a place, then capture it in relatively few words. Done properly, the article will evoke nostalgia for a world the reader has not yet experienced.

HUMOR

Culture clashes fuel many comic travel writers. Language barriers, foreign customs, and blundering tourists are irresistible targets for a witty mind. Readers also enjoy comedy turns, especially when they conceal good advice or apt observations.

Be careful not to fall foul of political correctness, though. The days of sniggering at "heathen savages" and "quaint native customs" are long gone, along with whalebone corsets, top hats, and steamer trunks blazoned with stickers from distant lands, borne by porters. Many journalists make themselves the butt of the joke instead. Here, too, tread warily. As *South Florida Sun-Sentinel* Travel Editor Tom Swick argued, the innocents abroad routine can pall. He blasted this "light amusing style" in the *Columbia Journalism Review*: "Its sole purpose is to get a laugh, not to reveal interesting truths about national character."[21]

ADVENTURE

Travelers are increasingly bold, venturing away from sanitized hotel rooms to bungee-jump, white-water kayak, hot air balloon, rock climb, excavate at archaeology sites, master cavalry secrets, or protect the nests of endangered loggerhead turtles. Writers, as usual, are leading the way, reporting back from Amazon jungles and the Outback on increasingly extreme holidays.

---

21. Tom Swick, "The Travel Section: Roads Not Taken," *Columbia Journalism Review*, May/June 2001.

Prior knowledge helps here, but isn't essential. After all, many readers might be newcomers to active vacations as well, so a beginner's perspective—call it the "I survived" article—is often welcome. Remember that adventures don't have to be sporty: you could cover a sushi class, an art tour of Florence, or a week spent in a Scottish lighthouse.

Most adventure travel articles are written in the first person, using "I" or "we." The style veers toward informal, as if the author is breathlessly recounting an exciting trip to his or her friends. The nuts and bolts—contact details, how to get there, and recommendations—should be banished to a sidebar or tacked onto the narrative's end, otherwise the "tall tale" can lose momentum.

ADVICE ARTICLES

The "do's and don'ts" of travel are a rich seam of material. These how-to stories are continually recycled, as each traveler ponders the same questions. Can rolling your clothes actually decrease wrinkles? What is the safest way to carry valuables? Are air miles worth the bother? What guidebook is best? Keep a list of such notions as they occur during your planning and trips. Some travel writers even carry a notebook with a page for "Things I've Done Wrong," which later can be spun into advice articles.

Budget tips are always welcome, as are health-and-safety checklists. The question-and-answer format is popular as well. Consider your expertise again. Someone handy with a needle might opt for "Ten Emergency Wardrobe Repairs," while a seasoned sailor might be able to dash off "Are You Really Ready to Cruise the Aegean?" Wherever possible, weave in comments from other experts, which lend weight to your work.

Advice articles tend to be light and parental in tone. Think "Dear Abby": concerned, caring, but not too technical. Never overwhelm readers with jargon or make them feel ignorant. Use straightforward, simple language. Remember that most newspapers aim for a thirteen-year-old's reading level.

SPECIALIST ARTICLES

Personal experience and expertise also can spark travel stories, aimed at people with the same interests. Are you a newlywed? Write about honeymoon destinations. Traveling with children? So are many of your harried readers, who might love to hear about kid-friendly destinations. In your free time, do you throw pots, train spot, hunt wildflowers, practice yoga, or collect antiques? Any hobby could be the focus of a spellbinding trip—and a smashing travel story.

Trade magazines are good forums for this type of story (many pay quite well, comparable to national publications). Journals aimed at minority groups—ethnic, sexual, and disabled—are another option. When writing for a like-minded audience, you don't have to explain every technical term. Authors often adopt a congenial, clubby voice for such pieces, telling the readers: "We're all in this together. I'll show you what's best in my experience."

ARTICLES THAT FOCUS ON HOW YOU GET THERE

"Getting there's half the fun," the old saying goes. Pick an unusual mode of transport, then enthrall the reader with your odyssey. Ride across the plains in a covered wagon. Recline regally on the Orient Express. Prod your stubborn, stinky, spitting llama up the rocky pass. Lounge on the decks of an international steamer. Soar through fields of bobbing sunflowers on a mountain bike.

Usually such articles are scripted in first person, relating your personal experiences. Enrich the piece by talking to fellow travelers, interweaving their anecdotes and reactions. For example, a writer might take an uneventful bath in a North Cascades glacial stream, while a fellow hiker is swept away on the green foaming torrent, caught at the end of the safety rope like a novelty balloon bobbing on a string. Such misadventure makes a far more entertaining tale.

Always keep an ear cocked for evocative legends—like the Phantom Conductor or Buffalo Bill—that could spice a piece. And don't forget to solicit interviews from the field's leaders, who've seen it all over the years. Expert comments give weight to the story and often provide critical insight. Maybe that hill you huffed and puffed up is an afternoon stroll to an experienced mountaineer: an important perspective. Then you discover it's notorious for lightning strikes. Best of all, the climber explains how to stay safe. Now a well-rounded, complex story is emerging, not just a tired recital of each muddy stretch, knee-ache, and granola snack of your hiking trip.

FOOD AND DRINK ARTICLES

Wining and dining are two of the most sensuous aspects of travel. Freed from the confines of the kitchen, your overly familiar recipes, and your limitations as a chef, you can savor foreign cuisine, imprinting another culture onto your taste buds. Readers are always eager for meal recommendations. What dishes are typical to the area? Where are they best sampled? What beverage will perfectly define a golden moment on holiday: caustic ouzo in Athens, tea in Sri Lanka, a fizzy lager on Bondi Beach in Australia?

Dedicated food writers are usually quite accomplished cooks, but most authors—however hapless behind a stove—can eat and, therefore, are qualified to comment on restaurants for a general audience. Research the establishment's history and reputation, plus the chef's background. Include detailed descriptions of your meal, its presentation, and prices. Don't forget to set the scene for readers: describe the decor, the ambiance, the other patrons, and the wait staff. Lead them through it by all five senses: Does the dining room smell of wood smoke or incense? Are the seats of worn, nubby velvet or molded plastic? Is there alarming modern art hovering over the table or discrete lithographs? Is Buena Vista Social Club burbling over the speakers or a sports match?

Most importantly, describe the exact sensations and tastes you encounter. A dish should be feisty with chili or languidly bathed in cheese sauce, not just "good." What memories does the food evoke? What metaphors? Does the meal symbolize an aspect of your trip or the local character? Writing about food gives great scope for imaginative language. Have fun with it.

HISTORY

Sometimes a journalist simply can't wax rhapsodic about a destination. So don't. Take Messolongi, the battlefield where Greeks defied Ottoman rule and the poet Byron perished. The modern town is a cracked pile of concrete, but the area's allure persists, thanks to the heroic resistance. The past is what draws visitors, so delve deep into the dramatic episodes, weaving a vivid picture.

An *Athens News* travel article began thus: "Messolongi's soil is stained by the blood of heroes. The area is famous for dramatic deaths: Suliot mothers hurling their children off crags, the [guerilla chief] Markos

Botzaris crumpling in battle, Lord Byron's fatal fever, and the slaughter of the Free Besieged. The town is mighty, but morbid and marshy: Not the most obvious choice for a carefree holiday, in other words.

"Yet Messolongi is finally clearing away the rubble, wedging atmospheric cafés into the shattered spaces and allowing hipsters in army chic to dance where freedom fighters once clawed through icy mud. Greece's sacred city is re-emerging from the ruins."[22]

Create a theme, a thread, to lead you through the labyrinth of dates, names, and places. Don't smother the story in facts, sprinkle them through the narrative. Carefully verify all information, as this is a more scholarly style of travel writing. Colorful tales are fine, as long as they're clearly attributed to "local legend." Weave in quotes from other travel writers—past and present—to add texture. The Messolongi piece, for example, included this fantastically pompous account:

"J.L. Stephens, visiting a decade later [in 1835], was stunned by the wreckage. The whole was a mass of new-made ruins—of houses demolished and black with smoke—the tokens of savage and desolating war." He passed miserable one-story shanties washed by the sea, piles of skulls, and a crude cairn over Botzaris's grave. "It had no connection with the ancient glory of Greece, no name or place on her historic page, and no hotel where we could have breakfast," he concluded, building up to the most serious atrocity."[23]

Historical articles are often timed with anniversary dates (the *Timeline of History* is useful for forward planning). Remember to pitch stories three-to-twelve months in advance if you're relying on a seasonal angle, such as "Colonial Christmas Traditions Enduring on Cape Cod" or "Spaghetti Western: The Italian Cowboys Annual Rodeo in Tarquinia."

DAY TRIPS AND SHORT BREAKS

These tiny jaunts usually center on a well-known destination: "Venturing Outside Chicago's Loop," "Easy Hikes Near Budapest," "Atmospheric B&Bs to Soothe Your Nerves Around Mexico City." National

---

22. Amanda Castleman, "Messolongi: A sacred city re-emerging from the ruins," *The Athens News* (April 7, 2003): A24.
23. Ibid.

publications crave these twists on hotspots (editors eventually grow tired of the perennials like "Shopping in London" and "Dining in Paris"). Regional papers often insist that travel destinations are within an eight-hour drive of their metropolitan hub. Write for weary workers, escaping the nine-to-five grind for a long weekend.

Lard on the details here, as you may be covering ground not included in guidebooks. Readers should be able to retrace your journey from transport options to hotels, restaurants, sights, museums, and shops. Always give your audience "news they can use." Is there a tricky turn off the highway? A novel that's essential reading for the region? A café selling perfect, sticky cinnamon buns, which sadly over-sugars the lemonade? Tell all.

ROUNDUP ARTICLES

This category is less flamboyant, more matter-of-fact. Select five or ten items with a common link, such as "Cheap Continental Spas," "Weekend Escapes from Singapore for New Lovers," "Canine-Compatible Hikes," or "Antique Deals in Tunisia." The possibilities are endless. You might even be able to recycle several old stories into a fresh, breezy overview.

Written from scratch, such articles rely heavily on research, as it's often difficult to visit, say, "A Blushing Bride's Top Twenty English Manor Houses." Try to push beyond the publicity material: though useful, it won't provide a well-rounded image. Read as many reviews and articles as possible. Canvass locals for their thoughts. Many writers send out surveys to clubs or groups immersed in the topic (e-mail is a fantastic tool for this, as are bulletin boards on Web sites). Ask everyone you know, too. A friend of a friend of your aunt might just have attended an elegant wedding in the Cotswolds.

Lists can take another tact: soliciting celebrity and expert opinions. Where do screen divas hide away in the Riviera? Which mountain resorts charm the Finnish Olympic skiers? What destinations attract architects? Where do the Daughters of the America Revolution celebrate the Fourth of July?

Roundups should be simple and light in tone, sometimes playful. Don't bog down with excessive details and descriptions. Paint with a very broad brush. Give the reader a sketch of the options—and how to pursue them farther—then move along.

TRAVEL NEWS

Staff writers have the edge in this category, as they receive press releases about travel industry news, like new airline routes, hotel and restaurant openings, last-minute bargains, and the launch of new attractions. Freelancers can ask for inclusion on companies' press lists, but this is a time-consuming process. It's often easier to just monitor local newspaper reports.

Tourism stories often appear on the business pages long before they hit the travel section. A dry planning-approval notice now may be a timely tip in a year. Also keep an eye on world events, then ponder their impact. Did the European Union expansion lure more tourists behind the defunct Iron Curtain? Will Greenpeace persuade visitors to boycott Iceland until it bans whaling again? Are more or less people coming to London after the terrorist bombing—and how do they feel about it? Is Disney threatened by the popularity of Universal Studios theme parks? Try to keep a file—paper or electronic—of potential ideas. Follow them up during dry spells.

News pieces generally use a more detached tone and the inverted pyramid format. Publications often require you to follow the *Associated Press Stylebook*, a worthwhile investment for any writer keen to break into the American newspaper market or international wire services.

MORE THAN WRITING STYLES AND TYPES

It all starts with the germ of an idea, as we discussed in chapter 6. That idea can come from one of the two tracks noted by Rumbaugh. It could come from a more direct approach, honed concepts, angles, writing about what you know, sourcing ideas or research as suggested by Castleman. Perhaps the idea will originate from the news and the trade press as suggested by Poynter. A travel journal frequently is the source for a good travel idea (see Papay's chapter 7) or from article ideas picked up on press trips as Lemmon suggests in chapter 8. Once an idea has surfaced, its practicality is tested by bouncing it off of editors through query letters or phone calls (chapter 11). Next you identify the travel writing style and type that you feel will best fit your article. But a good article is made up of more than style and type.

In the next chapter, you will learn the process of writing your article from the first rough draft to the polished third final draft. You will learn how to develop a "hook," the lead, and the key paragraphs that make up the body. You will learn how to write transitions, the negatives, a sidebar, and a good close. And finally you will learn how to package what you send to the editor so that you present your writing in the best way possible. In later chapters, you will learn about photos so that you can include these to make your writing even more impressive.

End-of-Chapter Questions

1. Travel journalism splits into three broad groups. One is commentary. Another is feature-style, also called narrative writing. What is the third group?
2. Can the travel genre stretch to include food, science, technology, and environmental topics?
3. According to Chip Scanlan, why does the inverted pyramid still survive?
4. According to the author, in writing commentary with what should one support well-reasoned arguments?
5. According to Peter Clark, in what way is a sharp focus like a laser?
6. What percentage of all U.S. newspaper stories use the inverted pyramid style?
7. Are destination pieces normally written as feature stories?
8. Are most adventure travel articles written in the third person?
9. In writing a food and drink-oriented travel article, should the travel writer lead the reader through the article by all five senses?
10. According to Castleman, what kind of travel writing should be simple and light in tone, sometimes playful?

WRITING ASSIGNMENT TWELVE
SOPHISTICATING THE TARGET MAGAZINE SEARCH

Assignment Introduction

You have now found ten magazines that you feel will be a good match for your contract travel article. Ideally it will be a good idea to know exactly who to pitch (sell to) at each magazine, the phone number and e-mail for that person, the mailing address of the magazine, and the writing guidelines for the magazine. In addition, you should have at least one recent (the latest, if possible) issue of the magazine.

Assignment Activity

To know who to approach at each magazine, it will be best to telephone and ask the person who answers the phone for the name, phone number, and e-mail address of the person at the magazine who buys travel articles. While on the phone, request a sample issue of the magazine (tell them you are a travel writer, and it will probably be sent free) and the magazine's writer's guidelines. Please complete the fill-in-the-blank information on the Targeted Magazine Information form on page 210.

Final Step: Add your name to the Instructor Comment Sheet for Writing Assignment Twelve in appendix 5 and staple it to your completed Targeted Magazine Information sheet. Then turn in both sheets to your professor.

Targeted Magazine Information

Magazine Title	Date Info Requested	Name of Travel Article Buyer	Phone Number of Travel Article Buyer	E-mail of Travel Article Buyer	Address of Magazine	Date of Sample Issue Request	Date of Writers' Guidelines Request
1.							
2.							
3.							
4.							
5.							
6.							
7.							
8.							
9.							
10.							

CHAPTER 13

The Process

James Poynter
Amanda Castleman
Sue Rumbaugh

A MAGIC WRITING NUMBER

Three seems to be a magic number in writing. Certainly three is a magic number in developing an article. There are three parts to a good article: 1) an introduction, 2) a body, and 3) a conclusion. Usually there are three drafts of a manuscript: 1) a rough first draft, 2) a second more finished draft, and 3) a finished third draft. Within the introduction, body, and conclusion there are three components. These are: 1) the lead, 2) key paragraphs, and 3) the close. All of these triples will be explored in this chapter plus much more. But as you undertake your travel writing, think in terms of three. It is a magic writing number.

BEFORE YOU WRITE THE FIRST DRAFT

Before sitting at your computer to compose the first draft, several preliminary tasks need to be undertaken. If you have pre-sold your article concept and you are working with a letter of agreement, you have already undertaken research, and you have substantially narrowed the writing project. Research and narrowing are not finished, however, and for most travel writers this is the next step.

Which should come first? To some extent both come together. While most travel writers will want to do as much narrowing as possible before leaving on the trip, many find that the narrowing process continues all the way through to the final draft. However, the more you have narrowed your target audience and your article concept before you leave on the trip, the easier it will be to undertake the necessary research.

Narrowing

Initial narrowing for your article will come down to two areas: the letter of agreement or contract plus any other communication from the editor who will be buying your article and a clear understanding of the target audience, i.e., the reader of the magazine. Most travel writers find it useful to simply jot down the parameters set down in the letter of agreement and/or other communications with the editor. These may include such things as the viewpoint you will take, the person you will use (first, second, or third), and the tense in which you will write. Of course, your agreement will also include the number of words, columns, or pages (usually words) for the article and a carefully defined description of the subject of your article.

Target Audience

Try to visualize your reader as a specific person. Are you writing for a big-game hunter or a quilting enthusiast? For an active retiree, frazzled young parent, or burnt-out executive? The slant and tone of your article should reflect the audience's character.

Don't rely purely on imagination. Most publications provide reader profiles and demographics as part of their advertising sales brochures. Request a copy—or track one down online. This information can prove invaluable. For example, if the average reader earns $75,000 a year, you may wish to omit hostel recommendations, concentrating on mid-range and luxury hotels.

Study the advertisements as well, when forming an impression. Are they pushing posh perfume? Chances are good that the reader buys and wears expensive perfume. Therefore, including wording in the article that appeals to the sense of smell might be wise. Are there advertisements plugging fair trade coffee? Perhaps your article might touch on ecotourism.

Research

Different writers research in different ways. Major areas of research include library research, i.e., a review of what has been written about the destination in the past; reviews of your travel journal (the journal kept while you traveled abroad); guidebook entries regarding your specific destination; determining what will be used from the interviews you conducted during your trip; a review of tourist bureau material you have written for and received; and frequently a review of material received from other sources.

Interviews

Before leaving for the trip, prepare yourself. Determine what interviews you will want and try to set them up in advance. Doors open for journalists, especially those with assignment letters. Don't just wander aimlessly in the museum, when a curator could give you an interview and conduct a tour. If you are writing an article on the unknown museums of London, work with the tourist board and get a listing of all of London's museums. Select the ones you want to focus on. Always choose more than you can include in your article so that later on you can narrow to include only the ones of greatest interest. Then write each museum, and ask for a day and time for an interview while you are there.

Setting up interviews, however, can be a time-consuming task, particularly abroad. Be prepared to chase people politely, sending letters with your credentials, then calling to confirm on arrival.

Don't be shy about interviewing. Most folks love to discuss their work—and will treat a journalist with cordiality and respect. Remember: bold investigation is part and parcel of the job. Quite often the trouble runs contrary to expectation: people are so excited to speak with a travel writer that they babble incessantly.

Before meeting with the person you will interview, conduct research to formulate intelligent questions. Before you left, you reviewed books (guidebooks and other publications), tourist board information, and perhaps pamphlets. As you review these materials, jot down key queries. Even during the interview, you may want to jot down questions so they don't slip away during a good conversation. Avoid questions with a simple yes or no answer; try to get subjects to elaborate. Remember to listen, not talk, advised Christopher "Chip" Scanlan, author of *Reporting and Writing: Basics for the 21st Century*.

You must ask permission to capture the conversation on audio or video tape (and, in some areas, even record the assent). Mini-cassettes—palm-sized models, also called dictaphones—make for carefree interviews, but the transcription process is a hassle. The standard 2.5-inch tapes don't fit a traditional player, so you rewind and replay to extract accurate quotes: endlessly punching small buttons while typing.

Some travel writers invest in a model with a pedal, which eases the process (and—even better—sometimes a contracting publication will provide secretarial transcription assistance). Digital equipment and voice-recognition software may further improve this situation. However, the prices are high, so most travel writers still rely on mini-cassettes and good solid notes. A paper copy is quicker to refer to anyway.

Remember, too, that technology can easily fail. An *Oxford Times* features writer once interviewed a haughty Noble Prize laureate, only to discover the recorder was on the wrong setting. The two-hour conversation was captured on high speed—creating a super-soprano, chattering, Alvin and the Chipmunks effect. Poor Reg Little spent long, long hours interpreting the tinny squeal. Background noise, battery failure, and tampering also can ruin recordings.

Travel writers typically prefer reporters' notebooks, also used by stenographers—narrow pads with spiral bindings at the top. In the U.K., many still learn shorthand for speed and accuracy. The Teeline system is easier, but the Pitman style is faster, allowing up to three hundred words per minute. Regardless of style, don't fixate on the notebook, as it distracts from the conversation (if the subject is mesmerized by the pen, throw in a few pleasant giveaway questions, stop scribbling, and make eye contact).

Start with easy, confidence-building queries, and then weave in tougher material—if any—toward the end. Always conclude with: "Is there anything you'd like to add that we haven't covered?" and "What elements would you emphasize in an article?" Often the best comments arise then.

Dig deeply. Weave in cultural context questions. Bolster the observations of your interviewee with observations made by other interviewees, and ask each interviewee to expand on his or her thoughts.

Then talk to people. Do not float through. Take advantage of the impromptu chats that arise during your travels, which can be far more illuminating than the formal encounters with tourism professionals. Seek out gritty "color" opportunities—an outdoor market, quirky museum, or sporting event. Hop on the tram or ferry. Go dancing. Walk in the park. Scan the local newspaper for rallies, performances, festivals, and other events. Ask the waiter about the Buddha's birthday. Where does the Bedouin guard drink tea? Why did the Italian grandmother buy pecorino rather than parmesan? Remember that many English-speakers are delighted to practice and showcase their language skills. Advance research aids all this, of course, but any decent guidebook can provide a springboard in a pinch.

"Off the record" means the subject is imparting sensitive background information not for print. Strictly speaking, they must specify this before the statement, but use your discretion. "Not for attribution" means you cannot use that person's name, just a vague description like "a Johannesburg shopkeeper" or "a Syrian homemaker." Avoid this whenever possible, as it weakens your credibility.

The interviewee has no right to preview the article. With extremely technical subjects, some authors fact-check the tricky bits, however, without reading back whole quotes or surrounding material. Always record the person's full name and title, spelled correctly, and contact details, in case a follow-up is required. Some elite publications demand copies of all notes, cassettes, and research material; make sure the fee is worth such laborious and expensive methods.

Sidebars

Sometimes your contract will call for one or more sidebar. This is typically a boxed section that is headed with the words: "If you go." If it is about a restaurant, it will include the name, address, and phone number. Special menu items will be listed and a range of prices (in U.S. dollars) will be provided. Helpful hints will be noted. For example, you might write: "Get there after eight at night. That is when the locals display their 'burning' desire to join the professionals in flaming sword dancing."

Editors sometimes want more than one sidebar. The time to get the information is when you are on-site. If you do not get it then, there is a chance that you will never get it.

If the editor does not require a sidebar, think of one or more yourself. You may decide to discard it before the final draft of the article is complete. But you may also find that having a good sidebar will help you sell the article to an editor.

Get Photo and Other Releases

The time to get photo and other releases is while you are on-site. As you take pictures, ask every person who is in the photo to sign a release. Most travel writers travel with a supply of photo releases and automatically get signatures as they take their photos. Many magazines and newspapers have lawyers who will not allow the use of a photo or a quote without a signed release form. Without it, the photo cannot be used, and often, if the photo cannot be used, the editor will not run the article. Most magazines have their own photo release forms. If you are writing a contract article for a magazine, always ask for a copy (or a supply of) the magazine's photo-release form, and use one for every photograph. If you are writing a spec article or an article for newspapers, use a standard release form. See chapter 8 for a sample photo-release form.

THE FIRST DRAFT

For the first draft, you will need a title that sells, a hook, a lead that draws them in, all the paragraphs that make up the body of the article, good transitions, and a close. After determining the person (first, second, or third) and a tense in which to write, many travel writers start with an outline, draw heavily from their travel journals, and tape record an initial rough draft in a manner that resembles talking to their great-aunt. Of course, it is important to include humor, if at all possible, and the travel writer should always include at least one negative in their travel article.

A Title That Sells
The title is as far as many readers get. As they skim through the newspaper or magazine, a large number of readers actually read only a small percent of the articles. The title will either get them to read more or reinforce their tendency to not read further. The title must not only catch the readers' attention, but it also must peak their curiosity enough to get them to read further. Which of the following would get your attention and encourage you to read further: "Little Dix Cay" or "The Third Most Beautiful Beach"? We are all inundated with superlatives. Even the title, "The Most Beautiful Beach," would probably not get our attention or encourage us to read further as well as, "The Third Most Beautiful Beach." But just naming the beach, as the first title did, those who are unaware of it will have no reason to stop and read the article. Try several titles, and you might bounce the list of titles off of several friends asking them to choose the title that most likely gets them to read further.

Talk to Your Great-aunt Bessie
One of the easiest ways to write a first draft of a travel article is to dictate it, pretending that you are telling a story to your great-aunt. Simply turn on your tape recorder, look at a picture of your great-aunt (Bessie or whatever her name is), and talk to the picture. "You should have been there, Aunt Bessie. They had the most amazing . . ." As you talk on the tape recorder to your great-aunt, don't worry about tense or person. Don't think about the lead that you will use or the body of the article. Don't worry about transitions or whether or not you are being too formal or too informal. Just talk as you would if your Aunt Bessie were sitting across from you and you were telling her about your most recent trip. By transcribing your talk with your Aunt Bessie, you will have a first, but rough draft of your article. Yes, it will need much more to be considered an acceptable first draft. But it is a good start as an initial rough draft.

Adopt a Person And A Tense

Now go back to your transcribed talk with your great-aunt, and decide whether or not you want your article to be in first person, second person, or third person. You may not have a choice. Travel editors like third person, and your contract may well call for you to write your article in third person. If so, simply change everything so it is now in third person. However, if the editor did not choose for you, review the articles in past issues of the magazine, and see how they were written. The chances are good that most will be in third person, but some may be in first person and some in second person. It is usually wise to adopt the person most prominently found in other articles in the magazine.

As you are changing the person in your rough draft, give some thought to what tense you want to write in. Most articles are in present tense, but there are many that are in past tense. Again, if the editor specified which tense, you have no choice. However, just as you did in selecting the person in which you write, do the same in determining the tense. Look at other articles in the current and previous issues of the magazine, and adopt whichever tense is used in most of those articles. Now you will have a refined rough draft, but it still does not qualify for a real first draft.

Consider Developing an Outline

You could prepare an outline for your article before you had the conversation with your great-aunt. However, in real life we do not tell people about our travels holding an outline in front of us. Your tape recorded tale of your trip is far more natural, and, generally, it will fit what magazines and newspapers want far better than a piece that was outlined in advance. Nevertheless, at this stage, by outlining the article, you can go through your rough draft and identify the key elements: the lead, each key paragraph in the body, and the close. If any of these are missing, you can add them in to your outline. When you are satisfied that the outline has all the basics, then you are ready to move toward refining the rough draft so that it will become a completed first draft.

Draw from Your Journal

You took the trip. Therefore you remember it. You told your great-aunt about your trip. However, there may be some special things in your journal which will add substantially to the article which you may have forgotten. Skim through the journal, and see what is there that will make the article even better. Especially look for anecdotes, quotes, humor, and pieces of history or geography that might intrigue the reader or give more strength to your article. When you come across something, add it into the draft without paying too much attention to how many words you use or how formal or informal your writing.

What Is Your Hook?
A hook is what captures the attention of the reader and gets him or her to read further. Many times the hook and the lead are the same. However, there can be more than one hook. As you read through what you have written, ask yourself what is particularly intriguing and how you can write it in such a way that it not only draws the reader into the article, but it encourages reading further. Some well-written travel articles will include a hook at the beginning or the end of almost every paragraph, but this is hard to do without sounding stilted.

If you want a good idea about what hooks are and how they work, watch television, especially the soap operas. Notice at the end there will be a hook to encourage you to watch tomorrow. The announcer will say something like, "Find out tomorrow if Johnny will propose" or "Did Alice die in the explosion? Tune in tomorrow to find out."

The Lead
While the lead and the hook may be the same, a good lead is frequently more than just a few words. More than one editor has been known to say to travel writers, "Make them (the readers) feel like they are there. After reading the first sentence they should have a sense of being there—feeling it, smelling it, hearing it, living it!" Of course, that may be impossible in one sentence, but the travel writer who can draw in the reader right away has accomplished writing a good lead.

But the lead also needs to be capable of providing an easy transition into the body of the article. After writing the lead and the body, go back and see how easily they transition from one to the other. It may be that they do not, and you will need to rewrite either the lead or the body.

The Body—Key Paragraphs

In reworking the rough draft of your article, concentrate on the body. These are key paragraphs, and each one should not only be interesting but should make the reader want to continuing reading. Do this by drawing liberally from anecdotes about people, word strings that draw on the senses, accurate details, quotes, colorful prose, and both history and geography. As you describe a person or a place, try to show the reader rather than telling him or her about the person or place. This task can be difficult in the beginning, but if you go back to your descriptions and rewrite them in several ways, you will start gaining the ability to show rather than tell.

Anecdotes Make Articles Memorable

It is frequently the people that we remember best about a trip. In a foreign capital city, the tourist stops at a crosswalk and looks at his map. Three natives come up, and with varying degrees of faltering English, each one asks if they can help him find his way. This incident becomes the tourist's most endearing memory of the city. There are many ways the travel writer can describe the incident, but it is our job to make the reader come away with the same strong feelings about the friendliness of the natives as the tourist who experienced the incident.

Initially, write about the anecdote in whatever way you want just to get it down in black and white. Then go back over what you have written, making sure that you *show* the incident rather than *telling* the reader about it and making certain that your presentation of the incident stands out. It may take two or three different drafts before you get it the way you feel it should be.

Draw on the Senses

A string of colorful words allows the reader to smell and taste the swarma offered up by the Athens street vendor, or the reflection of the setting sun on an ocean of open water as you descend to your gondola down the steps of the Venice rail station sets a visual tone for your arrival in this memorable ancient city. The cacophony of silence broken only by the flapping wings and the occasional cry of one bird to another helps you witness for the reader another return of the swallows to

Capistrano. Draw on the senses. Write the sounds, the aromas, the feel, and the visual feasts that guide you to helping the reader experience the destination.

Include Accurate Details

Details are important, especially if they will make a difference in how the reader experiences the destination. If you tell the reader that the hotel will accept check-ins as early as six in the morning after flying all night from New York to London and the traveler arrives counting on your promise only to learn that the standard check-in time is two in the afternoon and the desk check-in agent will not waiver from that hundred-year-old rule, you can be sure the editor will hear about it. Make absolutely certain that your facts are correct. Check and double-check. But do not leave out facts just because you want to avoid the work of confirming them. Sidebars especially are crammed with facts, and they all need to be correct.

Quotes Can Add

Get a copy of *Bartlett's Quotations* and get to know the publication. Unfortunately, not all the quotes that you will want to use are there. As you review transcriptions of your on-site interviews, take a big red marker and circle interesting comments that can be used as quotes. You will not include all of them, of course, but it is nice to have a large supply of good quotes from which you can draw. Do not overdo the use of quotes. A few memorable quotes sprinkled throughout your article can add as much taste as salt and pepper sprinkled on your salad.

Colorful Prose

On each review of your rough draft, look for an opportunity to make your writing more colorful. Slip in an intriguing word or two. From time to time, change the sentence structure so that the reader is slightly shocked, even though she or he may not know why. Find better ways of saying things. Try subtlety and understatement. As in some well-refined jokes, try placing the most important word in one of your sentences in the position of being the very last word. All of these techniques will add to an overall sense of a more professionally written travel article.

History and Geography

Some travel articles have too much history, but a taste of history, throwing in a tidbit from time to time, can liven up a travel article. And geography is important to give readers a sense of where they are. The geography rarely needs to be detailed, but you do not want readers to finish the article and say to themselves, "It sounds like an interesting place, but I don't quite know where it is." So balance the geography so that the reader is comfortably centered, but do not go overboard.

You will build a strong article foundation if you work the key paragraphs that make up the body of your article by including anecdotes, drawing on the senses, adding quotes, putting in accurate details, making your prose colorful, and including tidbits of history and geography.

Transitions

Transitions provide a smooth movement between ideas. They can be single words such as: but, however, and nevertheless. They can be short strings of words: on the other hand, in spite of, the next day. Usually it is better to consider all transitions at the same time. In this way, you will avoid overusing one word or one group of words, and you will be able to make sure that there are good transitions throughout. Remember that the major transitions need to be between the major parts of the article. This means between the lead and the body and between the body and the close. However, transitions need to be placed between each major concept or idea presented in the article. That does not mean after every paragraph. Sometimes there are two or three paragraphs for each major idea. You goal is a smooth flow from one thought to the next throughout the article so that the reader is never conscious of moving from one idea or concept to another.

The Close

The close should be definite and final. While it does not say it in those words, it should subtly let the reader know that this is the end of the article. For longer magazine articles and sometimes for shorter articles a summary is a good close. It is probably used more than any other. However, this is a place where quotes can also be effective. Experiment with writing several paragraphs that can be used as final paragraphs, and then select the one with which you are most pleased. Keep in mind that some editors, especially magazine and newspaper editors, still cut articles from the bottom. Therefore, the more that you can make your article appear logical, even if the last paragraph or two is cut out, the better. This means that your task is to make the last one or two sentences of each of the last two paragraphs in the article a logical close. Then if the editor has to chop, it will be easy enough to simply chop off the last paragraph or the last two paragraphs.

The Negatives

Good destination travel articles always include at least one negative about the place. Editors look for the negatives, and, if they do not find at least one, frequently they will return the article to the author so that the writer can rewrite and include one or more. The negatives should be real, but if you can suggest a way to mitigate the negative, that will be even better. For example, you might say: "The transfer service worked extremely well, and the limousine they use is luxurious. However, it consistently arrives between ten and fifteen minutes late. Therefore, to keep from worrying about not being met, it would be wise to bring a cell phone and to call the limo service as soon as you get off the plane to confirm your arrival and to confirm the pickup time." Always look for a way to overcome a negative, but recognize that sometimes there are simply no ways to overcome them. Nevertheless, the negatives should be included in your destination article.

Humor

True humor can make your travel article memorable. Few people write humor well, so, if you are able to do it, you should. Avoid humor based on sex, religion, or politics, however. Subtle humor used once or twice in the article is frequently the most effective. Experiment with humor, but if after writing it you do not think it is funny, the chances are good that your readers will not think it is funny either.

THE SECOND DRAFT

The first draft is really a well-worked version of the rough draft. In other words, it is not a first writing. After finishing the first draft, most travel writers will set the article aside and not look at it again for at least forty-eight hours and preferably for a week or two. When preparing a second draft, it is important that a rereading of the first draft appear to you much like the first reading of the article. It should seem to be fresh material. If you write it too soon after completing the writing of the first draft, you will be too close to it and not able to work with it as well.

The second draft is an opportunity to make certain that the article meets expectations. This means that you need to check to be sure that the article slant is directed to the reader. It also means that you need to actually count the words and make sure that the word count is reasonably close to the maximum word count provided by the editor. At the end of the first draft, most travel writers attempt to have between 150 percent and 175 percent of what they plan to include in the article. They know that cutting is much easier than adding.

You need to be able to review the article and ask yourself if you cut out the last paragraph will it still make sense. Then ask yourself if you cut out the last two paragraphs or the last three paragraphs will it still make sense. Remember that most editors today still want authors to give them writing they can easily cut from the end, i.e., an inverted pyramid.

The second draft is a time when all facts need to be checked if that was not completed during the first draft. Many travel writers will rewrite rather than leave any fact in the article that they are unable to check for accuracy. This is the time, too, when you may want to make certain that you are using the exact "right" word in each case. As you go through the draft, circle any words where you feel a synonym or another word might work better. Then go back through the draft, and change those words that need to be changed.

THE THIRD DRAFT

The third draft is the final draft. It is the finished article. Again, it is wise to put the article away for a week or longer and then come back to it to work on the final version. This is the time to "polish" your article.

If you are working on a contracted article, the editor gave you a preferred length. If it is a spec article and you have identified publications to send it to, you will have done a word count on recent issues and determined the number of words that will be ideal for the publications to which you will be sending the article. Now is the time to make absolutely certain that you are within the word-count constraints. Many in the industry say that it is not important to have exactly the number of words that the editor requires or the average number of words of articles in the publication. That is true. However, editors rightfully complain that articles are frequently far from their required or preferable word count. Therefore it is recommended that you count each word of your article and make certain that the final draft which you submit for publication is no more than ten words over or under the required or preferred number of words.

This draft is also the time to read through the article and make sure that it reads smoothly from the beginning sentence to the final sentence. Consider changing transition words or sentences if the flow is not smooth.

Finally, ask yourself if both the editor and the reader will like the article. That is, of course, the single most important factor.

PACKAGING AND DELIVERY

When you send your final manuscript to the editor, it is better to send it as part of a flat package. Do not fold it up and put it into a standard size (number ten) envelope. Usually a 10-inch by 14-inch insulated or bubble-protected envelope is best. In addition to the manuscript itself, the package should include a cover letter, appropriate photographs, and an invoice. Increasingly editors are asking for electronic copy as well. This means sending them a 3.5-inch floppy disk in a standard disk mailer. These disk mailers can be purchased at any office supply store.

Cover Letters

As a professional travel writer, you should have professionally printed letterhead with your name and return address on it. The cover letter basically states that you are enclosing the completed manuscript as specified in the editor's letter of agreement. Some writers review the highlights of what the editor asked for and indicate that all of the requirements have been met. A separate paragraph in the letter should discuss photographs that are enclosed. Finally, have a paragraph that says that an invoice is enclosed and that you will appreciate receiving payment as rapidly as possible. The last paragraph in the cover letter is one in which you thank the editor for the opportunity of working with the publication and ask that he or she contact you in the future for any additional travel writing needs. After your signature, list the enclosures.

Photographs

A photograph that is bent is useless. Therefore, photographs should be enclosed in a photo mailer, or sheets of cardboard should be placed in the front of and behind the photographs so that the photos are sandwiched in between the cardboard. Simply tape the cardboard so that it is secure and write in bold letters using a marker the word PHOTOGRAPHS. Remember to stamp the envelope and print clearly the words: PHOTOGRAPHS ENCLOSED—DO NOT BEND.

Invoice

The last component of your package is an invoice. It is better to have these professionally printed as standard invoice forms so that, as with your letterhead, your name and address will appear on the invoice. At the top section of the invoice form will be a place for the name and address for the publication that you are billing. Before the name and address, however, you should put in the name of the editor and his or her title. There will be a date block to be filled out, and you should enter the current date. The body of the invoice is where you should describe the work that you have done and, to the right of that description, put in the amount that is owed. Many invoice forms will have a section at the bottom where you total the amount that is billed.

Make sure that you prepare the invoice in at least two copies. Some travel writers prefer three copies. The first copy should be sent as a part of the package that goes in the mail to the editor together with your photos, cover letter, and manuscript. A second copy is normally kept in the file of the publication that is buying your article. Most travel writers keep an "Unpaid Invoices" file with invoices filed by date. It is in that file that the third copy is placed. Typically when payment is received, the outstanding invoice copy is pulled from the file and marked paid together with the date of payment. Then it is placed into a "Paid Invoices" file.

COMPLETION

The final manuscript represents completion of the three-part cycles. You now have a good introduction, body, and conclusion. You have completed a rough first draft, a more finished second draft, and a final polished third draft. Your travel article has an introduction, a body, and a conclusion; it also has a lead, key paragraphs, and a close. You have successfully closed each of the three-part circles, and your job with this article has been successfully completed. Congratulations!

But wait. You really are not finished. In this chapter and others, we have touched on photographs. And providing good photos to go along with the article is an important part of travel writing. Photos should relate directly to the article. They should complement the article and direct the person who is scanning a newspaper or magazine to stop and read the article. In the next two chapters, you will learn how to add photographs to your travel writing to not only make the package more attractive to potential readers but also to get editors to want to publish your work as compared to the work of others.

End-of-Chapter Questions

1. What is the magic number in writing?
2. Do most publications provide reader profiles and demographics as part of their advertising sales brochures?
3. Does the travel writer have to get permission to tape interviews with audio or video equipment?
4. Does an interviewee have a right to preview an article before the interview is printed in the newspaper or magazine as a part of the article?
5. Are you required to use a magazine's or newspaper's own photo release, or is it okay to use a standard photo release form?
6. Is it better to outline a travel article before or after writing the first rough draft?
7. Is it usually better for a travel writer to tell the reader about a place or for the travel writer to paint a word picture and show the place to the reader?
8. Is it possible to include too much history in a travel article?

9. Must a destination travel article always include at least one negative?
10. What words should be stamped or printed in bold letters on the outside of the envelope in which your article, cover letter, and other items are sent to a publisher?

WRITING ASSIGNMENT THIRTEEN
DRAFT TWO OF YOUR SPEC ARTICLE

Assignment Introduction

Now that you have written the first rough draft of your spec article and you have had an opportunity to let it sit for awhile, it is time to go back and prepare a good second draft of the article. This draft should be close to the quality level of what you are prepared to send to editors. It will probably need a little more polishing, but it should be in a reasonably finished state by the time you set it aside waiting to finalize it and mail it to editors.

Assignment Activity

It is usually better to prepare the second draft in stages. First, get a red pen and reread your first draft, making changes in red as you go. This is usually a fast first read, but your markings should be concerned with improving the flow of the article and making sure that it is an easy read. Don't be too concerned with grammar or spelling mistakes. Just circle them so that you will know to come back to them when you are doing a technical audit.

Second, document. Go through the article draft marking every statement of fact and every quote. You don't necessarily need to show footnotes documenting your facts, but you do need to have a factual record. That way if an editor calls or e-mails you saying he thinks the mountain you said was a mile-and-a-half high really is not, you will have a fact source confirming your statement. You will need to show documentation for any quotes or references from other book or magazine sources.

Next, make sure you have included the essentials of good travel writing. Your article should probably be an inverted pyramid (see chapter 12). The first sentence of the first paragraph should set the tone of the article, and it should make the reader feel as if he or she is at the destination. The first sentence will probably be your "lead," and it is the most important sentence in your article. In fact, usually the first sentence either turns on the reader (and gets him or her to continue reading), or it turns off the reader (who stops reading). Toward the beginning, there should be a "hook" (see chapter 12). If possible, you should include humor, quotes, and a little of both history and geography. Short anecdotes and colorful prose can also spice up your story. Before leaving your review for essentials, make sure your article includes at least one negative about the destination.

The technical audit is usually done next, though there is no rule that the reviews/audits must be done in the order listed here. Nevertheless, a technical audit is important. Do not rely on spell-check. Make sure there are no errors in spelling, punctuation, and grammar.

Your final review for a quality second draft should pay attention to transitions and potential cuts. Make sure you have well-thought-through transition words, phrases, and sentences. And then try to make the last paragraphs of your article material that can easily be cut without losing the logic.

After you have finished the final for the second draft of your article, set it aside until it is time to prepare the polished final manuscript to be sent to editors.

Final Step: Add your name to the Instructor Comment Sheet for Writing Assignment Thirteen in appendix 5 and staple it to a copy of draft two of your spec article. Then turn in both items to your professor.

CHAPTER 14

Provide Photos

Amanda Castleman

GOOD TRAVEL PHOTOS—NOT AS EASY AS IT LOOKS

Marcel Proust once wrote that "the real voyage of discovery is not in seeing a new landscape, but seeing it with new eyes." A lucky few are able to capture that vision—in words or images or both—to share.

Good travel photography conveys the essence of a destination, argued *National Geographic* contributor Bob Krist in *Spirit of Place: the Art of the Traveling Photographer*. "Besides the ineffable quality of beauty," he wrote, "four defining characteristics are always present: interesting composition, great light, a sense of movement, and . . . good color or a range of gray tones."[1]

---

1. Bob Krist, *Spirit of Place: The Art of the Traveling Photographer*, (New York: Amphoto Books, 2000), 8.

The recipe is easy to recount, hard to reproduce, he stressed. Shooters on the road must also contend with strangeness, "overcoming language and cultural barriers to create insightful photographs of a place where you might not even be able to read a street sign." Like most things in life, he concluded, it's nowhere as easy as it looks.

"An exotic locale may pique your interest, but doesn't immediately add value to your photographs," wrote Susan McCartney, author of *Travel Photography: A Complete Guide to Shoot and Sell.* "It's just as easy to take boring pictures in Bangkok as it is in Brooklyn."[2] Like Krist, she seeks a "sense of what makes a place unique" but also "what makes it universally appealing."

In an ideal universe, a professional author and photojournalist would collaborate on every story. Sadly, this only happens at quite a high level, so fledgling or mid-career writers should be able to supply or source images.

Photography demands a large amount of specialized knowledge, expensive and heavy equipment, and chutzpah (can you bribe an amputee beggar in Delhi? Approach a fierce fur-swathed babushka in Moscow? A Buddhist monk?). "Hone your photographic skills until they become second nature," McCartney wrote. This permits concentration on "the important things, which are aesthetics and logistics."[3]

Yet she acknowledged that almost anyone "with luck" could sell the odd picture occasionally. So it follows that any intelligent and dedicated journalist can produce images to accompany his or her articles. Granted, the photographs may not be Ansel Adams or Walker Evans quality, but a functional snap may tip the scales in your favor. And travel writers have an edge over other amateurs: an eye for the defining scene. They're already looking for the patterns, the evocative moments, the memorable slice of time and space.

COMPOSITION

Entire books have been written on the subtle art of photographic composition, which can't possibly be summarized in one chapter. However, here are ten tips for improving travel images.

---

2. Susan McCartney, *Travel Photography: A Complete Guide to Shoot and Sell* (New York: Allworth Press, 1999), 2.
3. Ibid, 3.

1. Get Close—Then Get Closer

Strong, bold images catch the eye, so charge right into the middle of the action. The traditional advice is "go as close as you dare, then advance three more feet." Portraits especially benefit from this intimate approach. What's more striking: a snapshot of granny on the couch with her dog, the molting Christmas tree, and a tepid cup of tea—or a full frame of her noble, wrinkled face?

Shy shooters fret over the "invasion of space," especially when the language barrier makes explanation impossible. Politely ask anyway, advised McCartney, who often talks and photographs for half an hour before reaching her favorite setup: three or four feet away with a 28mm lens.

Approach cautiously, and monitor the subject's expressions, gestures, and posture. "Approach slowly, as though they were small frightened animals (which most of us are, deep inside)," she joked.[4] The camera can erode inhibitions on both sides. "It's rather like wearing a mask—and with the camera's protection you can approach, talk to, and photograph most people quite easily."

As war photographer Robert Capa famously put it: "If your pictures aren't good enough, you're not close enough."[5] He followed this advice to the end: the forty-year-old stepped on a land mine while covering the French Indochina War in 1954. So get close, but tread softly and safely.

"Open the other eye occasionally," recommended photo editor Marcus Donner of the *King County Journal* in Seattle, Washington. "Maybe you're missing some interesting element . . . or maybe you're about to be whacked with a croquet ball. Don't let the camera give you a false sense of invulnerability."

2. Dominant Element

Your photo should clearly be about something. Direct the observer's eye—and don't distract the observer with too much clutter (like the poodle and the gift wrap). A useful trick here is the "rule of thirds."

---

4. Ibid, 4.
5. Alex Kershaw, *Blood and Champagne: The Life and Times of Robert Capa* (New York: Da Capo Press, 2004), 6.

Imagine a tick-tack-toe grid over an image. Good pictures have a "center of interest" where the lines meet.

When photographing people with objects, place the person in the extreme foreground, the object far in the background (this works well with large objects, such as St. Peter's and the Washington Monument. Otherwise you wind up with a camel driver against a biscuit-colored wall, instead of a camel driver with the Sphinx). Add even more depth with a relevant or interesting element in the middle ground, too. Make the viewer's eye move in the frame, transforming a two-dimensional object into a three dimensional-one.

Landscapes pose a particular problem, according to Michael Busselle, author of *Travel and Vacation Photography* and a fellow of the Royal Photographic Society. "There is often a temptation to include too much in the frame," he observed. The image "has no immediate focus of attention and too many conflicting details."[6]

3. Prime Time

Early morning and early evening light are warmer (the syrupy gold hue before sunset is nicknamed the "magic hour," much exploited by catalogue designers). Looking at a magnificent sunset? Without filters, the splendor is hard to capture. But spin around; all that gorgeous light may illuminate a more intriguing scene.

Avoid shooting at midday, when the sun throws harsh shadows. Eye sockets, in particular, recede into gothic gloom. The human brow really serves a purpose: it shades the eye. A fill flash softens the contrast. Slightly overcast days provide nice, soft tones for portraits (while landscape photographers gnash their teeth).

Take notice of the shadows in a composition. Is there a better time to return and try again? Ansel Adams was famous for stalking light, returning time and time again in different seasons, until the conditions optimized. Much of good photography is patience: composing a frame, then waiting for conditions to perfect (for the purple light of dusk, for a flock of birds in a certain quadrant, for the hunter-gather to pry open the trap or the Indonesian washerwoman to collect the linens).

---

6. Michael Busselle, *Travel and Vacation Photography* (Hove, England: Rotovision, 2002), 3.

This time-consuming process can clash with a reporter's restless quest for information. *National Geographic* staffer Jodi Cobb recommends that teams touch base—say, be in the same country and region—but not dog each others' footsteps.[7] Travel writers doing double duty should expect conflicted loyalties—and even compromised coverage at times, sad to say.

4. Work the Angles
Search out unusual angles. Climb up a column and shoot down. Lie on the cobbles and shoot up. Tilt the camera. Vary your perspective to produce an unusual effect. Also, look for natural "frames," which add depth and interest to an image. Try shooting through a doorway or an archway of branches. Place a palm-leaf umbrella in a corner, then photograph the sandy beach and surfline. Finally, compose with "leading lines," elements that draw in the eye (like a woman standing on the center line of a road, along a fence line, or atop a staircase).

5. Avoid Posing
"Photo faces" make for poor images generally. The artificial stiffness doesn't convey the sense of scene (professionals call this unnatural look "camera-conscious"). Shoot real people doing real things. Put subjects at ease by chatting—or shoot them unaware with a telephoto lens. Another technique is to "blow frames": keep the shutter firing until they grow accustomed to the experience and relax. Digital technology makes this option more affordable now.

6. Pound the Pavement
Remember those boots were made for walking. A common amateur mistake is monotony; dozens of shots where the people and backgrounds remain in the same ratio. Gathered together, the images are dull. Mix it up. Vary the distance between the subject and camera. Change lenses. Zoom in and out. No flashy technology? Wear down the shoe leather and simply walk closer to avoid visual redundancy.

---

7. Jodi Cobb, "Inside Secret Worlds," *National Geographic Live!* (February 23, 2005).

7. Outside the Box

Get one in the can, to borrow some Hollywood lingo. Take a middle-of-the-road, good-enough "safety shot," then push for riskier, more artistic compositions. The subject needn't be dead center in the frame—as long as it's still clearly the subject. A runner, for example, could race into the right side of a photograph, giving a sense of movement and speed. A portrait might emphasize someone's soulful eyes, by eliminating the subject's hair and chin. Likewise, not all photographs need to be the classic rectangle shape. Publications crop images into squares, panoramic strips, or thin columns. Keep this in mind when composing—and suggest edits with submissions (draw lines onto a photocopy or printout).

8. Silhouettes

Play around with shapes, especially distinctive ones (a pregnant woman, a child in a cowboy hat, a man with an Afro). Place the shadowy figure against a bright background (a person standing in a doorway on a sunny day does the trick). Adjust the exposure for the light area.

9. Avoid Distractions

Don't let unwanted elements destroy your images. Is a tree behind the shaman? That palm will sprout from his head in the photograph. Try to minimize signs, telephone wires, garbage cans, and other clutter. Shooting from a higher or lower angle often hides the mess. Blurring the background helps, too (limit the depth-of-field with a large aperture like f-2.8).

10. Bracket Exposures

Fancier cameras allow the photographer to set the exposure. The light meter displays the optimum setting. Take a shot at the recommended f-stop, then one above and one below (some models have auto-bracketing now). And don't hesitate to take multiple pictures of the same scene. Professionals use a rapid-fire function—and easily blast through several rolls of film or hundreds of digital frames perfecting one image. If in doubt, underexposure is always preferable, as it makes the color slightly richer.

PHOTOJOURNALISM VERSUS SNAPSHOTS

Photojournalism, called reportage photography in Europe, pushes beyond holiday snapshots and article illustrations. An image—or carefully chosen series—tells a story about a place and its people. Interpret the scenes; don't just photocopy Uluru or Angkor Wat. Make the tale compelling; the viewer has no obligation to examine the photo (or proceed on to the headline, captions and . . . finally to the text itself).

Here's the difference: a hiking tour company wins an award. The jaded local newspaper photographer herds the employees together with their plaque, producing a hideous "grip and grin" shot. A dynamic photojournalist shoots them camping by a lake or cresting a mountain in full outdoor regalia. She's gone to more trouble, but the active image captures the essence of the tour company, rather than a tired lineup.

Try to think like a photojournalist. Vary your images—horizontal and vertical, interesting crops—so that six or seven could be used on a spread. Take overview shots that set the scene, workplaces, landmarks, food bazaars, houses, signs, and flags. Capture groups of locals, faces close-up (or other details, like hands, feet, or one aspect of ceremonial costume), piles of souvenirs, and plates of food. Consider how the images work together. What do they convey?

"Shoot a range of different themes so you can capture a good all-around impression of the place,"[8] Busselle advised.

Sunsets, small furry animals, and postcard views aren't the goal, stressed David Hurn in *On Being a Photographer*. "Most great photographs displaying beauty reveal a sensation of strangeness, not predictability. . . . They are the opposite of clichés; they have a quality beyond the visually obvious."[9]

Such storytelling often involves contrast. This stretches far beyond light and shadow, however. Look for contextual friction, which adds emotional depth. For example, shoot a solemn person's portrait with gregarious diners in the background. The bubbly background adds information: the subject is withdrawn even in a boisterous environment. Similarly, some of the most poignant developing-world illustrations may not depict poverty per se, but may focus on the persistence of

---

8. Michael Busselle, *Travel and Vacation Photography*, 2.
9. Bob Krist, *Spirit of Place: The Art of the Traveling Photographer*, 8.

human spirit despite it, such as a child building a rope swing in a refuge camp. Link the familiar and unfamiliar to help viewers connect.

As in writing, seek the universal theme. Can you evoke an emotion—nostalgia, awe, or tenderness—from a single image or series? A well-composed photograph captures a time and place, conveying a message. You don't illustrate a story, you *tell* it, Peter Turnley once urged his colleagues.[10]

PHOTO RELEASE

Permission to use a person's image is called a "model release." Typically, travel editors demand these legal documents.

Here is an example:

> Date
>
> Photographer's name
>
> I give to _____ the irrevocable right to use my name and any photographic or illustrative depiction of me in all forms and for all purposes associated with the publication or transmission of works, including advertising and promotion. I waive the right to inspect or approve the finished version(s) and any requirement for payment.
>
> Name:
>
> Address:
>
> Phone:
>
> Signature:
>
> Guardian signature for minors:

EQUIPMENT: GETTING STARTED

Select a comfortable, nonthreatening camera, suited to your work. Filing a regular column for a webzine? A three-megapixel digital model might suffice. Snapping for a small community newspaper? A solid single lens reflex (SLR) could suit best. Aiming for the cover of *Travel & Leisure* or *National*

---

10. Peter Turnley, *Biography*, http://peterturnley.com/bio02.html.

Geographic? Plunge your life savings into lenses, and learn to shoot 35mm slides.

A point-and-shoot is a good place to start (most folks have one already). These standard snappers are small, light, and simple to use with a built-in lens and flash. Though convenient, they have limited manual override, so it's difficult to take good slide images. However, no travel writer should leave home without one. Even accomplished photographers carry point-and-shoots as backup equipment. Highly portable, these "toys" can be easily thrown into a purse or satchel, for times when you don't want to risk theft or lug thirty pounds of camera gear to a cocktail party. And under certain conditions, a discrete camera is key.

Professionals prefer 35mm rangefinders and SLRs (single lens reflex), which let the user change lenses and adjust the exposure. These cameras are more complicated and generally bulkier. Most have full automatic settings though, so beginners shouldn't shy away from a serious purchase. Midway between disposable cameras and professional rigs lies the "prosumer" market (futurist Alvin Toffler coined this phrase in 1979, but lately it's grown popular among dedicated digi-dabblers who prefer high-quality, high-tech gear[11]). A prosumer model can cost just a few hundred dollars more than a quality point-and-shoot, but it takes far superior snaps. Select equipment to grow into, as your skills expand.

Quality optics matter most, so it's worth investing in reputable brands such as Canon, Nikon, or Leica, even for a point-and-shoot. Buy the best lenses possible; if you must skimp, opt for a cheap camera body. "Always go for good glass," is the popular wisdom. Richard I'Anson stressed this heavily in *Travel Photography: A Guide to Taking Better Pictures*. "Lens quality determines image sharpness, color, and the light-gathering capacity of the lens, which can determine how you shoot in various lighting conditions," he wrote.[12]

Examine the warranty carefully, especially if shopping abroad. Some companies won't honor repair contracts outside the country of purchase. Test-drive the technology before returning home, and search for English-language manuals before any trouble arises.

---

11. Scott Kirsner, "Are you a prosumer?" *The Boston Globe* (June 13, 2005).

12. Richard I'Anson, *Travel Photography: A Guide to Taking Better Pictures* (Footscray, Australia: Lonely Planet, 2000), 25.

Finally, consider taking a class or working through a reputable book like *Basic Photography* by Michael Langford[13] or the less comprehensive *Teach Yourself Photography* by Lee Frost.[14] I'Anson's excellent and user-friendly Lonely Planet guide is also highly recommended.[15]

Lenses

Different sizes alter the image. A wide angle is good for landscapes and architecture, but it distorts the scene, curving it (18mm, 21mm, and 24mm). These lenses exaggerate the distance between objects, making the foreground and background seem farther apart. Achieve a more natural perspective with a 28mm or 35mm (the normal point-and-shoot size). A 50mm is close to what the human eye sees.

Invest in a macro for close-ups, say of wildflowers or butterflies. Telephoto lenses magnify, allowing you to shoot from far away. They also compress images, so objects seem closer together. Sports photographers charge around with huge 600mm the size of fire hydrants. For travel purposes, opt for a daintier 200mm. Zoom lenses are popular, but budget models can be slow to focus or just plain blurry.

Aside from sharpness, the other consideration is speed. The shutter determines how long light floods into the camera. The f-stop regulates how wide it opens. Confusingly, lower numbers allow *more* light. So f-2.8 is better for shooting in a shadowy church that doesn't permit flash photography to preserve frescoes. But f-22 is the ideal for a sunny landscape, where you want as much in focus as possible.

Photographers calculate the interplay between film speed, shutter speed, f-stop, and depth of field. This science takes time and practice to perfect. As McCartney admitted: "I am one photographer who had to work hard to understand the mysteries of f-stops and reciprocity and flash synchronization, and, after exposing many thousands of rolls of film, I still need to shoot all the time to keep in peak practice."

The most important f-stop lesson to absorb, while selecting equipment, is this: look for lower numbers. The 1.0–4 ranges usually indicate "fast glass," great for shooting in dim conditions. In fact, each f-stop

---

13. Michael Langford, *Basic Photography* (Oxford: Focal Press, 2000).
14. Lee Frost, *Teach Yourself Photography* (Columbus, Ohio: McGraw-Hill, 2004).
15. Richard I'Anson, *Travel Photography: A Guide to Taking Better Pictures.*

down *doubles* the amount of light inside the camera. So ignore the illogic of the numbering—1.4, 2.0, 2.8, 4, 5.6, 8, 11, 16, 22—and shop for lenses that are both sharp and speedy.

Accessories
Darkroom pundits insist that lens caps are for amateurs, while filters are for professionals. Overcautious camera-owners can miss critical shots, while struggling to remove a cap. A skylight or ultraviolet (UV) filter protects equally *and* cuts down haze in scenic shots, too. As I'Anson said: "Lenses are expensive; filters aren't. It's much better to clean a dirty big fingerprint off a filter than off a lens."[16]

Filters—which screw onto the lens' front or slip into a holder—are an art unto themselves. Travel writers' standards, however, are the UV and the polarizing, which deepens the color of the sea and the sky. It also eliminates most reflections: important if you're documenting an exotic storefront. However, this filter reduces the light coming into the camera, so remember to remove it. A host of others exist, among them the 81a and 81b, also known as "warm up" filters, which lend a cheerful hue to photographs.

A tripod is useful for longer exposures. Travelers usually prefer a lightweight, tabletop model with 15cm collapsible legs and Velcro straps (to cling to a tree, fence, etc.). A cable-release lets you fire the shutter without touching—and possibly shaking—the camera. A self-timer propped on a stable object can work just as well, cutting down on luggage and paraphernalia.

A flash is useful for low-light situations. Remember: it doesn't always need to be pointed directly at your subject (producing the dread red eye). You can "bounce" the light off a white wall or surface nearby, producing a softer effect.

Always carry extra batteries, as these can be difficult to find or just plain expensive at tourist traps (pack more for colder climates, where their efficiency dips). Digital cameras use proprietary rechargeable batteries, usually of lithium ion. New ones can last a week, but bring backups and also a charger. Remember to pack a plug adaptor or transformer, when abroad.

---

16. Ibid., 30.

Number your films—or files—then record the opening and closing shot of each roll in a notebook. Jot down caption information as well. (Some professional digital cameras encode this information.)

Pack everything in a nondescript, soft bag with a wide shoulder strap (to prevent theft and back strain). Many professionals prefer more comfortable back packs or waist bags: Domke is a popular brand. Keep close records of equipment, supplies, and processing fees, which may be tax deductible. And make sure your travel insurance covers all this expensive equipment. Look into journalist homeowner policies, designed for globe-trotting freelancers. Regular content-insurance may not apply if you are working.

FILM AND SLIDE

National Geographic photographers take two thousand images for each photograph used in the magazine.[17] Travel writers doing double-duty rarely have the time to amass such a stockpile. But permit yourself a margin of error; say a 1:10 ratio of published images to discards. The ironclad rule here is: snap a lot. Don't hold back; don't skimp. Traveling is expensive and time-consuming, often there's no second chance. So burn through those rolls or memory cards.

Slides—also known as transparencies, trannies, or chrome—are the industry standard, because they have the highest reproduction quality. The tones are richer, the images crisper, the grain fainter. Color and black-and-white prints can be made from slides, if need be. All this goodness comes at a price: it's more expensive than regular film and harder to work with, as the exposure must be absolutely correct (bracketing helps). But many publications only accept transparencies, so aspiring travel photographers should work in this medium or high-quality digital.

Fujichrome Velvia is good for landscapes, while Kodak Porta creates richer skin tones. Use Ektachrome 400 in low-light conditions. Plus-X film or Tri-X are recommended for black-and-white prints. Match your film speed to the conditions. Slow films are ideal for bright days: the standards are 100-200 (many photojournalists praise Fuji

---

17. Bill Allen, "From the Editor," *National Geographic* (June 2000).

Provia 100f as "virtually grainless"). Use 400 speed in a point-and-shoot. Higher-speed films—up to 3200—are key when there's not much light. Color negative can be more forgiving in dark situations. Try Fuji 800, "pushed" once (exposed and custom-developed as 1600 speed).

Consumer film is engineered to sit on the shelf and withstand a wide variety of temperatures. However, professional film is more delicate. Brought to its color-reproductive prime at the factory, it requires refrigeration. Fastidious photographers check the date on the box, to make sure the roll hasn't lingered for years, unsold and crumbling. Likewise, they never leave film in the camera for long, as it deteriorates. Store rolls in the fridge—or another cool, dark location—if there's a delay before processing.

Keep both camera and film out of the sun. Avoid shooting at midday in a hot climate (turn your back to the sun, while loading film). Likewise, cold makes the film brittle and can freeze the electronics in newer cameras. (Mountaineers opt for chunky old mechanical models, like the Canon AE1, which is cheap and fantastically solid. No bells-and-whistles like auto-focus and motorized film advancing, but it's a tank.)

Always carry rolls onboard aircraft, as the X-ray machines for baggage are much stronger and fog film (print a sign-wave, creating streaks or haze). Kodak estimates that low-speed rolls—400 and below—can survive 16 passes through hand-luggage inspection in western countries (the intensity may be higher elsewhere). A lead-lined pouch sometimes encourages officers to turn up the wattage. Instead, ask for a manual inspection. Remove rolls from their individual containers, and then repack them together in a clear plastic bag or box. Be early, as well as patient and polite. Some professionals prefer simply to express mail film home, registered and insured.

Travel writing instructor Louise Purwin Zobel offered a soothing tip for paranoid photographers: "Make the first shot on each roll a sheet of paper with your name and address, so there's no way it can be misplaced."[18]

---

18. Louise Purwin Zobel, *The Travel Writer's Handbook 5th Ed: How to Write and Sell Your Own Travel Experiences* (Chicago: Surrey Books, 2002), 176.

DIGITAL

Digital cameras entirely avoid those film and processing fees, not to mention X-ray worries. They also offer instant gratification. View images immediately and reshoot, if needed. Discard worthless efforts. Speed the learning curve. And electronic transfer avoids the palaver of scanning images into Adobe Photoshop (the best consumer program for electronic manipulation). The industry norm is already digital, outside the finest art and reportage efforts. Few photographers would recommend investing in anything else.

Here's the catch: the camera bodies and basic accessories are slightly more expensive on average. Popular prosumer models run between $700–$1,000 and require several silicon-chip devices, such as memory sticks. The best recording media are compact flash (CF) cards. These quarter-inch-thick squares are bombproof: some function after trips through the laundry or falls that produce visible denting. A 1GB card costs $75–$200 (Costco often has good prices on generic ones). Ideally, a travel writer-photographer dumps images to a hard drive, then burns CDs for backup—posting home copies and scattering others through their baggage.

The most popular SLRs—for travel writers moonlighting as photographers—are the Nikon D70 and Canon Digital Rebel XT. Whatever the brand or make, don't dip below six megapixels for print: photo editors prefer large RAW or JPEG files. For the same reason, avoid backup gadgets such as Apple's iPod Photo, which saves images in a proprietary format. A storage viewer like the Epson P-2000 is a better bet—and still plays music.

"Don't get hung up on megapixels," warned Yossi Fogel, digital sales manager for New York's B&H Photo, in *Wired News*.[19] "[Consumers] should focus on optical zoom and ease of use." Digital zooming inflates the pixels, which can blur the image. Professionals prefer a 1.x magnification factor.

While easy on the eye, a liquid crystal display (LCD) screen saps battery life and fades under bright light. Some models now have an electronic viewfinder (EVF), much like those in camcorders: an

---

19. Elisa Batista, "Digital Cameras: Where to Start?" *Wired News* (December 5, 2002), www.wired.com/news/gizmos/0,1452,56683,00.html.

eyepiece reveals a video image. Aimee Baldridge, CNET's camera columnist, explained: "Instead of providing a little window to squint into, it essentially gives you a second LCD that's shielded from bright light, uses less battery power, and offers a through-the-lens view of your whole image frame that shows both exposure and focus changes."[20]

Carry-on luggage bulks up quickly, as delicate electronics can't be checked. Little room remains for toiletries and spare clothes, once you've loaded the camera, lenses, laptop or hard drive, batteries, power cords, adapters, and transformers. The LowePro Roller usually accommodates some clean socks around the gear and fits in overhead compartments.

SUBMISSIONS

Transfer prints in a 5 x 7 or 8 x 11 format. Never write on photo paper, which is very delicate. Print labels instead with the following information: name, contact details, publication, caption—with all names spelled correctly—and permission, usually "one-time editorial use in one issue only."

Use a dedicated photo mailer or create your own (a large envelope, two slices of corrugated cardboard, rough side out, with the "grain" at 90-degree angles to each other). Mark the outside "photos, do not bend." Don't send originals. Chances are, they will be lost.

Slides should be sent in clear, plastic archival sheets, available at camera shops. Label each as well (a felt-tip marker works okay on the plastic or cardboard mounting, but a printed tag looks better). Should you insure the package, opt for "consequential loss" coverage, which insures the content, not just the cost of the physical film.

Some editors prefer proof (contact) sheets, 8.5 x 11 pages of tiny prints, which labs supply for a small charge. Send the original or a color photocopy. Another tactic is to post thumbnail images on a Web site. Simply supply the URL, rather than e-mailing photos, which could clog and crash in-boxes. Additionally, this allows for selective presentation of the best shots, hiding the backstage mess.

Digital submissions should be in the RAW or JPEG format. These

---

20. Aimee Baldridge, "Sights for sore eyes: a critical look at viewfinding," *Cnet* (May 4, 2004), http://reviews.cnet.com/4520-6501_7-5134913-1.html?tag=txt.

large, high-resolution files are best burned onto CD or sent via FTP (file transfer protocol), which uploads images onto a server.

REFERENCES

References are of two types. The first is books. There are a large number of photography books, but relatively few are written on travel photography. Some of the better travel photography books and one excellent photojournalism book are listed. The second type of reference relates to photo agencies and photo archives. These are good sources of photographs for travel writers. Several are listed.

Photography Books

Lonely Planet Travel Photography: A Guide to Taking Better Pictures (How to Series)
Richard I'Anson
Lonely Planet Publications, 2004, second edition
262 pages

Spirit of Place: The Art of the Traveling Photographer
Bob Krist
Amphoto Books, 2000
160 pages

Travel Photography: A Complete Guide to How to Shoot and Sell
Susan McCartney
Allworth Press, 1999, second edition
360 pages

On Being a Photographer: A Practical Guide
David Hurn and Bill Jay
Lenswork Publishing, 2001, third edition
95 pages

Photojournalism: The Professionals' Approach
Kenneth Kobre
Focal Press, 2000, fourth edition
384 pages

Photo Agencies and Photo Archives

Andes Press agency: www.andespressagency.com
Black Star: www.blackstar.com
Corbis: www.corbis.com

Getty Images: www.gettyimages.com
Magnum: www.magnumphotos.com

YOU DO NOT HAVE TO DO DOUBLE DUTY

The reality is that it is hard to be an excellent travel writer and at the same time be an excellent travel photographer. Yet travel writing buyers want both—good articles with good photographs. If you would prefer not to take the photos, there are several options open to you. In the next chapter, you will learn where you can get photos without taking them yourself. And you will be pleased to know that some "other source" photos will be of a quality that you probably cannot match yourself.

End-of-Chapter Questions

1. According to Bob Krist, what does good travel photography convey?

2. Any intelligent and dedicated journalist can produce images to accompany his or her articles.   A) True B) False

3. At what time should one avoid taking pictures?

4. The technique of keeping the shutter firing until a subject grows accustomed to the experience and relaxes is called "blowing" what?

5. To create a silhouette, place a shadowy figure against a background that is how well lit?

6. What is "photojournalism" called in Europe?

7. Shooting a solemn person's portrait with gregarious diners in the background is an example of what kind of friction?

8. What legal documents do travel editors demand?

9. Popular wisdom is to always go for what kind of glass?

10. Does your camera always have to be pointed directly at your subject?

WRITING ASSIGNMENT FOURTEEN
SELLING YOUR CONTRACT ARTICLE AND WRITING THE OUTLINE

Assignment Introduction

Once you have prepared yourself to sell your article, it is time to do the hard part, to call travel article buyers to sell your article proposal. This is telemarketing, and most people hate telemarketing. However, when you have prepared, there is no logical reason to fear it. We all hate rejection, however, and the potential for rejection can make us procrastinate. Arm yourself by knowing that your article concept is a good one and that the readers of the publication that buys your article will love what they read.

Assignment Activity

Prepare for your phone calls by deciding when you will make the calls. Avoid Monday morning and Friday afternoon. Also avoid lunchtime in the city or cities where you will be calling. Make sure no one else is home so there is no noise or disturbance during your call. Have a copy of the latest issue of each magazine whose travel article buyer you will be calling. Know the average lengths of the articles in each of the magazines, a little about who reads each magazine, and the writing styles preferred by the publications.

Call each travel article buyer one after the other until a buyer says he or she is seriously interested in your article concept. Ideally, the calls are over only after someone says, "Yes, I will buy it." Discuss the parameters of what the buyer wants, what he is going to pay, and when he wants the final article. The travel buyer will normally prepare a letter of agreement and send it to you. If the buyer does not say anything about the letter of agreement, you should ask for it. Getting an advance check is normal. It is usually between 10 percent and 50 percent of the agreed-upon total compensation.

Start the conversation by complimenting the magazine's travel article buyer about something having to do with recent travel articles that have appeared in the publication. Make it a genuine and unique compliment. Then say you are a travel writer and you would like to write an article that readers will like a lot. Give reasons why readers will like your article. In your conversation, let the travel article buyer know that you understand what the readers want because you have studied the publication and its writer's guidelines. Don't ask the buyer to buy your article, ask the buyer to make an either/or decision. For instance, "Your average articles run 1,200 words and 1,800 words. I can write the article for either length, but feel I can do much better justice to it if I write it at 1,800 words. Which length do you feel would be best?" If the buyer answers that question, you have a first commitment, and it will probably lead to agreement to buy the article concept from you.

Don't expect the buyer to ask you what you have written before. It is rare for a buyer to ask such a question if you, the writer, are full of self-confidence. Keep in mind that, if your article concept is one the buyer really wants, he can make changes to the copy if what you submit is not what he wants. After all, that is why most travel article buyers have the title of "editor."

After a travel article buyer says "Yes," stop calling. Do not call any more of the editors (travel buyers) on your list. You have made the sale. Your telemarketing job for the day is over. The next job is to write the article.

Start with an outline. It is often good to bounce the outline off the travel article buyer. However, avoid doing so until you have the letter of agreement and an advance check in your hands and you have cashed the check. If the buyer hates the outline, you do not want him to back out on the agreement.

Once you have the outline finished, prepare a first draft of your article. Try to prepare the outline within a week of the telephone call during which you obtained agreement from the travel article buyer to purchase your article concept.

A Sales Report Form is provided on the next page. Use this form for every article idea you are trying to sell. Fill out the Sales Report Form.

Final Step: Print your name on the Instructor Comment Sheet for Writing Assignment Fourteen in appendix 5 and turn in the following to your professor: 1) the Instructor Comment Sheet for Writing Assignment Fourteen, 2) the completed Sales Report Form, and 3) an outline of your contract article.

Sales Report for Selling Contract Article

Magazine Title	Date of Call	Person Contacted	Follow-up Needed or Results of Sales Contact	Comment
1.				
2.				
3.				
4.				
5.				
6.				
7.				
8.				
9.				
10.				

CHAPTER 15

Other Photo Sources

James Poynter

OPTIONS

If you are unable to take the photographs you want, there other options that might work for you. Sometimes travel writers take trips with travel photographer companions. This may be a spouse or a friend, but the travel writer does the writing, and the travel photographer takes the photographs. The arrangement works well for some in the industry. You might also obtain photographs from large, specialized photo libraries. Many state and national tourist bureaus and a large number of chambers of commerce have well-stocked photo libraries. Simply call or write, tell them the kind of photograph you want (a picture of people frolicking on South Beach, for example), and frequently they will send you several from which to choose. If you are sending your article out to newspapers, each travel editor will want at least one of each photo, and for this type of mailing you can request as many as you need from tourist bureaus. In most cases there will be no charge, but, if they do charge you, it will be a small charge.

CRUISE PHOTOS

You can stand at the end of the pier, point your camera toward your cruise ship, and possibly get a decent picture. Alternatively, you can contact the cruise line, tell your contact there that you want a top-quality photo of the ship on which you are sailing, and he or she will send you excellent photos prepared by professional photographers. Again, there is usually no cost.

When writing about a cruise that you have sailed on, you will need photographs to accompany your article. High-activity, people-oriented pictures will help to sell your article, especially if you are selling to newspapers. On most cruises, ship photographers can be your best photo suppliers. They are everywhere all the time. Consider meeting with the photographer at the start of the cruise. Explain to him or her the types of photos you want. And negotiate a compensation agreement that is fair to both of you. The photographer's first asking price will usually be more than you will be willing to spend. However, in most cases, you can negotiate so that you will get what you want at a reasonable cost. Ship photographers will take not only quality photographs, but they will get the needed photo releases as well.

OTHER VENDOR SUPPLIED PHOTOS

A few of the major resorts have photo libraries specifically to supply their public relations needs—including the requests they receive from travel writers. A few have professional photographers on staff as well. Others will have a roster of photographers who will sell their photos, which have been taken at the resort. Before you go, ask the public relations director of the resort to brief you on what is available.

All of the established airlines have public relations offices, and these are an excellent source for airline "stock" photographs. These are photos used by the public relations office for day-to-day needs. Often multiple prints of these photos will be made available to travel writers either on a gratis basis or at a low cost.

Other Photo Sources

MIX AND MATCH

Most experienced travel writers match photo sources to their needs. In most cases, the best photo for the article will be one that you take yourself. However, there are times when a tourist board photo or a vendor photo will be much better. It is usually best to give some thought as to exactly what type of picture will best help sell the article. If you can take that photograph, fine. If not, consider getting it from another source. Whatever you do, please remember that a good photograph can sell the editor on buying your article. Therefore, taking the time and making the effort to make sure the photos you send with your article are of the best possible quality makes good business sense.

End-of-Chapter Questions

1. Do travel writers sometimes travel with a friend or spouse who is a travel photographer?
2. In addition to local chambers of commerce, what state and national government entities sometimes have large, specialized photo libraries?
3. Will government entities normally charge a fee for the photos they provide?
4. Will cruise lines normally provide travel writers with photos of the ship on which they are sailing?
5. Who can be your best photo suppliers on most cruise ships?
6. With whom might you want to negotiate for photos on board cruise ships?
7. Do resorts have photo libraries?
8. With whom should you talk about photo resources before you go to a resort?
9. For what kind of photographs are airline public relations offices an excellent source?

10. In most cases, what is the source of the best photo for your article?

WRITING ASSIGNMENT FIFTEEN
THE FINAL DRAFT OF YOUR SPEC ARTICLE

Assignment Introduction

Our articles never seem to be good enough. However, to make money we must get them out the door. Therefore, your next draft should be your final draft of your spec article. Once you have done this final draft, prepare to send it to editors. You will be doing that in just a short time.

Assignment Activity

As you have with other drafts, start with red pen in hand reading and marking any changes that you feel will make the article better. There should be few or no red marks at this point.

It would be good to have others read your article at this stage. Avoid asking family members or close friends. They will say it is good and rarely will they give you constructive criticism. If you belong to a writing group, consider asking a couple of the other members to read it. You might contract with a professional editor to read it. You will find that several advertise in *Writer's Digest* and similar publications.

Once you are satisfied that your article is ready to submit, make enough copies for each publication to which you will send it. If you are submitting to magazines, normally articles are not sent to more than four or five select publications. If you are sending it to newspapers, you will probably want to send it to a large number of noncompeting papers, usually between fifty and two hundred. Make sure the copies are of top quality. A self-serve professional copying place is usually both inexpensive and able to provide the copy quality that you need.

Final Step: Add your name to the Instructor Comment Sheet for Writing Assignment Fifteen in appendix 5 and staple it to a copy of the final draft of your spec article. Then turn in both items to your professor.

SECTION V

TRAVEL BOOKS

While one normally thinks in terms of newspapers and magazines when considering travel writing, an increasing number of travel books are being published. Guidebooks are growing in number, in coverage, and in specializations. Years ago when John Q. Public visited his local bookstore, he was lucky to find one shelf of travel guidebooks available, and there were no books on most destinations outside of Europe and some parts of the United States. There are probably no countries or areas of the world for which a guidebook has not been written today. In addition, the shelves of bookstores are beginning to groan under the weight of specialized guidebooks. New specialized books are needed, and new authors need to be found for destination-oriented guidebooks. In chapter 16, Andrew Hempstead provides an excellent introduction to guidebook writing. He tells us what the editors are buying, how to approach editors, and how one goes about writing a guidebook that sells.

A second rapidly growing area of travel books is commonly called the "how-to" book. These include such titles as *How to Pack*, *How to Travel with Children*, and *How to Select a Cruise*. But there are also how-to books written for people in or just entering the travel industry. These carry titles like *Travel Writing* (this is a how-to book), *Tour Design, Marketing, and Management*, and *Incentive Travel*. Jim Poynter, editor and contributor to this book and author of the other two books just mentioned, spells out how to write a "how-to" book in chapter 17.

Some travel writers start their careers writing travel books, but most move into it after they have written newspaper and magazine articles. It can be a lucrative segment of travel writing, and, whether a writer starts with authoring books or moves to books after writing articles for newspapers and/or magazines, most travel writers who author a book stay with books after they have tasted the process and the income from writing travel books.

ANDREW HEMPSTEAD has been writing guidebooks since the late 1980s, when, after leaving a career in advertising, he took off for Alaska on assignment to update an existing guidebook. In the ensuing years, he has focused on writing about Canada, authoring guidebooks to Alberta, British Columbia, the Canadian Rockies, Western Canada, Vancouver, the Maritimes, Newfoundland, and Nova Scotia. He also has coauthored guidebooks to Australia and New Zealand and written on travel for a wide variety of magazines and other media. Following his own advice, he uses his time on the road as a tool for building a stock library that now exceeds twenty-five thousand images. These are then marketed to corporate, editorial, and advertising clients around the world.

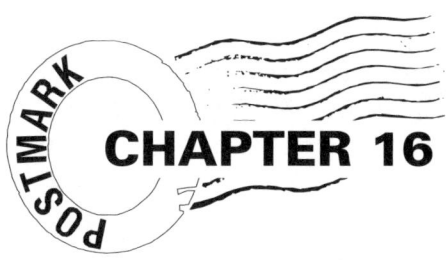

CHAPTER 16

Guidebook Writing

Andrew Hempstead

MULTIPLE REWARDS

Writing a guidebook is a massive undertaking. It is also incredibly satisfying. The rewards come in many forms. The most obvious is seeing your name on the cover of a guidebook as the author. The others are more subtle but equally important. Guidebook writers are forced to immerse themselves in different cultures for extended periods of time, to meet interesting people, and to see their writing in print for an extended period of time. Guidebook writing also has its practical virtues—some authors actually make a living from writing and updating guidebooks, while many more use their guidebook writing travels to research for magazine pieces or take photographs for extra income.

While much of the advice about writing travel for magazines and newspapers applies to guidebook writing, there are also some major differences. The most important of these is the ability to stay committed to a writing assignment that may take a full year or longer.

Writing skills also differ from other forms of travel writing. Guidebooks are branded by a publisher to appeal to a segment of the market. For the writer, this means following style and formatting guidelines while striving to capture the feeling of a destination.

THE GUIDEBOOK MARKET

Thousands of travel guidebooks are in print at any one time. The best known of these are part of a series (also known as an "imprint") that publishers target to a specific sector of the guidebook market. The trust and respect of readers is gained through a familiar format, reader-friendly writing, and up-to-date information. These factors contribute to the success of a series, but savvy marketing is also a major component.

Buy a variety of books to the region where you live or vacation, and field-test them. It will soon become obvious how up-to-date and comprehensive each book is, as well as what the target market for each series is. Be aware also that the most recognizable brands may be only one of many series published by the same company. Use the Internet or order catalogues to see which part of the world each series covers and—equally importantly—what part of the world the publisher doesn't cover.

Major travel publishers are continually reinventing their series to keep the brands fresh. It is an interesting exercise to peruse secondhand stores for old guidebooks and note the changes in look and feel over time.

MAJOR GUIDEBOOK PUBLISHERS

These are the major guidebook publishers:

- **Berlitz:** The Berlitz name is most often associated with language teaching systems, but the company also publishes various guidebooks and maps, including the compact Pocket Guides. The series is kept current by a team of updaters who live in the regions they write about. Check www.berlitzpublishing.com for contact details.

- **Best Places:** Published by Seattle-based Sasquatch Books, this series concentrates on the best and most unique places to stay and eat, with detailed reviews and symbols such as "Family Fun." Contributors are local writers. Contact information is online at www.sasquatchbooks.com.

- **Blue Guides:** Renowned for their solemn approach to describing history, culture, and architecture, this series of sixty books is published by Somerset Books (www.blueguides.com), based in London, England.

- **Bradt:** This British publisher offers titles to out-of-the-way places and brands such as the Eccentric series. Authors are generally experienced writers and always experts on the regions they write about. Book proposal submission details are at www.bradt-travelguides.com.

- **Cadogan Guides:** Published in Great Britain and covering all of Europe, this series has a reputation for high-quality writing that delves into history and culture. Authors write about where they live or have a strong connection to specific destinations. Contact information can be found at www.cadoganguides.com.

- **Eyewitness Guides:** Launched in 1993, Eyewitness has quickly grown to become one of the world's premier guidebook series. Color pages, 3-D maps, cutaway diagrams of famous buildings, and high-quality paper are defining features. The publisher is Dorling Kindersley (www.dk.com).

- **Fodor's:** Best known for its Gold Guides brand, Fodor's publishes over a dozen other series, including Exploring Guides, Compass American Guides, and See It Guides. Gold Guides are updated annually. Information about researcher positions and submitting book proposals is online at www.fodors.com.

- **Footprint:** A series that covers the world but is best-known in Europe. Readers are generally low to mid-budget independent travelers. Visit www.footprintbooks.com for information about joining the existing pool of authors and updaters.

- **For Dummies:** The most successful and recognized brand in the publishing world has an ever-increasing number of guidebook titles. The Web site www.dummies.com describes the acquisition process.

- **Frommer's:** Encyclopedic in detail, especially when describing hotel rooms and restaurants, Frommer's guides offer writing that is more readable than Fodor's but maps are scarce. The original Europe on $5 a Day (it's now up to $70) is now part of a series that has expanded to cover the world, along with other imprints under the Frommer's name. The Web site www.frommers.com describes the application process for registering as an updater.

- **Globe Pequot:** Based in Connecticut, this company publishes three guidebook series: Insider's Guides, which cover the United States; Falcon, a brand that concentrates on specific outdoor recreation; and Traveler's Companion, full-color guides to destinations around the world. The Web site www.globepequot.com encourages the submission of book proposals.

- **Hunter Adventure Guides:** This series details outdoor recreational opportunities in thirty titles that cover all parts of the world. Hunter Publishing (www.hunterpublishing.com) is one of the few travel publishers that encourages proposals from first-time writers.

- **Insight Guides:** These guides provide solid background reading on destinations worldwide through first-rate writing and stunning images. Contact information can be found online at www.insightguides.com.

- **Let's Go:** A favorite with budget travelers since the 1960s, this series covers the entire world, and every title is comprehensively updated each year. Although researchers are all students of Harvard University, it is worth being familiar with this popular brand. The Web site www.letsgo.com has information about the series and publication process.

- **Lonely Planet:** The world's best-known backpacker guidebook series had humble beginnings with a single self-published book to

Asia. The company now publishes more than six hundred titles in a variety of imprints. Visit www.lonelyplanet.com for details on joining the company's pool of writers who are commissioned as updaters.

- **Michelin:** The tall Green Guides are best known for their coverage of Europe but are also published to major North American destinations. Many editions are translated from French to English, including Red Guides, which cover Europe's best accommodations and restaurants. The Web site www.viamichelin.com describes the series and related electronic products.

- **Moon Handbooks:** Renowned by independent travelers for information that goes beyond the usual tourist trail, this series is strongest in its coverage of the Americas and Asia. The publisher is Avalon Travel Publishing (www.travelmatters.com), with future acquisition plans online.

- **Rick Steves:** This series offers thirty titles, including Europe Through the Back Door, North America's best-selling guidebook to Europe. Steves and a team of researchers concentrate on the best things to see and do without spending a fortune. Contact details at www.ricksteves.com.

- **Rough Guides:** Based in England, Rough Guides are aimed at young travelers on a budget. The series contains lots of detail on getting around by public transport. Information on applying to be an updater and submitting book proposals is online at www.roughguides.com.

FINDING A PUBLISHER

There are two ways to get started as a guidebook writer—either by updating a book that already exists or writing a new title from scratch. Publishers are constantly on the lookout for freelance writers to update existing guidebooks. Often, writers of the previous edition are hired, but new contributors are always needed somewhere. The idea for a new title usually comes from in-house, with a commissioning editor searching for an author through freelancer writers that the company has worked with previously. Regardless of how a publisher goes about the search for freelancers, experienced writers with expertise in specific regions are preferred, although sometimes writers may be hired simply on the basis of a résumé that shows deep knowledge of a particular region.

Unlike the world of fiction writing, a literary agent is not necessary when searching out a publisher for a guidebook.

Getting On File

Many guidebook writers start out by updating an existing book for a publisher who has their details on file. Simply sending out form letters or e-mails to every publisher is a waste of time. On the other hand, the approach doesn't need to be outrageously memorable. Submit a cover letter that is straight to the point; outline writing experience and knowledge of specific destinations. Publishers that employ teams of updaters for their larger guidebooks often look for local talent. Keeping this in mind, unless you have strong ties to another part of the world, the city or state where you live should be at the top of your list of areas of expertise.

If communicating by e-mail, provide links to examples of previous travel writing assignments or, better still, to a personal Web site.

Address correspondence to the commissioning or acquisitions editor. If a name doesn't appear online, check the copyright page of a recent edition, or make a phone call to the publisher's switchboard.

Submitting a Book Proposal

A proposal must sell the publisher on two things: that the guidebook proposed will be a success and that you are the right person to author it. These two factors are inextricably linked and should form the main thrust of any book proposal. Extolling writing strengths and areas of travel expertise is straightforward. Convincing the publisher that your idea will translate to a bestseller requires research.

Guidebooks have been written about all corners of the globe, so chances are the region that you propose to write about is already covered by one or more series. Even if the proposed guidebook has competition, a publisher may be interested in the idea, especially if its brand is targeted to a different market or specializes in a recreational activity, such as hiking. In a proposal, don't shy away from discussing the competition. Talk about the competition's strengths and weaknesses, explaining why the proposed book will be different and better.

Tourism numbers should form an important part of every guidebook proposal. Most state or national tourism offices have these statistics. Although a high number of visitors to a region may seem to bolster the case for a guidebook, statistics can be deceiving. Details of where visitors are coming from and the type of travelers they are should be included. For example, a Caribbean island may receive millions of visitors a year, but if most are arriving from the United States, a British publisher may not be interested in producing a book about that region of the world. Acknowledge the source of the statistics. Not only is it professional, doing so provides an easy way for the publisher to do its own research.

It is important to remember that, although writing a guidebook is an expensive and time-consuming endeavor for the author, the publisher will be using even more resources to create a successful title. You may think the proposed guidebook will be a bestseller, but, if the publisher doesn't think it will be economically viable, it won't consider publishing it.

Publisher Responses

Guidebook publishers receive a constant stream of writer pitches and book proposals. Many are rejected on the spot, most often due to the applicant not researching the type of books the company publishes. In the case of pitching for update work, a résumé may remain on file with the publisher for many years, along with dozens of others in a folder marked "Florida," or whatever region is tagged as a specialty. For this reason, asking for update work "because I like writing and traveling" doesn't work.

If the guidebook market has been researched and the correct publisher approached, the book proposal should at least pique the interest of an editor. If this is the case, a commissioning editor will make contact for further discussions.

Regardless of whether you have approached the publisher to work as an updater or with a full book proposal, the most common response will be a form letter stating that the information will be kept on file. The publisher may not reply at all.

Correspondence may be held at the publishing house for many years. Therefore, if you think you may be moving in the future, use a post office box as a contact. If you do move cross-country (it's a trait of travel writers), send a follow-up note with the new address.

COMPENSATION

Contracts for writing a guidebook vary greatly between publishers, with potential returns that range from very poor to occasionally good. Payment is either as a flat fee or royalties. Although there are advantages and disadvantages to both methods of payment, publishers pay either one way or the other.

Guidebook authors have traditionally been paid royalties, but, in the last decade, more and more publishers have been changing over to paying a flat fee (also known as writer-for-hire). The switch to paying a flat fee is ongoing for some publishers. Therefore, authors contracted on the same series may be paid in different ways.

Flat Fee

Working for a flat fee means knowing that an agreed upon payment is paid regardless of how well the book sells. Fees vary greatly between publishers, with other variables including how experienced the writer is, how well the book sells (or is projected to sell), the book's page count, and, to a lesser degree, the cost of travel to the destination. The fee for authoring a regional guide for a small publisher may be as low as $2,000 while a guidebook to an entire country may pay $50,000 or more. Larger books are often written and updated by a team of writers (contributors), each under contract to complete a section of the book. The fee for updating an existing guidebook is generally around 50 percent of what the publisher is willing to pay out for a first edition.

Earning Royalties

Signing a royalty contract means that the writer's payment is linked to the number of books sold—i.e., the writer receives a share of every book sold. Earning royalties means the writer can make more money if the book is a success. But the opposite is also true. If the book doesn't sell well, both parties stand to lose money.

Royalty rates can be calculated in one of two ways. The first is as a percentage of the cover price (the price printed on the cover). The second is as a percentage of the net amount the publisher receives for each book sold. (The latter is also referred to as the "wholesale price," "price received," or "net invoice.") As publishers sell books to distributors and the like for up to 60 percent off the cover price, it is important to be clear which type of royalty the publisher is offering—a royalty rate of 10 percent of the cover price is better than 15 percent of the wholesale price.

An "escalator" is a royalty rate that increases when an agreed threshold of books has been sold. For example, a royalty rate of 10 percent may be paid on the first 10,000 copies, with 12 percent paid on any additional copies. Escalators were common in royalty contracts fifteen or more years ago, but few publishers offer the option today. If negotiating with a smaller publisher, this option is worth discussing.

Working out how much each book will earn in advance of signing a royalty contract is simple but not precise. For example, if the guidebook has a cover price of $20, the publisher may sell it to a distributor for a 50 percent discount. This means a royalty paid on the wholesale price would be calculated on $10 per book. A 12 percent royalty rate would equate to the author receiving $1.20 per book sold.

If contemplating a royalty contract, it is important to have an idea of projected sales. One way to do this is by asking the publisher how many copies will be in the initial print run. Another is by contacting other writers who have authored books in the same series.

Additional money can be earned from subsidiary rights, such as another publisher purchasing the right to print a foreign edition or a Web site owner negotiating to use the guidebook text online. Royalty contracts will include a clause that details the split of subsidiary rights; 50/50 is common.

Royalties are never paid on books the publisher uses for promotional purposes or gives away free to book reviewers.

Each publisher has a different schedule for royalty payments, with variations from monthly to annually. The actual payment is usually made up to one hundred days from the end of the reporting period. In most cases, payment schedules are nonnegotiable.

CONTRACTS

A guidebook-writing contract is a legal document that specifies the terms under which the work will be undertaken, payment, and other issues. Publishers generate most contracts from their own boilerplate (template), but many clauses are similar throughout the guidebook-writing world.

Becoming skilled at the craft of guidebook writing is important, but the most important part of the learning curve is understanding the difference between a good and bad deal before signing a contract. It is important to read and understand the entire document. Discuss specific clauses with the commissioning editor. A lawyer will clarify any further concerns.

Copyright

The copyright owner is the legal owner of the text. As a general rule, authors who are paid royalties retain the copyright to what they have written, while writing for a flat fee means that the publisher owns the copyright. (Check the front or back copyright pages of the major guidebook series to get an idea of which publishers own the copyright and those that don't.)

One of the main advantages in owning the copyright is that, when it comes time for the next edition, the copyright owner (the writer) will be the first considered to work on the update. This is written into the contract as part of a clause that includes a timeline for submitting updated manuscripts and the amount of future advances. In effect, this gives the stability of knowing that every two or three years (the usual time between editions) a new edition is due to the publisher.

If the publisher owns the copyright, the author has no control of how the text is used nor does the author gain financial reward for subsidiary rights.

Right of First Refusal

Some flat-fee contracts include a right of first refusal clause; many don't. In simple terms, it means that the publisher must offer the writer the first right to a contract for the next edition. If, at that time, the writer refuses, the publisher will go about finding someone else to do the update.

Although the right of first refusal is built into royalty contracts as the new editions clause, in reality there is nothing preventing a publisher from terminating the original contract. This may occur if the author doesn't live up to his or her part of the agreement (such as submitting the manuscript after the deadline) or the publisher decides the guidebook is no longer economically viable. Whatever the circumstances, the author will always own the copyright to the text.

Advances

An advance is a nonrefundable sum of money paid by the publisher to the author before the book has been published. It can be paid upon signing a contract, upon acceptance of the manuscript, or, most commonly, split between the two. An advance is especially important for guidebook writers, who are able to use the money as capital to pay for travel expenses. An advance may be as little as $3,000. Advances over $10,000 are rare and usually only offered to well-established authors tackling a new book that the publisher feels will be a success.

When a guidebook is published, the advance is deducted from the royalties. For example, if it is estimated the writer will earn $1 per book and an advance of $5,000 is paid by the publisher, the writer will begin to receive actual royalty payments once 5,000 copies have been sold. In this example, the advance is known to have "earned out" after 5,000 copies have been sold.

In the truest sense of the word, an advance is an advance on royalties. But if the publisher pays a flat fee to a writer-for-hire, often part of the remuneration may be paid up-front, upon signing the contract, and this is commonly called an advance.

Regardless of whether the publisher is offering a flat fee or royalties, an advance will be built in to the contract. As an advance is deducted from royalty payments (or subtracted from the total fee in the case of writer-for-hire), aside from handing over money earlier, the amount and payment schedule doesn't affect the publisher's bottom line. Therefore, advances are one part of the guidebook contract that is negotiable.

Maps and Photos

It is important to discuss mapping and photographic needs with the publisher before signing a contract.

Maps are an important part of a guidebook. Guidebook maps are generated by in-house cartography departments or contracted to outside agencies by the publisher. The author's role ranges from supplying mapping materials marked up with references from the text to simply proofing a completed map set.

Guidebook series such as Insight and Eyewitness, which stake their reputations on top-quality photography, source images from stock libraries or commission photographers on a per project basis. Publishers that include black and white photos often require their authors to supply images. This doesn't necessarily mean the author must be the photographer, but that the final submission must include images.

All-important cover images are the domain of the graphics department, with images sourced from stock libraries and photographers that specialize in that particular region. While the editor may appreciate subject matter suggestions, rarely does an author have a say in the final choice of a guidebook cover.

Noncompeting Books

A noncompeting books clause is commonly added to guidebook contracts. If royalties are paid, it is usually all encompassing, while a writer-for-hire deal may set an amount of time. The main reason it is included is to prevent the author from writing books about the same destination for more than one publisher. This clause is negotiable to an extent—the fact that the writer already authors a book about the region can be noted, and exceptions are often made for specialty guidebooks.

Free Copies

Upon publication, the publisher may provide anywhere from one to fifty copies of the finished work to the author, often with an option for the writer to purchase additional copies at a discount.

Subcontracting

In the context of guidebook writing, a subcontract is an agreement between an author who has signed a contract with a publisher and a third party. The third party is subcontracted to write or update a section of the guidebook. The publisher's contract should include a clause detailing whether or not the author is permitted to subcontract work. With royalty contracts, subcontracting is usually allowable.

Expenses

The vast majority of guidebook writers cover their own expenses. Therefore, it is important to know how much the research trip will cost before signing a contract. Some publishers build their writer-for-hire fee around a per diem (an allowance for daily expenses), a practical option for destinations that are expensive.

Receiving freebies is an age-old dilemma in the travel-writing world. Some publishers forbid their writers from negotiating discounted or complimentary services. Other publishers don't, simply by not including such a clause in their contracts.

Deadlines

An important part of any guidebook contract is the deadlines clause, which includes information regarding publication dates and payment schedules. The contract will include a date on which the manuscript must be submitted to the publisher, with penalties for not meeting the deadline that may be as severe as voiding the entire agreement and the forced return of monies paid as an advance.

Deadlines are extremely important in the guidebook publishing industry. Not only does the publisher spend time and money in anticipation of publishing books on a specific date, most travel destinations are seasonal. For example, summer is high season for European travel, making spring the ideal time of year for publishing guidebooks to that destination. Using a six-month production cycle (from when the author submits the manuscript to finished books being shipped to bookstores) to illustrate the point, the publisher would require an author to submit the manuscript in September to ensure the book is on bookstore shelves by April, just prior to the main travel season.

It's important to note that finishing the manuscript doesn't necessarily trigger payment, such as the second half of an advance. Instead, acceptance by the publisher does. This could come a month or more after the manuscript has been submitted. Requesting a time limit on the payment, such as "upon acceptance or within thirty days of submission," is not unreasonable.

Warranties and Indemnities

Often combined into one clause, a warranty requires that the author asserts that the writing is the author's own work (in other words, it does not infringe someone else's copyright), it is not libelous, and it is true. The indemnity is the publisher's legal exemption from liabilities that breach the warranty, such as a lawsuit arising from something written.

Some contracts include the author in the publisher's liability insurance. This is the fairer alternative, as the editor and publisher have the final say as what does and doesn't go into the finished book.

Returns

Bookstores return unsold books to the publisher for any number of reasons but most often when the publisher announces a new edition of the same title. Some royalty contracts stipulate that a percentage of royalties (5 percent is normal) will be held in anticipation of returns, while others deduct returns from royalties earned on the following edition. It is important to discuss with the publisher the length of time returns will be accepted.

WILL IT PAY?

Even if the compensation for a guidebook writing assignment sounds tempting, it is imperative to work out how much money will be eaten up by travel expenses and how long the writing will take.

Estimating the time it will take to write or update a guidebook is difficult but important for two reasons—to decide whether the publisher's fee is reasonable and to request a sensible deadline for submitting the manuscript. For a first guidebook, generating one page per day is average. For an update, four pages is a reasonable guide. If you are a quick writer and have a deep knowledge of the region, it is possible to generate two and eight pages, respectively. It's good to get in the habit of tracking time. After completing one chapter, use the timesheet to gauge progress as it relates to the remaining chapters and deadline. If time is tracked on the first guidebook assignment, the next time around it is easier to gauge how long it will take. This will help in scheduling and in negotiating a fee.

Even though the earnings from a royalty contract are impossible to calculate in advance, making an estimate is vital. When a figure is arrived at, or if the payment is a flat fee, it's important to decide if the contract is economically viable. To do this, figure out how much travel expenses will be, add in an hourly rate, and leave plenty of room for error (traveling usually costs more than anticipated and writing takes longer). The other method is to work backwards, as in this example:

1. The offer is a flat fee of $15,000 to update a 500-page guidebook.

2. Travel expenses are calculated at $6,000

3. At four pages per day, it will take 125 days to update the book.

4. Divide the remainder of the fee, $9,000, by 125 days to calculate a daily rate of $72.

5. Using these figures, this assignment equates to an hourly wage of $9.

While this may seem a reasonable return, it doesn't include travel time or dealing with editorial and production queries, home office costs such as the telephone and a computer, or an overrun of travel expenses, all of which should be factored into the equation.

PUTTING THE "TRAVEL" INTO TRAVEL WRITING

The travel component should be the highlight of writing a guidebook, but it will certainly not be a vacation. Researching a guidebook is a massive undertaking that requires advance planning, focus, and strict budgeting.

Travel Time

Figuring out how long it will take to complete the research for a guidebook is a problematic but important facet of any guidebook-writing project. On one hand, it is impossible to set aside too much time for research, but, on the other, every day on the road costs money.

The first component when deciding when in the year to research a guidebook is to work backwards from the deadline. As discussed earlier, the publication date of guidebooks corresponds with the peak travel time to the destination. Taking a six-month production process into consideration, planning on researching the destination in the high season of the year prior to publication works well for an update. For a new guidebook, this leaves little time for writing. Instead, the period of time prior to the high season of the year before publication often works. The timeline for a guidebook to Canada may look like this: research in the spring, set aside summer and fall for an October submission. The book would then be published the following spring.

Researching major cities is more flexible. They can be visited year-round, with only participation in outdoor activities curtailed by the season. Therefore, if the commission is for a guidebook to one of the northern states, divide research into two trips, covering metropolitan areas in winter and leaving the rest of the state for warmer months.

If writing about where you live, not only are travel costs minimal, but it is possible to set up a schedule that coalesces researching and writing.

Depending on the scope of the guidebook and personal circumstances, relocating to the destination for the period of the project may be an ideal option. Not only will you be immersed in the local culture, it is possible to get a firsthand look at all four seasons.

The Pros and Cons of Traveling Incognito

Some guidebook writers travel incognito; others don't. It comes down to a personal preference and, to a lesser degree, the commissioning publisher.

Ethical issues aside, announcing what you're doing just for the sake of it wastes precious research time, especially when a motel owner wants to show off every room or a museum manager expects you to linger over every exhibit.

There are two common exceptions to the incognito rule—tourism authorities and people on the ground with whom the writer has built up relationships over many years of traveling to the same destination.

Tourism organizations are in place to help travel media, including guidebook writers. They are a source of information in advance of the research trip, often help out with travel costs, and are great for filling in any gaps or keeping writers abreast of changes as a deadline looms.

Make contact with the relevant office as far in advance as possible. Start at the top by approaching the tourism authority that markets the entire region about which you are contracted to write. (Many international destinations have representatives in the United States.) Most tourism Web sites have links for the media (also called travel trade or corporate sites), where contact information can be found. Writers should introduce themselves, offer to send through a letter from the publisher confirming the project, and request a media kit. At this point, the tourism office may offer to help out with travel costs or would expect the writer to enquire about having travel arrangements made for them.

Staff at information centers affiliated with national or state parks are usually extremely knowledgeable. If making contact, try to do so in advance by forwarding a list of generic questions that apply to all parks to be covered by the book.

Tourism offices and independent operators often contact publishers requesting to be included in guidebooks or outlining changes from existing listings. This type of correspondence, along with any relevant mail from readers, is usually forwarded to the author when signing on to update a guidebook. Don't take any of this information verbatim. Instead, include all that you think is necessary on pre-trip planning notes.

Pre-trip Planning

Planning a research trip can be overwhelming, especially if it centers on an extended road trip or the destination is unfamiliar. But don't let it be. If researching for an update, the region has already been broken down into chapters—the perfect starting point for dividing the trip into manageable sectors. If writing a guidebook from scratch, a good starting point is to work out a chapter list of regions to be covered (this is usually done as early as the book proposal) and to divide your travel time accordingly.

Do as much research as possible before leaving home. If working on an update, finding out what has closed in advance saves time once on the road.

Getting Around

The type of transportation you decide to use is mostly dependant on the destination to be researched. This usually corresponds with how readers will be traveling (by train in India, rental car in Scotland, for example).

Clear and concise information about city public transportation is an important facet of any guidebook, and the best way to understand local systems is to use them to get around when researching.

TOOLS FOR GUIDEBOOK WRITING

Packing for a research trip is no different than getting ready for any other type of travel. Start by packing everything you think you'll need. Then put half of it back in the closet. The airlines have generous baggage limits, and you can always upgrade to a larger rental car. But that's not the point—you just never need as many things as you think you do.

A surprising number of guidebook writers travel without a laptop computer, feeling it slows them down by not allowing them to focus on the job at hand—research. The theory is this: after ten or more hours researching, capped by dinner that doubles as research, the last thing the writer wants do to is start inputting notes to a computer.

If updating an existing guidebook, it is much easier making relevant notes on an actual book page rather than in a notepad. If the publisher supplies text files laid out in the format of the book, it is simply a matter of printing out the files. Marking up text files can be confusing, so, if supplied with Word or similar files, cut the spine off the most recent edition and photocopy each page, leaving ample white space all around for notes made in the field. Make two copies of each map—one for fieldwork and one for the final submission.

Initial guidebook writing assignments may include subcontracting to update a section of existing text for an established author who has the contract with the publisher. If this is the case, the author will often request that photocopied book pages are marked up with notes. Make two copies—one for use in the field and a second to mark up for the final submission.

Of course, the longer the research trip, the more notes that will accumulate and the more important organization becomes. Making photocopies of marked-up pages and keeping them somewhere safe or posting them home at regular intervals is a sensible safety net.

COLLECTING INFORMATION

The key components of a guidebook—things to see and do, where to stay and eat, and transportation—vary greatly between series. It is therefore vital to become familiar with other books in the same series before beginning a research trip. Obviously it's impossible to stay in every accommodation and dine at every restaurant, but you must do your best to visit as many options as possible—even if you simply ask to see a room or order a coffee. If readers want to stay in a Holiday Inn or eat at McDonald's, they can usually find these chains themselves. Instead, concentrate on researching options that are unique to the destination. Gather more than just the facts, making notes about the ambiance and the views. If an accommodation has no outstanding features but needs to be included (if, for example, it's the only choice in town), get creative and note its location in relationship to nearby attractions. Researching can become tedious, especially if you're collecting information on banks, Internet cafes, and the like. But it is all important and done most easily while on the road, especially if every text reference needs to be tagged onto a map.

Even if the writer is not a professional photographer, using a digital camera to record information found on interpretive boards, restaurant menus, and the like saves time jotting down notes.

While traveling, the evening is a good time to get organized for the following day. If updating a guidebook, read through the existing text, highlighting sections that will need to be visited. If working on updating a larger city or park, divide the destination into manageable sections that can be comfortably covered in a day.

INFORMATION CENTERS

Reading local literature is a good way to find out the basics—such as a list of local attractions—but to get a feeling for the atmosphere it is important that every establishment is visited, regardless of whether it is being written about for the first time or it is included in existing text. Even a quick walk through a museum or a coffee at a café will provide a feeling for the place. Using the phone and

Internet is useful for changeable information such as hours of operation and prices.

Tourist information centers are an excellent place to begin on-the-ground research. They operate under a number of different models, and it's useful to understand which is which. Some, for example, are operated by a local organization that promotes only member businesses (and they'll never suggest "a great new restaurant" that isn't a member). Others are run by the town or municipality, and, although the information supplied is unbiased, there is no guarantee that the staff are as knowledgeable as they should be. Often, some of the best information is tucked away under the counter, so go beyond the brochure racks to ask about heritage walks, hiking trails, bird lists, and the like.

Information center staff are generally not permitted to suggest one restaurant over another but often do. (I once had an older lady explain she wasn't allowed to recommend any restaurants, but then she smugly whispered across the counter "but I can tell you where *I* always eat out.")

Many smaller information centers close in the off-season. At this time of year, head to the local town hall building for tourist literature.

MAKING A LIVING AS A GUIDEBOOK WRITER

Making a living from writing guidebooks is possible, but it usually requires an income flow from other sources. Typically, full-time writers would use their guidebook travels to research articles for newspapers and magazines and to build a collection of photographs to sell as stock images. Guidebook writing may also be a sideline to other forms of writing or working as a newspaper travel editor.

Each guidebook writer has his or her own reasons for choosing the profession, and, therefore, each sees profit in a different light. For some writers, often those starting out with no big overheads, simply seeing something they've written in print is good enough. Down the road, when there are children to support and a mortgage to pay, the threshold for what is a good deal will have changed dramatically.

In the first instance, taking on a small updating assignment that can be combined with time spent earning a regular income is a sensible way to get a feel for the industry. Some jobs are ideal for combining with guidebook writing in the longer term. For example, a teacher could sign a royalty contract in which every second summer was spent researching and writing about the destination.

Working with a recognized publisher provides the best chance of making money as a guidebook writer, but there are many regional and specialist travel publishers that provide a foot in the door to a career as a guidebook writer.

Royalty Contracts

Signing onto a royalty contract gives the stability of knowing that every two or three years the book will need to be updated, and in return you'll receive another chunk of money as an advance. In most cases, it's difficult to justify the royalty returns on a first edition, but, for the second and successive editions, the time and costs involved in updating will be minimal in comparison to the first time around.

Specialization and Branding

Having written a guidebook, the author is assumed to be an expert by other publishers and the general public. So, while traveling the world writing more books may seem like the ideal lifestyle, building a reputation around a specific destination is an excellent way to convert expertise to monetary returns. Using a guidebook as a "business card" opens doors throughout the industry. Submitting travel articles to magazines and newspapers is the most obvious option, but writers can also sell their skills as copywriters for travel companies and, as discussed previously, can build up a specialized collection of stock photography images. Another income source for authors who have achieved name recognition is to lead tours to the region of their expertise.

While travel writers like Bill Bryson and Paul Theroux sell books through name recognition, the guidebook industry is different—it is the publisher's brand that sells books, not the author's name, and guidebooks are marketed as such. (Some publishers display author names on the front cover and devote a full page to author biographies, while others include nothing more than a list of contributors.) Because publishers concentrate on promoting their brand, it is important for authors to create their own name recognition both within the guidebook writing industry and with readers. This is especially important for authors on royalty contracts, who can use name recognition as a marketing tool for selling more books.

A good foundation for guidebook author name recognition is to construct a Web site. The focus of the Web site should be well defined. If its aim is to market writing skills to editors, build the site around a personalized domain and writing examples. If the intention is to promote the writer's name as an expert to a particular destination, create a Web site that concentrates on that particular place. For an author who has signed a royalty contract, a destination-specific Web site also can be used as a marketing tool for selling more books.

Not all writers are comfortable doing slide shows or bookstore signings, but, if you are earning royalties, this type of event can help get your name out while also selling a few extra books.

THE BEGINNING OF A CAREER

Deciding on your specialty, finding a publisher, negotiating a contract, and, finally, receiving an advance can take a long time—up to six months just for the negotiations in some cases. Once confident things are moving forward, begin collecting information, planning a schedule, and laying out initial ideas for the guidebook. When the countersigned contract arrives, the first phase is over and a much longer but exciting one is about to begin.

End-of-Chapter Questions

1. Does guidebook writing require a longer commitment than most other travel writing?
2. Where do the "updaters" live who keep the Berlitz Guides current?
3. What are some of the defining features of books in the Eyewitness Guides series?
4. What is the most successful and recognized brand in the publishing world?
5. What guidebook series concentrates on specific outdoor recreation?

Guidebook Writing

6. What is the world's best-known backpacker guidebook series?

7. There are two ways to get started as a guidebook writer. One way is to write a new title from scratch. What is the other way?

8. In requesting an assignment, your cover letter should cover two things. One is your knowledge of specific destinations. What is the other?

9. In a guidebook proposal, should you avoid any mention of the competition?

10. Who is the legal owner of the text of a guidebook?

WRITING ASSIGNMENT SIXTEEN
PHOTOS AND THE FIRST DRAFT OF YOUR CONTRACT ARTICLE

Assignment Introduction

You are close to becoming a published travel writer. Congratulations. As you know, you will need to provide photographs to go with your articles. You will need 8 x 11 inch black and white photos to go with each copy of the spec article that you send out. The travel article buyer of your contract article will tell you how many photos and what type of photos are needed for that article. You also will be told how the publication wants you to submit the photographs that go with your contract article.

You also need to prepare the first draft of your contract article. By this time, you should have received the letter of agreement from the magazine that is purchasing your contract article. Details regarding article content will be specified in the letter of agreement.

Assignment Activity

After selecting the photographs to go with your spec article, take the negatives to a photo processing firm. In some cities, these are listed in the phone book as wholesale photo finishing companies. These firms tend to do a better quality job, and, for large numbers of photographs, they charge less money per photo. If you are unable to locate a photo processing firm or a wholesale photo finishing company, a quality retail photo finishing company can prepare them for you.

Find out from the editor what photographs are needed for your contract article, and get the number of photographs needed to supply their requirement. Normally, editors want just one of each of the photographs that will go with your article, but they may want slides or they may prefer something other than standard prints.

Either purchase or prepare photo mailers. If you purchase them, try a paper supply house. It will probably sell the mailers at a lower cost than you will be able to get them anywhere else. If you prepare them, purchase 9 x 11½ inch padded mailing envelopes at the paper supply store, and also get twice the number of pieces of cardboard as the number of envelopes that you will mail. The cardboard should be cut to 8¾ x 11¼ inches. Insert the photographs for each envelope between pieces of cardboard and tape the four sides so they will not fall out. Put the photos surrounded by cardboard into each envelope. Do not seal the envelopes because you will want to add your article and a cover letter before putting the envelopes in the mail.

In drafting your contract article, follow the same guidelines you used in preparing the first draft of your spec article. However, you should pay special attention to the requirements specified in your letter of agreement and to the magazine's writer's guidelines. Also review your recent copy of the magazine itself to make sure you are writing for that magazine's readers.

Final Step: Label the cardboard mailers "Photo(s) for (name of article)" for one print of each photograph that will go with your spec article, and do the same for one print of each photograph that will go with your contract article. For the instructor-submitted photos only, also indicate either "Spec article photo" or "Contract article photo" on the cardboard mailer labels. Attach these and a draft of your contract article to the Instructor Comment Sheet for Written Assignment Sixteen in appendix 5. Print your name on the Instructor Comment Sheet and turn in the entire package to your professor.

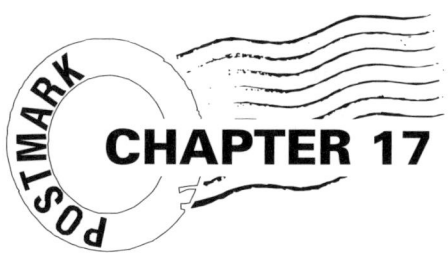

CHAPTER 17

How-To Travel Books

James Poynter

TWO TYPES—SIMILAR APPROACH

How-to books in the travel writing genre are of two types. The best known are the consumer how-to travel writing books. These are books sold in retail bookstores and are designed for customers who come in and ask, "Do you have a book on how to . . ." Some examples of this type of how-to books are *How to Travel With Children, How to Pack a Suitcase, How to Plan a Two-Week Motor Home Trip*, and so forth. The second type of how-to book is for the current or would-be industry person. *How to Start Your Home-Based Travel Agency* is one of the most popular. But there are books on how to put together tours, how to get a job in inflight services, and there are even books on how to make your hotel or motel ecotourism friendly. These books sell to people who want to get into the travel industry and to people who want to move up in their current travel industry jobs. Both consumer-oriented and industry-related how-to books are growing in both the numbers that are published every year and the scope of coverage. Many major publishers and an increasing number of smaller publishers are contracting with authors to write how-to travel books.

HOW MUCH DOES IT PAY?

The pay for the authors of how-to travel books can range from very little to quite substantial. David Howell, the author of *Passport*, was reputed to have earned more than $90,000 in royalties the first year the book came out. *Passport* was adopted as a textbook by many colleges and universities, but it also sold well in retail bookstores. Most authors make far less than Howell made, however. It is common for publishers to pay a first-time book author as little as 5 percent of the net price of the book. Net is usually between 45 percent and 50 percent of the retail price of the book. This means that if a book sells in a bookstore for $20, the author is likely to receive a royalty of about fifty cents per book sale. Of course, the actual royalty amount, the actual price of the book, and the bookstore discount from the published price are all variables, but the fifty cents per book royalty is a good guestimate from which to work.

This, of course, means that the author's actual income can vary considerably depending upon how well a book sells. The vast majority of books are here today and gone tomorrow. In many cases, a book is sold as a "remainder" after eight or nine months from its publication, and many books are never listed in a publisher's annual catalog more than once. How-to books, however, seem to sell much longer than the average book. Those that are geared toward people in the industry or who want to get into the industry tend to have a longer life cycle than those that are sold primarily to the retail consumer. *Passport* is still being sold well after ten years from when it first came on the market. One of the books on how to get a job in inflight services has been on the market for more than five years. Excellent and popular retail-oriented how-to books can also have a long life cycle. For many years Leila Hadley's book *Travel With Children* was almost the only book in the field, and it continued selling year after year for many years. The especially nice thing about authoring many popular how-to books is that you will continue getting royalty checks in your mail many years after you did all the work of writing the book. There are few feelings as good as pulling checks out of the mailbox year after year, but, if you write a popular how-to travel book, the chances are good that you will learn to love your mailbox.

START WITH THE IDEA—AND THE BUYER

The travel book idea or concept is perhaps the most important part of getting an editor to agree to publish your book. One of the best ways of getting a good book concept idea is to visit a well-stocked bookstore. Bring a pad of paper and a pen or pencil. Look at the titles of the how-to books that are there, but, far more important, look for the titles that are not there. For example, if you see a title, *How to Select a Cheap Cruise*, think of terms in the travel industry to substitute for the word "Cruise," and see if a book with that title (or a similar one) is there— for example, *How to Select a Cheap Resort*, *How to Select a Cheap Rental Car*, and so forth. What you are doing is looking for a book concept idea that will fill a need and for which there are either no books written or few books written. Another example might help. Although Leila Hadley had the first major book on travel with children, ask yourself how many books you see on the bookstore shelf on "travel with . . ." and fill in the blank for the last word. There are a few books showing up now on "Grand Travel" (grandparents traveling with their grandchildren), and this is one of the most rapidly growing segments of the travel industry today. But what about books like *How to Travel with Your Pet*, *How to Travel with Your Nephew or Niece*, or even *How to Travel with Your Rich Old Aunt*? After a couple of hours at a bookstore jotting down ideas, even fantastic ideas, you will come back with many book idea concepts.

Of course, you will need to narrow down your ideas. One of the best ways to do that is to work with a book buyer who is associated with a large bookstore. The buyer you want will be the person who buys travel books. Retail bookstore buyers are busy and rarely will take the time to gratuitously provide an evaluation of new book concept ideas for authors. Ask, however, and you may be surprised at the results. For many years I was able to bounce book ideas off of Gordon Pierce, the travel book buyer at that time for the Tattered Cover Bookstore, which is the largest freestanding bookstore in the United States. Unfortunately, he has now retired. Gordon never charged me for his evaluations, and although many times he told me the book title ideas I approached him with would not sell, from time to time, he responded to a title idea by saying something like, "Yes, we have customers wanting that title all the time, and there are no books filling that need." You cannot get that kind of response from a retail bookstore buyer unless you come up with a large number of ideas for them to consider.

Once you have a positive response from the travel book buyer at a retail bookstore, reconfirm your book title concept with other bookstore buyers in other parts of the country. If you are fortunate enough to find that each of the retail bookstore travel book buyers gives you a positive response, ask the book buyers to put it in writing. Editors are impressed when they receive multiple letters from retail travel book buyers who say that the book concept is a good one and a number of their customers would buy the book if it is well written.

MULTIPLE BUYERS

While retail bookstores are the number one sellers of books and letters from travel book buyers at bookstores will impress editors, there are also other target buyers for travel how-to books. For example, the book *Home-Based Travel Agent*, 4th edition, by Kelly Monaghan is sold to and through the major association for home-based travel agents, the Outside Sales Support Network. If you plan to write a book for people who are currently working in the industry or who want to get into the industry, bounce the book concept idea off appropriate industry association executives. If they give you a letter which essentially says that, if the book is published according to the specifications that you have provided, they will order it in quantity (normally at a 50 percent discount from the retail price) and resell to their members. This type of letter will impress the editor as well.

THE COLLEGE AND UNIVERSITY MARKET

David Howell was associated with Niagara University at the time that he authored *Passport*. At that time Niagara University had the largest enrollment in a travel program of any college or university in North America. Of course, they adopted *Passport* as a textbook as soon as it came out, and many other colleges and universities did as well. If the how-to book that you want to write can be used as a textbook, contact the International Society For Travel and Tourism Educators (586-294-0208 or joannb@istte.org) and purchase a membership list. Write to either a sampling of the members or to all of them, and tell them about your book idea. Ask them to e-mail you and let you know whether or not they would consider adopting the book if it is written according to the specifications that you outline.

WILL IT SELL?

After you have done your preparatory work, it is time to approach editors. Keep in mind that the single most important consideration for an editor regarding a travel how-to book is the question: "Will it sell?" The more that you can do to convince an editor that the book concept you are proposing will sell, the better. If you are making phone calls to editors, tell them that you have X number of letters from retail bookstore travel book buyers, Y number of letters from associations within the industry, and Z number of letters from educators who are textbook adopters at colleges and universities. If you are approaching editors with a query letter, your letter to them can say the same thing, but it will be even better if you enclose copies of the letters from bookstore travel book buyers, association executives, and educators.

ANOTHER APPROACH

While book editors are busy people and rarely take the time to "chat" with potential book authors, if you have some good book ideas, you will be surprised at how many of them will talk with you. However, it can be frustrating if you provide them with two or three good book concept ideas backed up with letters from book buyers, and they are not interested in any of your book concept ideas. If that happens to you, one of the best approaches is to say to them, "If you don't like any of my book concept ideas, tell me what kind of how-to travel book you really want and are unable to find an author to write?" It may seem flip to ask such a question, but I have been surprised at how many editors do have one or more books in mind that they would like to publish, but cannot find someone to write. This is how I got my first how-to travel book writing assignment. I telephoned the owner/editor of a small, specialized how-to travel book publishing company. A number of book ideas were thrown out, and he said "No" to all of them. Finally, I asked, "What book do you want written but can't find an author?" He responded immediately, "foreign independent tours." I did not think it would sell. Nevertheless, I wrote the book. Indeed, it took many years to sell all of the small number of books that were printed. But it is amazing how many additional books editors will contract with you to write once you have successfully completed your first book.

WHICH EDITORS?

But how do you know which editors to approach? While you are at your local bookstore getting ideas for the how-to travel book you want to write, jot down the names of the publishers of each of the books in the how-to travel book section. When you run across the same publisher a second time, put a checkmark next to the name on your list. Each time you run across a publisher's name on a different book, put a checkmark down. When you leave the bookstore, you will know which publishers you will want to approach.

If you want a listing of industry-oriented how-to travel book publishers, you will find some of their books in your local bookstore as well. For example, the companies that publish books on how to get a job in inflight services or how to be a home-based travel agent will be in the retail bookstore, and you will be able to pick up those names as well. However, your local retail bookstore will probably not carry titles such as *Corporate Travel Management* or *Incentive Travel*. You can find the publishers of specialized industry-oriented how-to travel books in two ways. One of these ways is to approach the associations in the field. The major book in most libraries on associations is *Gales Encyclopedia of Associations*. Go to your library, and look up the associations by key word based on the how-to travel book you plan to write. Then contact the associations, and ask the executive director in your letter or e-mail if he or she will send you a listing of the publishers that publish books for people in that segment of the industry. For example, if you wanted to write something on corporate travel management, you would find two major associations: the National Business Travel Association and the Association of Corporate Travel Executives. Send an e-mail to the executive directors, and they will be able to give you the names of the publishers that publish in that specialized area. The same approach will

How-To Travel Books

work for books oriented toward airlines, travel agencies, cruise lines, tour companies, car rental companies, and other segments of the industry.

A second approach is the International Society for Travel and Tourism Educators. For many years, the association published a booklet for its members titled *Travel and Tourism Books In Print*. That publication has been out of print for several years, and the publishers listed in the last edition will not be exactly the same as those that are actively publishing in the field today. However, most publishers of industry-related how-to travel books will attempt to market them to educators as either reference books or textbooks and, therefore, will either be full members or affiliate members of the association. The executive director can provide you with a current listing of publisher members.

TIMING IS IMPORTANT

Many years ago I thought of an idea for a how-to book on how to select a cruise ship. Every travel book buyer I approached told me that it would not sell. Some were nice and said that it was an interesting idea, but not a saleable book. I did not even approach an editor with the book concept idea. Today, books on how to select cruise ships are some of the best how-to books selling in bookstores. If you have a how-to travel book idea that you really believe in, but you find that the travel book buyers do not feel it will sell, do not shelve the idea permanently. Instead, go back every few years, and see if the market has caught up with your idea. Timing is important.

AFTER THE EDITOR SAYS "YES" OR "MAYBE"

After you have convinced an editor that your how-to travel book idea should be considered, there are several steps that all editors will follow. Unless the editor is also the owner of the publishing company, the probability is that the editor will not have the final say on whether or not to contract with an author for a new book. Consider the editor as a screener who says "no" most of the time but sometimes will say "maybe" or a qualified "yes" to your how-to travel book idea. With most publishers, the editor must have the approval of a contracting committee (other terms are used as well) before a contract will be signed. In addition to getting the contracting committee's approval, editors will be expected to get readers from outside the publishing company to review your materials and to make recommendations on whether or not the publisher should contract for the book.

It is a multistep process. The first step is a formal meeting with the contracting committee, during which the editor will present your book idea and committee members will consider it. In almost all cases, you, the potential author, will not be invited to attend the contracting committee meeting. Therefore, it behooves you to provide the editor with as much ammunition as possible to convince the contracting committee that they should consider your book idea. The editor will not even ask for a meeting of the contracting committee unless the editor believes that your book idea will be a good fit for the publishing company. That is in your favor. However, the editor will still have to sell the committee. At the very least, the contracting committee will expect the editor to provide them with: 1) a working title for the proposed book, and frequently they will want one or two additional alternative titles; 2) a complete outline of the proposed book; 3) at least one completed chapter, and many will require a minimum of two completed chapters; and 4) a marketing and sales analysis.

The Title of Your How-to Travel Book

For many how-to travel books, the title jumps out. For example, if you were writing a book on travel with children, you have limited options. You might try *Traveling With Children*, *Travel With Children*, or *How to Travel With Children*. But after these three titles, there is nothing left that clearly identifies what it is you are writing about. A large number of how-to travel books provide authors with a similar limited range of appropriate titles. But, after coming up with the logical titles, give some thought to innovative interesting titles that might peak the interest of the potential buyer. In hindsight, David Howell's *Passport* did extremely well. However, there certainly must have been people who wondered what the book was about when they heard the title. Certainly not everybody would jump to the conclusion that the book was an introduction to the travel industry. Usually, therefore, the titles that jump out are best. They clearly tell the potential buyer what the book is about.

A Complete Outline

The committee will expect to receive a complete outline of the book.

This will tell them that you have given considerable thought to your book concept. It will also tell them exactly what will be included as well as what will not be included. While the editor can and frequently will make changes to your outline if and when the publisher contracts for the book, at this stage the committee will want to know exactly what you plan to cover in the book.

Completed Chapters
Several years ago committees were requesting one completed chapter. Today almost all committees are asking for two completed chapters, and, once in a while, they will request three completed chapters. Part of the reason for wanting completed chapters is to see how well you write. Almost all committees have English language experts on them, and these people will look for what they consider to be well-written chapters. They want to see writing that will spark the interest of the reader in the first sentence and keep that interest throughout the entire chapter. They want a good and logical introduction, body, and conclusion. In other words, they are looking for "good writing."

In selecting the chapters that you will complete, it is recommended that you never select the first chapter of your proposed book or the last chapter. Because of their positions in the book, they are the two chapters that are most likely to be critiqued negatively. Instead, study your outline. Identify the chapters that you think will be of greatest interest to readers. After you have finished a draft of the two chapters you have selected, find a minimum of three readers who know nothing about your subject. Ask them to tear it apart. In reviewing the change recommendations received from these readers, pay special attention to any suggestions where two or all three of the readers make the same change suggestion. Some how-to travel book authors contract with professional readers and pay them for reviewing their manuscripts. You can find a listing of professional readers in the classified section of the PMA (Publishers Marketing Association) newsletter. Some libraries subscribe to this publication, but, if you are unable to find it in your library, you can call the association and request a recent sample issue. The phone number is 310-372-2732.

Your Marketing and Sales Analysis

The most powerful person on most contracting committees is the representative from the marketing and sales department. This person will want to determine the answer to the question: "Will it sell?" Sometimes every other person on the committee can say "yes" to a new book proposal, but, if the marketing and sales committee representative says "no," the contracting committee will give the editor a "no." Publishing companies make money by selling books. Unless it is a subsidized vanity or university press, knowing that the publishing company will make a profit on publishing and marketing the book is the single most important consideration in contracting for a book.

What the contracting committee will want is an analysis of your proposed book as compared to all other books like yours. For example, if you are going to write a book on traveling with children, the contracting committee will expect that you will have reviewed every book that is currently in circulation about traveling with children. They will expect you to explain clearly why the contracting committee can conclude that your book will sell better than the books offered by competitors. If your book is the first in the field, the contracting committee will want to know why you believe there is a market for the book. In both cases, the best ammunition for the marketing and sales analysis consists of letters from bookstore buyers, associations, educators, and others who commit to the book in advance and in writing.

Paid Reader Evaluators

After the contracting committee gives the editor their tentative approval, the editor will be required to line up a minimum of three qualified paid reader/evaluators for the proposed book. Since the editor will have to go back to the contracting committee for final approval, the editor will make every effort to find paid reader/evaluators whose qualifications will probably meet with the approval of the contracting committee. The vast majority of reader evaluators with whom editors contract are retail bookstore travel book buyers. However, depending on the book, they may contract with reader evaluators who are association executives or travel educators who determine which books will be selected for textbooks. Occasionally it will be someone else within the industry.

The publisher will pay the reader evaluators. The normal compensation will range between $100 and $250. Readers will be provided with a listing of questions to answer. These questions will be similar to the questions considered by the contracting committee. However, the most important question or set of questions will relate to whether or not the reader evaluator believes that the book being considered will sell in sufficient quantity to make a profit for the publisher. They rarely will be asked the question in that way. However, there are usually two or three questions designed to get to an answer to that question.

There will also be an open-ended part of the evaluation form. It will ask for recommendations for changes from what is proposed by the potential author. All readers will be given the list of potential titles, the completed outline, and the completed chapter or chapters.

Some bookstore travel buyers make a good add-on income by being reader evaluators. If they have done it often, they learn what editors want. One of the things editors will expect is a listing of change recommendations. Therefore, you can expect that, if the editor ultimately contracts with you to write the book, the editor will require you to make changes. Most of the time these changes are the ones that are recommended by the reader evaluators. Most editors will be adamant about your making the changes that are recommended by two or all three of the reader evaluators. Expect it.

After the reader evaluations have been received, the editor will make a decision as to whether or not to go back to the contracting committee. If the reader evaluators are generally favorable, the chances are probable that the editor will go back to the committee and present the written evaluations from the reader evaluators. If the contracting committee recommends going forward with the project, the next step will be for the editor to prepare a contract and to present that to you, the author.

CONTRACTING

In most cases contracting for how-to travel books is identical to the contracting process for other books. The editor will prepare a contract and send it to the author. The author can make change requests, but rarely will an editor consider any major change requests from first-time authors. The most important considerations for most authors are three:

1) the amount of the advance; 2) the percentage to be paid as royalty; and 3) the completed manuscript deadline.

Advance

Most publishers will offer to pay authors an "advance" on to-be-earned royalties. As noted earlier, when a book sells, a percentage of the net price of the book is normally paid as a royalty to the author. The advance is a way of giving the author some money prior to the time when a royalty would normally be earned. Usually the editor projects book sales, and most editors agree to pay authors an advance amount of money based on a percentage of projected sales. For example, if the royalty is 5 percent of the net price of the book and the editor projects that first year sales will be $100,000, the net amount accruing to the publisher will be from about $49,000 to up to $50,000 (net is normally between 45 percent and 50 percent of gross). This means that based on the $100,000 projected gross sales figure, the author's 5 percent of net would be $2,500 (5 percent of $50,000). Most editors will determine the amount of the advance that they are willing to offer by calculating 50 percent of projected first year royalties. This means that the advance that would be paid to the author based on these calculations would be $1,250.

It used to be that the term "advance" meant in advance of writing the book, and, whatever the advance figure was, it was paid to the author at the signing of the contract. In recent years, however, it has become more common to divide the advance payment into three parts. One-third is paid at the time of signing the contract. A second one-third is paid at the time the final manuscript is accepted by the editor. And the final one-third is paid when the first order of books is shipped to a retail bookstore.

Authors should expect to receive an advance, but rarely will a first-time author be able to negotiate the amount of the advance or the dates on which the money will be received. Nevertheless, the advance serves the purpose of transferring risk. The author has some protection in case the publishing company is unable to sell any copies of the book. In this case, the author would receive $1,250 even if only one bookstore order was shipped.

Royalties

As noted earlier, royalties are paid to book authors, and they are normally a percentage of the net price of the book. Typically in the first few months after the release of a book, the earned royalties will be considerable. However, because an advance has been paid, no additional checks will be issued to the author until the amount of the royalties earned surpasses the amount of the advance. Although the author may not receive any money in the first few months or even the first year after a book has been released because the royalties earned will not have equaled the advance, the publisher will still send the author a report showing the number of sales and the amount of royalties earned. The report will show the difference between the amount of advance money paid and the royalties earned. Therefore, the author can rapidly determine how soon a first royalty check (after the advance) can be expected.

If the book continues to sell over a period of years, sooner or later the author is likely to receive a negative royalty report. This means that during the reporting period bookstores have returned more books than they have ordered. Therefore, there is a negative figure. Authors are not expected to return royalty amounts that have been paid, but they will not receive an additional royalty check until the earnings outweigh the returns.

Deadlines

For most authors, the third major concern in a book contract is the deadline. This is the date by which the author agrees that the finished manuscript will be delivered to the editor. Normally this is twelve months from the date of the contract. Authors should take the deadline seriously. Publishing companies have a workforce dedicated to book manufacturing. These are the people who turn a finished manuscript into the final printed books. They work on a tight schedule, and the editor must request book manufacturing slot time. Normally, the scheduled date for initiating book manufacturing is just a few days after the manuscript completion deadline. If the author does not meet the deadline, it will mean that the book manufacturing schedule will be missed. This will be expensive for the publisher, and it will delay the printing and release of the book.

Authors who miss manuscript completion deadlines are normally never contracted with again. It is one of the major problems editors and publishers have with authors. However, when an author meets the publishing deadline or gets the finished manuscript to the editor ahead of time, there is a strong probability that the publishing company will seriously consider working with the author on additional books in the future. When you receive your contract, if there is any doubt that you will not meet the deadline, ask for an extension. Once a date has been entered into the contract and the contract has been signed, that date will be taken seriously by the editor, and the author is expected to meet it. Nevertheless, many editors will be willing to give an author fourteen to eighteen months to complete their manuscript, as long as that deadline is written into the contract.

MARKETING ASSISTANCE

Many first-time book authors believe that, once they have completed the final manuscript, their work is over. However, contracts will require them to make any changes that the editor requests after going through the final manuscript and to be one of the proofreaders just prior to printing. There is no additional compensation for this work. In addition, with many how-to books, authors are expected either to prepare a professional-quality index for the book or to pay a professional indexer. This is also normally spelled out in the contract. Most editors will offer to prepare the index for you, but they will charge the cost of index preparation to your royalties. Study the contract, and be aware if this is required of you. You can get professional indexing completed for you at a much lower cost than what the publisher usually charges by contracting with indexing specialists. The PMA classifieds normally list several good, low-cost indexers. The organization's phone number is 310-372-2732.

As the author, you will rarely be required by your contract to assist in marketing your book. However, because your income from royalties will depend on sales, your help with marketing can make a difference in the publisher's sales of your book and your royalty income from the book. If you are available to do so, let the editor and the publishing company's publicist know that you are willing to make guest presentations on local radio and television stations about the book, do book signings at bookstores, and greet bookstore and/or librarian buyers at trade shows. Often the publisher will pay your expenses, and the push your book receives from you can make a large difference in overall sales.

IF IT FITS

How-to travel books are not for all travel writers. However, some authors love to write this type of travel book. Try it, and see how you like it. One of the nice things about travel writing is that you don't have to get locked in. If you try how-to travel books and don't like it, there are many other areas of specialization for you to undertake.

End-of-Chapter Questions

1. How-to books in the travel writing genre are of two types. One type is for the current or would-be industry person. What is the other type?

2. Do how-to travel books seem to sell longer than the average book?

3. What is perhaps the most important part of getting an editor to agree to publish your how-to travel book?

4. Why might you want to bounce new book ideas off of retail bookstore travel book buyers?

5. Can a how-to travel book sell in the college and university book market?

6. How do you know which editors to approach?

7. What four things will the editor need to get from you in order to present your book idea to the publisher's contracting committee?

8. How many paid reader/evaluators will normally be contracted to review your book proposal for a publisher?

9. Are royalties normally a percentage of the published price of the book?

10. Will authors normally be expected to proofread final "typeset" manuscripts prior to the book being printed?

WRITING ASSIGNMENT SEVENTEEN
PACKAGING AND SUBMITTING YOUR SPEC ARTICLE

Assignment Introduction

Finally, you are getting your spec article in the mail. If you are submitting to newspapers, you should have identified the noncompeting papers to which you wish to send your article. If you are submitting to magazines, you should have selected the publications to which you will be submitting with the same care you took in selecting magazines for your contract article.

There will be several pieces to your mailing. These are: 1) a cover letter, 2) the article, and 3) two photographs. Each envelope you mail out should contain each of these pieces.

Assignment Activity

You have already purchased and inserted your photographs into envelopes. Get a bold stamp for the front of the envelope, and stamp each one with the words: PHOTOGRAPHS—DO NOT BEND.

It will be more professional if you purchase printed mailing labels. In the return address block, these will have your name followed by the words "Travel Writer" followed by your address. You can get these at a quick print shop, your local office supply store, or a company that specializes in labels. The Drawing Board (1-800-253-1838) is a good source. You might also buy blank mailing labels from your office supply store. You can have a stamp made up with your name, title (Travel Writer), and return address. Using this rubber stamp, stamp the return address section of each label.

Prepare a computer-generated peel-off label with the name and address of each person to whom you are sending your article (and other items). Avery white 1 x 2⅝ inch labels can be found in almost all office supply stores. Try using Avery size 5160. Instructions for preparing labels on your computer are on the inside of each box.

Once you have the PHOTOGRAPHS—DO NOT BEND message stamped on each envelope, an address label has been placed on each envelope, and you have inserted two photographs into each envelope, you are ready to add the final two pieces for the mailing. These are your article itself and the cover letter.

Make sure your name and contact information for you appear in the top right corner of your article before you photocopy the article.

Your cover letter should show the date followed by your name, your title (Travel Writer), and your address. Then it should show the name, title, name of publication, and address of the person to whom you are sending your article and related materials. The body of the letter should be brief saying something like:

> *Enclosed is a travel article that should appeal to your readers. If you run it, please send a tear sheet and a check to: your name, Travel Writer, and your address.*

Your letter should be brief. Many editors do not even look at the letters until they are ready to send a check to the author. You want their entire attention to be directed to your article. Therefore, do not distract by having a long letter.

After you have stuffed all envelopes with cover letters, a copy of your article, and the photographs, seal the envelopes and take them to the post office. It is better to get them weighed and get real stamps to put on each envelope.

Final Step: Prepare one envelope exactly as the ones you are sending to newspaper or magazine editors, and bundle it with or attach it to the Instructor Comment Sheet for Writing Assignment Seventeen (in appendix 5) when you turn in this assignment to your professor. Also include in that envelope a listing of the newspaper or magazine editors to whom your article has been submitted, and please make sure you have printed your name on the Instructor Comment Sheet.

SECTION VI

MAKING TRAVEL WRITING PROFITABLE FOR YOU

While some travel writers author just a few articles a year and look at travel writing as a nice add-on job that will bring in some additional money and travel benefits, others are in it for the money. For those who want to make travel writing pay off well, there are several approaches they can take which will help.

In chapter 18, the business of travel writing is presented. In general, the more that the author treats travel writing as a business, the better the chances are of reaching profitability and making good money. The sections on contracts, selling rights, accounting, financial recordkeeping, and mileage all have a direct bearing on profitability.

But the last chapter is totally oriented toward building profits. In this chapter, pay special attention to the strategies for becoming a top-paid travel writer and the section on well-paid travel writers. If you choose, you can determine to be among those who make the greatest amount of money as travel writers. Outline an individual development plan for yourself, and you may be surprised at how soon you will reach the top.

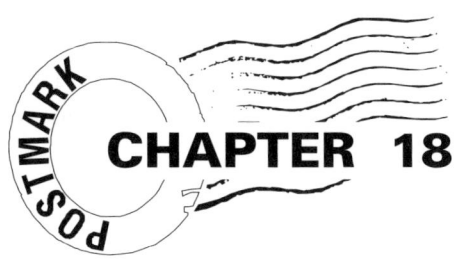

CHAPTER 18

The Business of Travel Writing

James Poynter

FINALLY A TRAVEL WRITER

You are first a marketer, then a business manager, and finally a travel writer. As Richard Cropp says, "Writing good prose may be your most important skill, but to be a success in this industry, it may end up being one of your least used."[1] That may be a little strong, but there is no question that, if you want to make good money in travel writing, it will be important to manage your business.

---

1. Richard Cropp, Barbara Braidwood, and Susan Boyce, *Writing Travel Books and Articles*, (Bellingham, WA: Self-Counsel Press, 1997), 3.

YOUR BUSINESS

The vast majority of travel writers are independent contractors and are paid for each article purchased, for each chapter authored, or for each book that is written. This means that you have a business of your own. Taxes will not be deducted from the checks you receive in payment for your writing. You will have to pay your own taxes. You will need to file additional income tax reports each year, and you will need to keep additional accounting records. You will probably want to set up an office, at least a corner of a room in your home that you consider an office, and you are likely to get more writing assignments if you come across to your clients as an established travel writing business. This means that you will have a telephone with an answering machine that provides a business-like recording when you are not there; that you provide magazine, newspaper, and book publishers with either an EIN (business identification number) or an independent contractor's SSN (social security number) on your bills; and that your invoices, letterhead, and envelopes are professionally printed with the name of your company (it can be as simple as Jane Jones—Travel Writer) and contact information. Since you will be in business for yourself, the more you can reflect a business image, the more likely that you will be taken seriously as a professional travel writer.

YOUR BUSINESS ENTITY

There are several types of business entities. The more popular ones are single proprietorship, partnership, corporation, and LLC (limited liability company). It will be beneficial to talk with a business lawyer to determine which type of entity you want to establish for yourself, but the default entity is a single proprietorship. In other words, if you do nothing, the government will consider you to be a single proprietor, and you will need to file end-of-year tax forms accordingly. This basically means that, for tax purposes, you mix the accounting for income and expenditures for both your personal finances and those of the company. You file one tax return, and it covers both you and the company. However, you should still keep good accounting records, because, if you are audited, the Internal Revenue Service will expect to see your records. Most people, when they first become travel writers, elect to be single proprietorships.

Whatever form of business you adopt, you have choices for filing the required documentation. You can work with a business lawyer. The lawyer will file all documents for you, but you will still be required to sign several of them. Another option is to file all the papers yourself. Contact your chamber of commerce; they will direct you to the right offices where you can pick up the forms and file them after they are completed.

LEGAL CONSIDERATIONS

While a variety of legal issues may arise from time to time, the major legal concerns for most travel writers are contracts and rights. It is beneficial to have a lawyer available with whom you feel comfortable working.

Contracts

When you receive a contract or a letter of agreement from an editor, read it thoroughly. Understand what the contract calls for you to do and make notes (on another piece of paper) if you do not understand a section of the contract or if you feel a part of the contract should be changed. It is okay to tell the editor that you want a part of the contract changed, and it is usually a good idea to do so, if there are no reasons to rush into an agreement. If you want to work on the project and the editor is not willing to change the contract, talk with your lawyer, and see if you can get wording that will give you most of what you want while still satisfying the needs of your editor. It is amazing what lawyers can do these days.

The Rights You Are Selling

If you are selling to magazines, normally it means that the magazine is purchasing the right to publish your article in North America. You retain the right to sell in other countries, and you can sell a revised version of your article within six months in the United States. Although you have the right to do that, it is recommended that you not resell a magazine story in the same country for at least two years. Many editors will take exception to your reselling the article—especially if you sell it to a competing magazine, even though you have a legal right to do it.

Some magazines may require exclusive rights to your article and will put that into their contract with you. Most travel writers will agree when exclusive rights are requested, but the magazine should pay more money when it asks for these rights.

Most newspapers purchase local or regional rights. This means that you can sell the same article to many newspapers. Most who write for newspapers do sell to multiple papers. However, newspapers with a large statewide or nationwide circulation will expect to have the rights for their entire circulation area even though that area may include the entire country. *The New York Times*, *The Washington Post*, and the *Christian Science Monitor* are all publications of this type.

ACCOUNTING AND FINANCIAL RECORDKEEPING

The primary reason for having good financial records is to determine if you made a profit or if you lost money—and if you made a profit, how much profit. Why not write for those editors who pay the most? Just knowing how much the pay per word or per page is not enough. In evaluating publications, editors, and projects, it is important to know how much profit is earned. Expenses can eat you up, and it is easy for travel writing project expenses to exceed income.

A second reason for keeping good financial records is the Internal Revenue Service. Because you have two reasons to keep records, there are two types of records that need to be kept. The record you will want to keep for your profitability measures is a Project Receipts and Disbursements Record. It shows for each travel writing project how much money was received and how much was spent as well as how much profit or loss occurred. For most writing projects, a simple record form can be kept. See figure 18-1 for this form. Just fill in the blanks, and, at the end, you should understand how much money you make per project.

Figure 18-1

**TRAVEL WRITING PROJECT
RECEIPTS AND DISBURSEMENTS**

Project Name: _____
Dates of Project: _____
Approximate Person Hours for Project: _____
Income total: $_____ Expense Total: $_____ Profit Total: $_____

RECEIPTS
Advance _____
Additional Payments _____
Total Receipts: _____

EXPENSES
Personal Expense (cost of my time)
    Person hours _____ x my cost per hour _____ = _____
Project Travel Expenses
    Air _____
    Car Rental _____
    Food and Beverage _____
    Lodging _____
    Parking _____
    Rail _____
    Tips, Luggage Handling, etc. _____
    Tolls _____
    Other _____
Other Project Expenses
    Automation _____
    Automobile _____
    Project (article or book) Production Expenses _____
    Project Marketing Expenses _____
    Project Photocopying and Printing _____
    Project Postage and Express Mail Costs _____
    Project Phone and Fax Usage _____
    Project Taxes _____
    Use of Office Supplies and Equipment _____
    Other _____
Total Expenses: _____

Recordkeeping for the IRS is more complicated. You need to show every expense and all income throughout the year. Therefore, a Receipts and Disbursements Statement completed on a monthly basis and extended to an annual basis is the type of form that you can complete and turn over to your accountant at the end of the year. See figure 18-2 for an example.

Figure 18-2

**TRAVEL WRITER'S MONTHLY
RECEIPTS AND DISBURSEMENTS STATEMENT**

RECEIPTS
Book Sales _____
     Advance Income _____
     Royalty Income _____
     Other Income _____
Magazine Sales _____
Newspaper Sales _____
Other Sales _____
Other Income _____
Total Income: _____

DISBURSEMENTS
Personnel Costs
    For me: Person hours _____ x my cost per hour _____ = _____
    For others: Person hours _____ x   cost per hour   _____ =
Trip Expenses _____
     Airline Tickets _____
     Car Rental Costs _____
     Other Transportation Costs (Rail, Bus, etc.) _____
     Lodging Costs _____
     Vaccinations _____
     Trip Insurance _____
     Maps _____
     Film _____
     Baggage _____
     Audiotapes _____
     En Route Research Publications _____

Other Expenses   _____
    Article and Book Production Expenses   _____
    Automation   _____
    Automobile   _____
    Bad Debt   _____
    Bank Expenses   _____
    Conference Expenses   _____
    Donations   _____
    Dues and Subscriptions   _____
    Legal   _____
    Marketing   _____
    Office Furnishings   _____
    Office Supplies and Equipment   _____
    Phone and Fax   _____
    Photocopying and Printing   _____
    Postage and Express Mail   _____
    Rent   _____
    Research Expenses   _____
    Taxes   _____

Total Expenses: _____

MILEAGE

If you will be using the same car for private (personal) and business purposes, the chances are good you can claim mileage credit at the end of the year as a business expense. You can only claim business miles driven, however, and your first and last trips of the day do not count. Talk with your accountant or tax filer about it. If you decide to claim mileage, you will need to record miles on a daily basis. Keep a large pad in your car, and use it just to record mileage. On the first day of January, put the current year in the top in big numbers.

You only need to keep records on days when you will be undertaking business expenses. On those days, record the day on the left side of the page. Working your way to the right, record: the starting mileage for that day, the designation for each trip (marking it personal or business), the mileage for each trip, the destination for each business trip, and the mileage when you return home.

At the end of the year, add up and determine the total miles driven (personal and business) by subtracting the mileage at the beginning of the day on January 01 from the mileage at the end of the day on December 31. Next, calculate all business miles driven (except from your home to the first business destination of the day and from the last business destination of each day back to your home). This will give you the total business miles for which you can claim financial credit.

FILES

What files will you need? For hard copy files, i.e., those that are kept in a file cabinet or other storage unit, at the least you will need a file of everything you have written that has been published, a tickler or reminder file, an industry vendor file, a research source file, a pending queries file, a photo file, a map file, and, most important, a file for each publication that might buy your travel writing. There are various ways of keeping records regarding editors and others who contract with travel writers for the material they author, but a good record of these valuable contacts is essential.

The file of your published work will usually be a collection of "tear sheets," i.e., torn out copies of the articles. Each should indicate the date of publication and the magazine or newspaper in which it appeared. Some authors make multiple copies of tear sheets and file one in a date file (by date of publication) and another in their file for the publication in which the article appeared.

A tickler file is a reminder file. It should be organized by future date. Have a file section for each year for the next five years. Within that have tabs for each month, and within the month tabs, have a file folder for each week. On the same day each week, open the file for the week, and act on the items in the file. When you run across a travel article and feel you could write something similar but with a different twist (perhaps the same idea for a different location), you know the editor would not want to run such a similar story next month. So perhaps you decide the best time to approach the author with your idea will be thirteen months later. Write a reminder note to yourself, attach it to a copy of the recently published article, and drop it in your tickler file for thirteen months out. Then when you open that file you will know to contact the editor with your now-timely article idea.

Your industry vendor file should be organized by type of vendor:

transportation companies, tourist boards, lodging companies, car rental companies, and so forth. Behind each tab in this file drawer you will have a file folder for each vendor company. For example, behind the car rental tab will be a file folder for Hertz, Avis, and each of the other car rental firms.

Your research source file drawers should include a file folder for every state and national tourist bureau, all major convention and tourist bureaus, research libraries, photo libraries, and so forth. You will probably want large flat drawers for your map and photo files.

The pending queries file is usually a date sequenced file folder containing all outstanding queries. Once you have heard from an editor saying "yes" or "no," the query letter or note-to-file should be removed from the outstanding queries file.

Rolodex or Computer Business Card File

More and more people are keeping business cards on computer files. You have the old-time option, of course, of a Rolodex, and obviously it works since people have been using it for many years. However, business cards scanned into a computer reference system can give you the ability to find reference names alphabetically (as one normally files them on rolodex cards) or by type: editors, transportation contacts (for airline, motorcoach, rail, and cruise), state tourist boards, national tourist bureaus, convention and visitor bureaus, lodging contacts (people who work at resorts, hotels, and similar facilities), and miscellaneous. An especially nice aspect of computerized business card files is that once the card is entered into the computer it can be scotch taped to the front of the file folder for the publication for which the editor works or the file of the appropriate vendor or contact company.

Computer Files on Disks

In addition to hard copy files, you will have many computer disk files. These serve two purposes: 1) backup to what you have generated on your computer, and 2) the originals of written articles, chapters, and books that you have authored. A good rule is to back up everything important that has been generated on your computer. There are several ways to do this, but many travel writers save their work to floppy disks (no longer floppy) or CDs and will never leave anything important stored on their computer that is not also stored on a computer disk. Because disks are so inexpensive, you can save each article and each book chapter to a disk of its own. It is good to have a variety of options. Being able to burn to a CD or a DVD disk gives you the space to send editors entire books on a single disk.

It is a good idea to print hard copy paper backups for everything that is on a disk. Then, if the disk is damaged or destroyed, you can run a scanner across the hard copy and generate a workable replacement disk in very little time.

LIST MANAGEMENT

Having a listing of publications that buy travel writing will become one of your most valuable assets. Start with the list in the appendix of this book, but make sure that you keep it up-to-date. The best source of current travel writing opportunities is the *TravelWriter MarketLetter* ($70 per year—P.O. Box 1782, Springfield, Virginia 22151; phone: 208-988-7672). It details what editors are buying currently. Even if you are not interested in meeting the current needs of a particular publication, add the names of each publication listed in the *MarketLetter* to your contact list and files. Make sure you capture the name of the person at the publication who buys travel writing. Listings for foreign publications that purchase travel articles can be found in *Editor and Publisher International Yearbook*.

Writers Market Online "has all the resources of the print edition combined with a yearlong subscription to its online database. It has excellent search capacity enabling you to search for publications in a particular genre, subject category, or location, or those with particular pay rates, those that buy reprints, pay upon acceptance, and don't demand all rights."[2]

But having a good list of editor contacts and publications is not enough. It is frustrating to think in terms of what you might consider an excellent travel article and then have to go to either a well-stocked bookstore or a large library to peruse publications in order to determine

---

2. Louise Purwin Zobel, *The Travel Writer's Handbook* (Chicago: Surrey Books, 2002), 44.

which editors to approach. Therefore, it would be best if your personal home or office library would include at least one copy of each and every magazine that might possibly buy articles on travel.

Start this library collection by going to *Writer's Market*. Identify appropriate magazines. As soon as you can, send a postcard to each magazine asking for a sample copy and their writer's guidelines. Have a stamp made up which says, "Please send your writer's guidelines and a sample copy of your publication as suggested in *Writer's Market*. Thank you." Be sure to leave a place for your return address and for you to sign.

You should have a file for each magazine by the title of the magazine. In almost all cases, the writer's guidelines will show the amount of money paid for an article. In many cases, it will be one level of payment for a smaller number of words and a larger amount of money for a greater amount of words. Leave room to the far right on the file folder tab to write in the compensation amounts in pencil. In this way, when you are considering the placement of an article and you have identified several different magazines, you will know right away what the compensation will be from each magazine. Of course, this will need to be confirmed when you discuss an agreement for a writing project, but it will help you to speed up your marketing efforts and to concentrate on the better paying magazines.

Prepare an address label for each publication. Since you will be starting a file for each magazine, one of the items in that file can be a full page of address labels. That way, when you want to send something to that publication, you will have the address label already prepared. For this project, you will need several boxes of labels. It is recommended that you try Avery's White Mailing Labels for Laser Printers, box category number 5160. These are 1 x $2^{5}/_{8}$ inch labels, and there are thirty labels per page. Preparing a page of address labels for each magazine is a tedious project. You may want to do labels for fifteen magazines per day so that you spread the project over a multi-day period. You might shorten the initial process some by looking through *Writer's Market* and identifying those publications that appear to be most oriented toward travel and going back to the less travel-oriented magazines to complete your library later.

After you have completed your daily quota of address labels, put one on each postcard and mail them out. You will start collecting a large number of magazines, and, of course, you will also have the writer's guidelines. It is suggested that both the magazine copy and the writer's guidelines for that magazine go in the file that you have created for the publication.

Some magazines will not send out free sample copies, but most that do not will send a sample at a cost. Usually the cost is between $1 and $3. After you have requested all that send free copies, you might go back to those that levy a charge, and change the message that you stamp on your post cards to say: "Please send a sample copy of your magazine and appropriate writer's guidelines. Enclosed is a check for the appropriate amount as indicated in *Writer's Market*. Sincerely, (and leave a place for you to sign your name)." Of course, you will want to have your name and address appear on this message as well. Please make sure that you pay using business checks. These are checks with your name followed by "Travel Writer" on them. By using a business check, the recipient of your letter will know that it is a real travel writer who is requesting the sample issue.

EDITOR CONTACT INFORMATION

Your editor contacts constitute one of your most valuable resources. Keep all of your editors on file with details on each individual. Note their idiosyncrasies, but especially note their specific editorial requirements.

COMPUTERS

Today most people have computer systems. For new travel writers a question comes up as to whether they will need a desk top or a laptop or both. In terms of hardware, travel writers have such a variety of equipment, it is safe to say that whatever you have now will probably work. For almost all writing projects, neither specialized hardware nor specialized software is needed. Some travel writers like voice recognition software, which allows them to dictate their articles and book chapters to their computers. The software is getting more sophisticated all the time, but it still requires effort to train the software to each individual's voice. There are several systems, and each of the more expensive ones is about the same as another. It is suggested that you wait for a few more years, however, until voice recognition is upgraded.

The major add-on that will pay for itself is high-speed Internet. So much research is now done on our home computers that anything less than high-speed Internet will slow you down considerably. It is also suggested that you get a dedicated e-mail address for your travel writing business. If possible, use the term "travel writer" in your e-mail address, for example: JaneDoeTravelWriter.com

OTHER OFFICE EQUIPMENT

Printer

Your computer printer should be a laser printer. Most of what you will be printing will be black and white. However, there will be times when you will want to print full four-color documents. Consider getting a computer printer that is built just for color rather than using a printer that switches between black and white and color. It is easy to switch from one printer to another these days, and most up-to-date computer systems come with sufficient ports for multiple printers.

File Cabinets

In considering file cabinets, there are several choices. If you live in a major city, office furniture outlets might well be your best source for inexpensive new and slightly used file cabinets. You might also want to consider mail-order sources. It is recommended that you utilize horizontal file cabinets rather than the standard four-drawer vertical ones. It is also suggested that you include a map file cabinet, a photo file cabinet, and a slide file. Because of cost, you might have to add these later.

Phones and Answering Machines

It will be much better if you have a separate phone for your business and not try to share your home phone. A professional answering machine should be attached to your phone. Select background music for your answering machine tape. One professional uses a tape of music from *Around the World in 80 Days*, but give some thought to what you select so that it comes across professionally.

A speakerphone is something you will thank yourself for adding. When doing research you will often be put on hold. When this happens, you can put your phone on speakerphone and turn up the volume control. Then do other work until you hear someone come on the line. This can save a substantial amount of time—and can avoid frustration.

A Copy Machine

It is suggested that you purchase a copy machine. Get one that takes standard paper as this will look much better. A reasonably good copier designed for a home office will cost between $800 and $1,500.

Fax Machine

Your fax machine should be capable of transmitting photographs. Spend the time to make up a fax template that clearly identifies your company as a travel writing firm. Of course, travel writing will be included in the name of your company, but having a template with a lightly printed travel scene in the back or something similar will clearly help to put across that you are a professional travel writer.

A dedicated line for your fax is almost a necessity. Yes, it is more expensive. However, you will get a large number of faxes, and you will want to send out a large number of them. This can interrupt telephone calls (both in and out) if you have to share a line for your phone calls.

YOUR TRAVEL WRITING HOME PAGE

Many professional travel writers are developing their own home pages. This is a great place to put together a portfolio so that editors who are considering working with you can go to your site and see copies of everything you have written that has appeared in print. It is also a good place to display your résumé. Instead of including an expensive portfolio and/or résumé in the documentation supplied to clients, give them your home page address so that they can easily access as much or as little information about you as they want.

YOUR TRAVEL WRITING LIBRARY

Your travel writing library should contain at least the following: a quality dictionary (the *Oxford English Dictionary* and *Webster's Dictionary* are good ones but the larger and more comprehensive, the better), Roget's *Thesaurus*, *Bartlett's Quotations*, Strunk and White's *Elements of Style*, a book on synonyms and antonyms, and the *Associated Press Stylebook*.

Somewhere you will need to store the multiple brochures and booklets you receive on various destinations. A good way to do this is in vertical file boxes, which can be purchased in any office supply store. Most find that labeling them geographically and then alphabetically is beneficial. For example, in the European section, you might start with Albania and continue alphabetically from there.

PROFESSIONALISM

Associations
Professionals in most fields belong to their professional associations. There are several associations for travel writers, but the one that is considered the elite of the associations is the Society of American Travel Writers (1500 Sunday Drive, Suite 102, Raleigh, North Carolina 27607). Its phone number is 919-861-5586, and its e-mail address is satw@satw.org.

The North American Travel Journalists Association has less stringent requirements for membership. You must submit ten clips from the previous twelve months and pay an application fee of $25. Annual dues are $125 as of this writing. Its address is 531 Main Street, Suite 902, El Segundo, California 90245. The phone number is 310-836-8712, and the fax is 310-836-8769.

Networking
We have all heard the axiom, "Who you know is more important than what you know," and, in travel writing, contacts can make a big difference. Many writing opportunities will ultimately come from the contacts you make. Therefore, be cordial, collect business cards, return phone messages and e-mail messages rapidly, and maintain your industry contacts.

Professional Tidbits
It is considered polite to copy tear sheets and send them to people who have been interviewed or who in some other way have contributed to your article. The same is true with books. If someone contributed to a book you have authored and that person did not charge for the contribution, it is considered polite to send them a gratis copy of the book when it comes out.

Always use spell-check, but do not rely on it totally. Read through your material to catch spelling and grammar errors, and use others who have excellent English usage knowledge to review your work before it goes to your editors.

A PROFESSIONAL BUSINESS

Having a professionally run business will help you gain the respect of other travel writers, provide you with the tools at hand to make travel writing easier, and, most importantly, help you get more travel writing assignments and be better able to complete assignments on time and to the specification of your editor. You may feel that adopting all the suggestions in this chapter might be too expensive. If so, do what you can and schedule implementation of the other things/activities over a period of months—or even years. What is most important, however, is that you set up your travel writing business in a professional manner and that you continue to grow in your professionalism over time.

End-of-Chapter Questions

1. According to Cropp, writing good prose may be one of your least used skills.   A) True   B) False

2. What type of business entity do most travel writers select for themselves?

3. Is it okay to tell the editor if you want a part of the contract changed?

4. What is the name of the form that is used to determine whether or not you made a profit on a writing project?

5. A "tickler" file is the same as what other file?

6. Is it better to back up travel writing to a computer disk, with a hard (paper) copy, or both?

7. Which publication should you consult to start your personal library collection?

8. In what way are postcards used to obtain writer's guidelines?

9. What type of computer printer should the travel writer have?

10. Should travel writers have a shared phone line for their fax machine?

WRITTEN ASSIGNMENT EIGHTEEN
COMPLETING AND SUBMITTING YOUR CONTRACT ARTICLE

Assignment Introduction

You probably received an advance check for your contract article. It is important that you submit your article on or before the date you and the buyer agreed upon. You may need a little more time after this assignment is due to finish it because of the research requirements of some contract articles. If so, the final completion and submission to the editor can wait until a week or so before your agreed-upon submission date. Meanwhile you can take preliminary steps to make sure the packaging is prepared in advance, and you can submit the best draft you have available to your professor with the Instructor Comment Sheet for this written assignment.

Assignment Activity

The packaging and submission of your contract article will be similar to the packaging and submission of your spec article. The main difference is that you will only be sending out one envelope instead of many envelopes. However, you should use the same size of 9 x 11½ inch padded envelope. You need to stamp the front of the envelope: PHOTOGRAPHS—DO NOT BEND. And you need to have a mailing label with your return address and the name, title, name of the magazine, and address of the travel article buyer.

As with your spec article, photographs should be enclosed in a photo mailer. And, as with the spec article, your name, title (travel writer), and address should be in the top right corner of each page of your article.

The cover letter should be a little different. You still need the same type of headings as you had with your spec article cover letter. However, the body of the letter should be more detailed saying something like:

> *Thank you for the opportunity to work with you. Enclosed is the manuscript for the travel article, (insert the title of your article). I have made every effort to write the article in accordance with your specifications, your writer's guidelines, and the guidelines discussed on the phone and in your letter of (date of the letter of agreement).*
>
> *Please feel free to edit in any way you feel will make the article more appealing to your readers. If you would like for me to make any changes, please advise accordingly.*
>
> *It has been a pleasure working with you. I hope to write for you again in the near future. Please send the final compensation check and a tear sheet to me at the address above.*
>
> *Sincerely,*
> *Your Name*
> *Travel Writer*
> *Enc. Manuscript for (title of your article)*

Keep in mind that, as you complete your contract article, you will need to prepare drafts in much the same way that you prepared drafts of your spec article. However, you should go through everything that is special and unique to the publication and to the travel article buyer, making notes of the requirements and checking off each one to make sure each and every requirement is met.

Final Step: Please print your name on Instructor Comment Sheet for Writing Assignment Eighteen in appendix 5, and staple it to a copy of your cover letter to the travel article buyer. Copies of the photographs that you will submit with your article and either the final draft of your contract article manuscript or the best draft to date of your manuscript should be included in the package that you send or give to your professor.

CHAPTER 19

Advance and Make Top Money

James Poynter

MORE FREELANCE TRAVEL WRITING

The days of the full-time, well-paid travel journalist roaming the world on a generous expense account are pretty much gone. Few are full-time anymore. Most employers have found it much less expensive to buy from freelancers or the syndicates or to add travel writing to the job of the editors. Not only are there fewer personnel expenses, but there are savings in benefits (retirement, life insurance, etc.) and office expenses (computers, rent, etc.). Even those few who work in the field on a full-time basis usually have to work with limited expense-account budgets.

But the opportunities for freelance travel writers are growing rapidly. Many newspapers have gone from a few columns in the Sunday edition to multiple pages on Sunday and either a Tuesday or Wednesday travel supplement. Every year there are more magazines devoted to travel, and an increasing number of magazines that never used to run a travel article are now adding travel pieces because their readers are asking for it. A few years ago, few how-to travel books could be found in bookstores. Today, the how-to segment is the most rapidly expanding part of the travel book industry. It has grown to the degree that in some bookstores these publications take up almost as much shelf space as do guidebooks. And when it comes to guidebooks, the numbers and the variety of guidebooks is greater than it ever has been—and growing. Meanwhile, trade publications are increasing in number, and more and more of the "trades" are demanding specialized travel articles and books.

GREAT PAY FOR SOME

But although the opportunities to get your travel writing in print have increased considerably in recent years, the pay has not kept up. Richard Cropp, Barbara Braidwood, and Susan Boyce put it well when they state: "The money in travel writing is lousy for most people, mediocre for a few, and spectacular for a tiny minority."[1] The reality is that the average freelance travel writer is not well paid. In fact, some say they are often lucky to get enough to cover expenses.

An increasing number of people are entering the field for the love of travel and the excitement of the job, not for the money. It is not unusual for a magazine to pay $100 or less for a two-thousand-word lead article, but some pay $1.00 per word and ask for articles ranging from one thousand up to five thousand words. Travel writers who write for the newspaper market rarely make more than enough to cover their costs— and many do not cover their costs. Newspapers can buy from syndicates for as little as $10 per article, so there is not much incentive for them to pay more to travel writers. Therefore, many newspapers will limit their pay for articles written by freelance travel writers to $15 per article.

---

1. Richard Cropp, Barbara Braidwood, and Susan Boyce, *Writing Travel Books and Articles* (Bellingham, WA: Self-Counsel Press, 1997), 1.

However, there are travel writers who are consistently able to sell the same article to between sixty and eighty newspapers in the U.S. and Canada, and those who write regular columns for large and/or international papers can and do command good incomes.

Most guidebook publishers pay on a per-word compensation basis, usually between fifty cents per word and one dollar per word, with the majority at the lower end. However, when it is a new title (not one that is being updated), many guidebook publishers will cover the airfare and the hotel costs. A number of them, however, will save on these costs as the preference for an increasing number of guidebook publishers is to hire American travel writers who are already living at the destination.

But if many travel writers are not being paid well, who is and what areas of travel writing should the writer who is seeking top pay avoid? Reasonably good money ($50,000 and up) is almost never earned by writing for newspapers. The papers are a great place to break into the field and get a first piece published, but the challenge to make any real money as a freelancer selling to the newspaper market it so great that most travel writers move to more lucrative markets rapidly in their careers.

The best incomes are earned writing for the better paying magazines, syndicates, some of the guidebook publishers, specialized travel book publishers, how-to travel books, and some of the trade publications. As noted in the chapter on how-to books, David Howell, author of *Passport*, told me he made about $92,000 in royalties the first year his book came out. Shortly after that first year, Howell was hit by a car while jogging, hospitalized for months, and died. However, I understand his widow continued to collect royalties on the book for many years.

Top names in guidebook publishing—Temple Fielding, Eugene Foder, and Arthur Frommer, for example—have done well financially. Some experienced travel writers who consistently write for *National Geographic*, *Islands* magazine, and *Condé Nast Traveler* are reported to earn $60,000 and more per year. And some travel writers who specialize in writing for trade publications make as much as $80,000 per year.

STRATEGIES FOR BECOMING A TOP-PAID TRAVEL WRITER

Rarely does a travel writer just arrive in the field, get paid well for his or her first piece, and make an excellent income the first year of travel writing. For the vast majority, it takes time. However, the amount of time required to move from beginner making very low pay to experienced author making top pay will be reduced considerably if the travel writer develops a money-making strategy.

One of the best strategies is to specialize in a top money-making area as rapidly as possible. For example, a new travel writer may initially write for newspapers to get a first few articles published. Meanwhile, the new writer is targeting book publishers. As soon as the ability to write travel articles is proven with the publication of newspaper articles, all attention is given to getting a book contract. Once the first book is written and published, top-paying book publishers are targeted. This approach can lead a travel writer from entry-level newbie to well-paid experienced writer is just a few years.

Another approach is to target the travel trades. Subscribe to *Travel Weekly*, *Business Travel News*, and other trade publications. Research the histories of Arnie Weissmann, Andrew Compart, and Alan Frederiks, CTC (recently deceased). Find out how they reached the pinnacle of income in travel writing. Go to the conferences, and meet Compart, Weissmann, and other well-paid travel writers. Talk with them. Then decide how you want to break into the top money. Write down what you will do, and then proceed to follow your strategy.

You might decide that syndicate writing is for you. Make it a habit to go to your library. Pull out the travel sections of major newspapers around the country. Read the syndicated articles each week. Identify the syndicates you feel you would best fit in with. Contact the syndicates, and ask where their travel writers are speaking. Not all of them are on the speaking circuit, but many are. Attend some of their presentations, and prepare well-thought-through questions to ask in the Q&A sessions. Take a few minutes after the presentation to talk with them. Survey their strategies, and then develop a strategy of your own. Try to get one or more to act as a mentor. It is surprising how many will take on the role of mentor when asked.

WELL-PAID TRAVEL WRITERS

There will always be well-paid travel writers. Most do not reach this level of accomplishment by accident or just because they were lucky.

Advance and Make Top Money

They got there with hard work and dedication, and most develop a well-thought-out strategy early in their travel writing careers. The chances are good that you can make top money, too—if you set your mind to it and if you pursue a well-developed strategy.

End-of-Chapter Questions

1. Why are there more freelancers and fewer full-time travel writers than there used to be?

2. For what reason is it easier to get newspaper articles published than it used to be?

3. What is the most rapidly expanding segment of the travel book industry?

4. Which segment of the travel writing industry is demanding more specialized travel articles and books?

5. Instead of entering the field for the money, why are an increasing number of people entering the field of travel writing?

6. Some magazines pay one dollar per word and ask for articles ranging from a low of one thousand words to a high of how many words?

7. Most guidebook publishers pay a compensation based on per what?

8. The best incomes are earned writing for the better-paying magazines, some of the guidebook publishers, specialized travel book publishers, how-to travel books, some of the trade publications, and what other group of travel writing buyers?

9. What might a travel writer develop to shorten the time required to move from a beginner making entry-level pay to an experienced author making top pay?

10. One of the best strategies for a travel writer is to specialize. In what area should the travel writer specialize?

WRITING ASSIGNMENT NINETEEN
YOUR INDIVIDUAL DEVELOPMENT PLAN

Assignment Introduction

Serious travel writers usually want to move from part-time travel writers to well-paid, full-time, professional travel writers. Developing and following an individual development plan should help you get to the apex of your travel writing career as rapidly as possible.

Assignment Activity

Prepare an individual development plan for yourself. Review the biographical data provided in major travel publications such as *Condé Nast Traveler, National Geographic*, and so forth. As much as possible, try to determine why each travel writer whose work was adopted and published in the publication arrived at the professional status whereby their travel article was picked up by a major publication. In many cases, the information published in the magazine will center on the article itself and not provide much data about the background of the author. However, frequently, with a little digging, you can get that information. For example, put the author's name into a computer search, and you probably will be able to find a home page for the author. Often it will give the background (biographical data) on the author, and many times it will list the author's credits.

Try to find detailed information on the background of at least five professional travel writers. As you develop that background, attempt to find similarities in terms of what they have done to be able to reach the professional status that they have attained.

Armed with the data you have compiled regarding professional travel writers, develop a plan for yourself that will identify what you can do to move from where you are as a student/travel writer to becoming a highly paid, full-time, professional travel writer. Prepare three to four pages of paragraph-style copy identifying a development plan for yourself.

Final Step: Add your name to the Instructor Comment Sheet for Writing Assignment Nineteen in appendix 5 and staple it to a copy of your individual development plan. Then turn in both items to your professor.

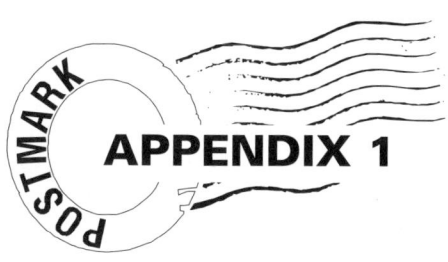

APPENDIX 1

Chronological and Alphabetical Lists

The following are lists of authors and works of travel writing shown on "A Map of the World of Travel Writing," the fold-out chart that accompanies this book. Due to space limitations, the map for the most part shows only titles, sometimes abbreviated. In this appendix are all the names of the authors and complete titles; they are listed chronologically and alphabetically by author. This is by no means a comprehensive list of travel writers or works. For further information on the map included with this book and the information in this appendix, see chapter 2, "Observations and Explanations Concerning the Map."

CHRONOLOGICAL

900 B.C.E.	*The Odyssey*	Homer
440 B.C.E.	*Histories*	Herodotus
1100	*Deeds of the Franks*	Anonymous
1298	*Travels of Marco Polo*	Marco Polo

TRAVEL WRITING

1568	*The Discovery and Conquest of Mexico*	Bernal Diaz del Castillo
1588	"Of Cannibals"	Michel de Montaigne
1611	*The Tempest*	William Shakespeare
1719	*Robinson Crusoe*	Daniel Defoe
1726	*Gulliver's Travels*	Jonathan Swift
1763	*Turkish Embassy Letters*	Lady Mary Montagu
1771	*The Expedition of Humphrey Clinker*	Tobias Smollet
1775	*Journey to the Western Islands*	Samuel Johnson
1786	*A Sentimental Journey*	Laurence Sterne
1794	*Travels*	William Bartram
1812	*Childe Harold's Pilgrimage*	George Gordon, Lord Byron
1839	*Voyage of The Beagle*	Charles Darwin
1855	"Song of the Open Road"	Walt Whitman
1864	*Journey to the Center of the Earth*	Jules Verne
1869	*The Innocents Abroad*	Mark Twain
1877	*The American*	Henry James
1885	*The Adventures of Huckleberry Finn*	Mark Twain
1900	*Sailing Alone Around the World*	Joshua Slocum
1902	*Heart of Darkness*	Joseph Conrad
1915	*Old Calabria*	Norman Douglas
1921	*Sea and Sardinia*	D.H. Lawrence
1924	*A Passage to India*	E.M. Forster
1929	*A Farewell to Arms*	Ernest Hemingway
1933	*Brazilian Adventure*	Peter Fleming
1937	*Out of Africa*	Isak Denison
1939	*Lost Horizon*	James Hilton
1944	*Brave Men*	Ernie Pyle
1949	*The Sheltering Sky*	Paul Bowles
1955	*Lolita*	Vladimir Nabokov
1957	*On the Road*	Jack Kerouac
1957–60	*The Alexandria Quartet*	Lawrence Durrell
1961	*The Lonely Land*	Sigurd Olson
1961	*A House for Mr. Biswas*	V.S. Naipaul
1962	*Under the Mountain Wall*	Peter Matthiessen
1962	*The Middle Passage*	V.S. Naipaul
1965	*Full Tilt*	Dervla Murphy
1965	*Questions of Travel*	Elizabeth Bishop
1968	*Desert Solitaire*	Edward Abbey
1971	*Fear and Loathing in Las Vegas*	Hunter S. Thompson
1972	*Among the Believers*	V.S. Naipaul

1972	*Invisible Cities*	Italo Calvino
1974	*Tristes Tropiques*	Claude Levi-Strauss
1975	*Far Tortuga*	Peter Matthiessen
1975	*The Great Railway Bazaar*	Paul Theroux
1975	*Going After Cacciato*	Tim O'Brien
1977	*Dispatches*	Michael Herr
1977	*A Time for Gifts*	Patrick Leigh Fermor
1979	*The Hitchhiker's Guide to the Galaxy*	Douglas Adams
1980	*Abroad*	Paul Fussell
1982	*Blue Highways*	William Least Heat-Moon
1982	*The Mosquito Coast*	Paul Theroux
1983	*Among the Russians*	Colin Thubron
1984	*Into the Heart of Borneo*	Redmond O'Hanlon
1985	*The Polar Express*	Chris Van Allsburg
1987	*The Songlines*	Bruce Chatwin
1988	*Holidays in Hell*	P.J. O'Rourke
1988	*Nothing to Declare*	Mary Morris
1989	*A Year in Provence*	Peter Mayle
1990	*Omeros*	Derek Walcott
1991	*Unquiet Days*	Thomas Swick
1991	*Road Fever*	Tim Cahill
1992	*Imperial Eyes*	Mary Louise Pratt
1992	*Dave Barry Does Japan*	Dave Barry
1994	*The Lost Heart of Asia*	Colin Thubron
1995	*A Small Place in Italy*	Eric Newby
1995	*Notes from a Small Island*	Bill Bryson
1996	*Love Thy Neighbor: A Story of War*	Peter Maass
1997	*Into Thin Air*	Jon Krakauer
1997	*Routes*	James Clifford
1998	*Ecotourism and Sustainable Development*	Martha Honey
1998	*Tourists with Typewriters*	Patrick Holland & Graham Huggan
1998	*The Art of the Pilgrimage*	Phil Cousineau
1999	*Round Ireland with a Fridge*	Tony Hawks
2000	*The Amazing Adventures of Kavalier & Clay*	Michael Chabon
2001	*Teach Yourself Travel Writing*	Cynthia Dial
2003	*Blue Latitudes*	Tony Horwitz
2003	*The Art of Travel*	Alain de Botton
2004	*Cooking with Fernet Branca*	James Hamilton-Paterson
2005	*Istanbul*	Orhan Pamuk
2005	*Writing the Journey*	David Espey

| 2006 | *Eating Europe: A Meta-Nonfiction Love Story* | Jon Volkmer |

ALPHABETICAL

Abbey, Edward	*Desert Solitaire*	1968
Adams, Douglas	*The Hitchhiker's Guide to the Galaxy*	1979
Anonymous	*Deeds of the Franks*	1100
Barry, Dave	*Dave Barry Does Japan*	1992
Bartram, William	*Travels*	1794
Bernal Diaz del Castillo	*The Discovery and Conquest of Mexico*	1568
Bishop, Elizabeth	*Questions of Travel*	1965
de Botton, Alain	*The Art of Travel*	2003
Bowles, Paul	*The Sheltering Sky*	1949
Bryson, Bill	*Notes from a Small Island*	1995
Cahill, Tim	*Road Fever*	1991
Calvino, Italo	*Invisible Cities*	1972
Chabon, Michael	*The Amazing Adventures of Kavalier & Clay*	2000
Chatwin, Bruce	*The Songlines*	1987
Clifford, James	*Routes*	1997
Conrad, Joseph	*Heart of Darkness*	1902
Cousineau, Phil	*The Art of the Pilgrimage*	1998
Darwin, Charles	*Voyage of The Beagle*	1839
Defoe, Daniel	*Robinson Crusoe*	1719
Denison, Isak	*Out of Africa*	1937
Dial, Cynthia	*Teach Yourself Travel Writing*	2001
Douglas, Norman	*Old Calabria*	1915
Durrell, Lawrence	*The Alexandria Quartet*	1957–60
Espey, David	*Writing the Journey*	2005
Fleming, Peter	*Brazilian Adventure*	1933
Forster, E.M.	*A Passage to India*	1924
Fussell, Paul	*Abroad*	1980
Gordon George, Lord Byron	*Childe Harold's Pilgrimage*	1812
Hamilton-Paterson, James	*Cooking with Fernet Branca*	2004
Hawks, Tony	*Round Ireland with a Fridge*	1999
Hemingway, Ernest	*A Farewell to Arms*	1929
Herodotus	*Histories*	440 B.C.E.
Herr, Michael	*Dispatches*	1977
Hilton, James	*Lost Horizon*	1939

Chronological and Alphabetical Lists 331

Holland, Patrick and Graham Huggan	*Tourists with Typewriters*	1998
Homer	*The Odyssey*	900 B.C.E.
Honey, Martha	*Ecotourism and Sustainable Development*	1998
Horwitz, Tony	*Blue Latitudes*	2003
James, Henry	*The American*	1877
Johnson, Samuel	*Journey to the Western Islands*	1775
Kerouac, Jack	*On the Road*	1957
Krakauer, Jon	*Into Thin Air*	1997
Lawrence, D.H.	*Sea and Sardinia*	1921
Least Heat-Moon, William	*Blue Highways*	1982
Leigh Fermor, Patrick	*A Time for Gifts*	1977
Levi-Strauss, Claude	*Tristes Tropiques*	1974
Maass, Peter	*Love Thy Neighbor: A Story of War*	1996
Mayle, Peter	*A Year in Provence*	1989
Marco Polo	*Travels of Marco Polo*	1298
Matthiessen, Peter	*Far Tortuga*	1975
Matthiessen, Peter	*Under the Mountain Wall*	1962
Montagu, Lady Mary	*Turkish Embassy Letters*	1763
de Montaigne, Michel	"Of Cannibals"	1588
Morris, Mary	*Nothing to Declare*	1988
Murphy, Dervla	*Full Tilt*	1965
Nabokov, Vladimir	*Lolita*	1955
Naipaul, V.S.	*A House for Mr. Biswas*	1961
Naipaul, V.S.	*Among the Believers*	1972
Naipaul, V.S.	*The Middle Passage*	1962
Newby, Eric	*A Small Place in Italy*	1995
Pamuk, Orhan	*Istanbul*	2005
Pratt, Mary Louise	*Imperial Eyes*	1992
Pyle, Ernie	*Brave Men*	1944
O'Brien, Tim	*Going After Cacciato*	1975
O'Hanlon, Redmond	*Into the Heart of Borneo*	1984
Olson, Sigurd	*The Lonely Land*	1961
O'Rourke, P.J.	*Holidays in Hell*	1988
Shakespeare, William	*The Tempest*	1611
Slocum, Joshua	*Sailing Alone Around the World*	1900
Smollet, Tobias	*The Expedition of Humphrey Clinker*	1771
Sterne, Laurence	*A Sentimental Journey*	1786

Swick, Thomas	*Unquiet Days*	1991
Swift, Jonathan	*Gulliver's Travels*	1726
Theroux, Paul	*The Great Railway Bazaar*	1975
Theroux, Paul	*The Mosquito Coast*	1982
Thubron, Colin	*Among the Russians*	1983
Thubron, Colin	*The Lost Heart of Asia*	1994
Thompson, Hunter S.	*Fear and Loathing in Las Vegas*	1971
Twain, Mark	*The Adventures of Huckleberry Finn*	1885
Twain, Mark	*The Innocents Abroad*	1869
Van Allsburg, Chris	*The Polar Express*	1985
Verne, Jules	*Journey to the Center of the Earth*	1864
Volkmer, Jon	*Eating Europe: A Meta-Nonfiction Love Story*	2006
Walcott, Derek	*Omeros*	1990
Whitman, Walt	"Song of the Open Road"	1855

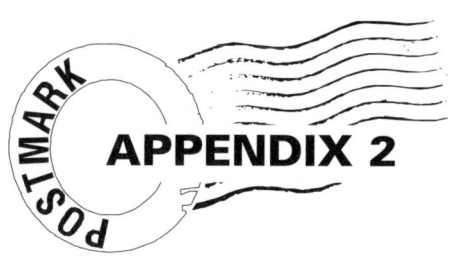

APPENDIX 2

Writer's Guidelines for Selected Magazines That Buy Travel Articles

WHY COLLECT WRITER'S GUIDELINES

Sources for writer's guidelines and a number of the guidelines themselves are provided in this appendix. These were current guidelines at the time of publication of this book. However, many guidelines change frequently. Therefore, it is wise to always check with the publication for which you are writing to make sure that the guidelines below still apply.

Professional travel writers, even part-time, freelance travel writers, obtain writer's guidelines from every publication to which they expect to submit a query. You are encouraged to add to this list of writer's guidelines by requesting up-to-date guidelines from a large range of publications. Then when you have a query to submit, you can match it to what specific publications are looking for. And, once you decide to submit your potential article for publication, you may study the needs of multiple editors before approaching their publications. Then, when you do submit a query, you will understand the focus of your target publication.

SOURCES OF WRITER'S GUIDELINES

The best source of writer's guidelines is the publication of the same name. Many publications have their guidelines on the *Writer's Guidelines* Web site. This is often the best and the easiest way to build a collection of current guidelines. If the guidelines you are looking for are not on the publication's Web site, try calling the editor's office and requesting the guidelines. In some cases, the Web site will show a phone number or an e-mail address for the publication. If so, this is probably the *best* way to request guidelines.

There are several published listings of writer's guidelines. Although not a reproduction of the guidelines themselves, Judy Mandell's book, *Writer's Guide to Magazine Editors and Publishers*, provides most of the information an author would want from the listings in the book. Unfortunately, the book has not been updated for several years.

GUIDELINES AND EXCERPTS FROM GUIDELINES

The following are guidelines, guideline sources, and excerpts from guidelines of a select group of publications that accept travel articles. As always, it is best to contact the publication *before* submitting a query to make sure its guidelines have not changed.

Alaska Magazine: Pays 32 cents per word with the average article length being 2,000 words. Therefore, the average pay is $760. An excellent online resource for writers provides answers to most questions. Go to www.alaskamagazine.com/about/writers.shtml.

American Cowboy Payment is negotiated, and roughly it depends on the number of pages of the article. E-mail Debbie Cruz for writer's guidelines for *American Cowboy*. Her e-mail is Debbie@cowboy.com. Article length will usually range from 400 words to 2,000 words. No phone queries accepted. E-mail a three- or four-paragraph query letter summarizing the article idea, with supporting facts and writing credentials. *American Cowboy* covers all aspects of western style and culture including upbeat and lively travel articles with unique angles. Multiple submitted article ideas are okay.

Arthur Frommer's Budget Travel To get current guidelines, e-mail David LaHuta at LaHuta@Newsweekbt.com. Longer stories are 600 to 1,000 words, but many shorter stories are also sought.

There are two categories for articles: Where and How. The Where editor is Nina Willdorf (nina.willdorf@newsweekbt.com). These articles are about destinations and include: 1) Eat Like a Local—a restaurant roundup usually written by a local; 2) My Hometown—a story about a place the way it was and the way it is as revisited today; 3) The Secret Hotels of… —a roundup of hotels, inns, and other lodging under $150 a night but worth more; 4) Top Shops—the best shopping in a city or country; 5) Time Out—spa and mind/body stories; 6) Fresh Air—adventure travel and other outdoor activities; 7) Cheapest Places on Earth—a cheap place and why it is so inexpensive (half-page max); 8) In the News—newer destinations but not war-ravaged places; 9) Why Haven't You Heard of… —little known and little publicized destinations and why budget travelers might want to travel there; 10) College Town—an insider's view on what to see and do that is cheap or free (half-page max); 11) Take My Word—short destination advice from someone whose taste you would trust; 12) You Only Live Once—a splurge experience that is well worth the extra money; 13) Crash the Party—how to experience a big event the budget travel way and at the last minute; 14) Hot Property—a great new hotel or resort under $150 a night; 15) Supermarket Souvenir—something cheap, easy to find, and especially interesting when brought back from a foreign country; 16) How to Buy a TK in TK—"a bikini in Rio, for example"—a unique, but inexpensive purchase that gives insight into a place; 17) Tour du Jour—"A short item on a tour that gives a unique view of a place"; 18) Now or Never—a place or event that is closing soon and should not be missed; 19) Face Lift—an updated building, museum, or neighborhood; 20) Call in Sick—a domestic two- or three-day weekend lesser-known destination and why readers should want to visit; 21) Landscape—"a map of a newly-interesting, developing neighborhood in a big city, with call-outs for places to stop on a walking tour;" 22) Happy Anniversary—a celebration of the birthday or anniversary of a place or person that will be a big bash, internationally; 23) Before It's Ruined—a place that tourists are beginning to go to in greater numbers but a place that "isn't yet overrun with tourist hordes;" 24) Sleep Tomorrow—how insiders "do" a place after dark; 25) Time Travel—a trip or visit with historical importance; 26) 2-Minute Guidebook—"a quickie guide to a region, best used in a pithy chart comparing several places in one (What's the Next Prague, for example)"; and 27) Opening Soon—a place or experience that will be opening soon.

The How editor is Brad Tuttle (brad.tuttle@newsweekbt.com). These articles relate to how "smart travelers learn to work the system. They don't have to be about how to save money—they'll be about smart travel as much as how to travel cheaply." Longer articles are in five categories: 1) 10 Questions to Ask Before You… —"What to ask before you book a cruise, rent a villa, swap houses, rent an RV, whatever. Then explain why each question is important (1,000 words)"; 2) The BT Handbook—"how-to stories on haggling, tipping, hiring a tour guide, etc. (800 words)"; 3) Easier Than You Thought—"an exciting vacation mode and how easy it is to arrange and accomplish, like RVing in New Zealand, trekking in Nepal, etc. (800 words)"; 4) A Step Ahead—"getting around new problems/costs associated with a recent travel trend, such as nickel and diming people for every little thing on cruises (600–800 words)"; and 5) The Long Answer—detailed and knowledgeable information about common travel issues such as, "When is the best time to book airfare?" (700–1,000 words).

Shorter articles for the How section generally run from 300 words to 1,000 words. These include: 1) Industry Watch—something that is going on in the travel industry that directly affects how you travel (300–500 words); 2) The Fine Print—"a dissection of complicated travel issues: taxes, insurance, cancellation policies, etc. (300–1,000 words)"; 3) In The News—"We reveal what's going on behind the scenes in travel, and explain how to put that knowledge to work for you (300–800 words)"; 4) Confessions of a… —a person in the industry (a cruise reservationist, for example) "tells the tricks of the trade (500 words)"; 5) How to Buy a TK in TK—a step-by-step guide on how to buy a

Writer's Guidelines   337

native item in a foreign country (300 words); 6) Dealbreaker—"packages that cost more than they would if purchased individually (100 words)"; 7) Debunker—"explain how a travel myth is wrong (200 words)"; 8) Cultural Etiquette—"do's and don'ts in situations known to cause outsiders anxiety: tea time in England, spas in Finland, dealing with footware in Japan (500 words)"; 9) Faux Pas—"a quick how-to or how-not-to behave, focusing on behavior that could be misconstrued, such as hand gestures (200–300 words)"; 10) Web Smart—"new tools and trends on the Web (200–800 words)"; 11) Say What?—"lighthearted, oddball stuff, curiosities from around the world that the reader might be able to put into action, or at least get a good laugh from (200 words)"; 12) Packing List—"new gear to bring on the trip (50–100 words)"; 13) How to Speak Travel Agent—"lingo that will tell your agent you know what you're talking about (75 words)"; 14) Books—"new Books that help you travel smarter (50–200 words)"; 15) Pet Peeve—"a gripe about something new in the travel world: new fees, removing a feature that travelers like (50 words)"; and 16) Kudos To—"We applaud the folks doing something good in the travel industry, stuff that makes travelers' lives easier and their experiences better (50 words)."

Backpacker As we go to press, new guidelines are being prepared. The new guidelines will be on the Web site or can be requested by mail (33 E. Minor Street, Emmaus, PA 18098), phone (212) 573-0209, or e-mail www.BACKPACKER.com/Guidelines. If you call, talk with Darlene at (610) 967-8296 or John at (610) 967-8746. Inquiries should be sent directly to the appropriate editor at editor@backpacker.com. Pay per article is negotiable.

Cross Country Skier Editor is Lou Dzierzak at (715) 798-5500. The guidelines are on the Web site on the left side of crosscountryskier.com. Go to info@crosscountryskier.com. Features should be essays on topics of interest to Nordic ski enthusiasts. Articles on personalities and gear are also sought. With your query send samples of previously published work to Editor, *Cross Country Skier*, P.O. Box 550, Cable, WI 54821. Allow six to eight weeks for a reply. Compensation is negotiable.

High Times Go to http://hightimes.com and click on Contributor's Guidelines. Features are 1,500 to 3,000 words and pay $500 to $1,000. Special Report segments are 1,200 to 1,500 words and pay $100 to $500. Reviews are 250 to 300 words, and the pay ranges from $100 to $150. Contact: edit.queries@hightimes.com or edit.submission@hightimes.com

Military Spouse For writer's guidelines, go to www.militaryspousemagazine.com, go to the *Writer's Guidelines* at the bottom of the home page, and click on *Complete Writer's Guidelines*. About 75 percent of the editorial content of the magazine is purchased from freelance writers. One of the departments is Travel. These articles require extensive reporting and interviewing. The preferred article length ranges from 800 to 1,000 words. Each issue also runs at least four feature articles. These should be approximately 1,500 words, and the pay runs from $100 to $400. Detailed queries are sought and can be sent by mail or e-mail. Response time is usually about six weeks, but there will be no response unless the editors are interested in purchasing the article. Send queries to Regina Galvin, Managing Editor, *Military Spouse* Magazine, P.O. Box 3447, Fort Leavenworth, TX 66027 or rgalvin@militaryspousemagazine.com.

Montana For writer's guidelines, go to www.montanamagazine.com, click on *Reader Submissions* at the top of the page, and then click on *See the Guidelines* at the bottom left side of the page. Written queries are accepted by mail or by e-mail and will be read and reviewed within two months. No telephone queries accepted. Provide a thorough outline of the proposed article. Start with the lead, then write a short summary of content, including specifics on whom you plan to interview, research sources, highlights, anecdotal information, and conclusion. Provide several samples of your writing. Include a return envelope and postage. Manuscripts must be typed, double- or triple-spaced. Include a return envelope and postage if you want your material returned. The basic pay is approximately 20 cents per published word. Additional pay is provided for photographs, and sometimes the pay is greater for articles requiring substantial expense. Send queries to: Beverly Magley, Editor, *Montana* Magazine, P.O. Box 5630, Helena, MT 59604.

Writer's Guidelines

New Mexico Magazine For writer's guidelines, go to www.mnnagazine.com, put your cursor over *About Us* at the top of the home page, click on *Contributor Guidelines*, and scroll down to *Writer's Guidelines*.

Travel is only one of the many areas covered by this magazine. The magazine pays on acceptance for manuscripts and normally replies to queries in four to six weeks. All articles should involve an aspect of New Mexico. Published writing samples should be sent with your query. The pay is 30 cents a word with $100 minimum, and article lengths run from 250 to 2,000 words. Use the AP Style Manual for writing guidelines and type your name, address, (including e-mail address), and phone number in the upper left corner of each page. Double- or triple-space text, and number your pages. Include a "tag line," a short paragraph about you and your related experience at the end of your query. If your article is published, the tag line lets the reader know something about the author. Provide contact information for all the people in your proposed article. Illustrations (usually photographs) will be required.

Before writing your query, "Study the magazine and know the departments, style, and what we have already covered." Only developed queries will be considered. Provide "at least a half-page pitch" for your article. Always include your contact information on each page of the query. Do not send e-mail or faxed queries.

Submit your queries to Emily Drabanski, Editor-in-Chief, *New Mexico* Magazine, 495 Old Santa Fe Trail, Santa Fe, NM 87501-2750.

Oklahoma Today To access the writer's guidelines, go to www.oklahomatoday.com, click on Editorial Department at the top of the page, and then click on Writers, Photographers, & Reporting Guidelines.

Seven issues are published each year. All have travel articles, but one issue is THE travel issue. Articles range from 500 words to 3,000 words. And payment starts at $25 to $50 for shorter pieces and $75 to $300 for major pieces. Payment is made upon publication, but $25 per day is deducted for manuscripts submitted after the agreed-upon deadline. "The magazine likes to give the readers information on not only the regular 'hot spots' to visit, but places that are 'off the beaten track' as well." Provide the history behind a place, but the focus should be on today. Answer two questions: 1) "Could the reader see or do what the article talks about?" and 2) "Will the story expand the knowledge of the readers' Oklahoma cultural knowledge?" Documentation is crucial. No statements will be published if they have not been documented to the satisfaction of the publication's editors. Primary sources are required for all previously unreported facts and for all other facts important to the story. Relying too heavily on secondary sources is discouraged. You must give credit to other publications for original reporting. Writers are expected to take responsibility even for "so-called common knowledge." Writers are expected to keep unpublished drafts of assigned articles confidential. And authors are required to supply an annotated fact-checking manuscript that reflects their guidelines. Specifically, the publication will require: 1) any notes, transcripts, or tapes of interviews; 2) all magazine or newspaper stories used in reporting; 3) all other supporting material, with relevant parts clearly marked; 4) phone numbers for sources; and 5) the annotated manuscript.

Submit manuscripts to: Editor, *Oklahoma Today* Magazine, P.O. Box 1468, Oklahoma City, OK 73101.

Porthole Cruise Magazine   This bimonthly magazine is 90 percent freelance written. Payment ranges from $400 to $1,200 for assigned articles and from $250 to $1,000 for unsolicited articles. In addition, the publication often pays the expenses of writers who are on assignment. It seeks cruise-related general interest, historical and nostalgic, how to pick a cruise, personal experiences, humor, and interviews and profiles with crew on board or industry executives. Articles should be 1,000 to 3,000 words. Send to Ralph Grizzle, the editor. His e-mail is rgrizzle@ppigroup.com, and his fax is (954) 377-7000. The phone number is (954) 377-7777.

SAIL   Go to www.sailmag.com. In the "Search" box in the column on the right side of the page enter *Writer's Guidelines* and click *Go*. Click on the *Guidelines for Writers and Photographers* in the middle left column. This is a magazine about sailing, and most of the articles are oriented toward sailing. However, "we are always on the hunt for good material about sailing the lakes, rivers, and coastlines of America. Keep in mind that you want to take readers onboard to share your sailing experience.

Many of our favorite features are simultaneously entertaining, practical, and instructive." A popular article length is 1,500–3,000 words, though it takes a strong concept to merit maximum length. Most stories in *SAIL* are shorter, and very, very short pieces are prized. Query *SAIL* about specific ideas. Send your story idea via e-mail. The general e-mail is sailmail@primediasi.com. Manuscripts should be sent to Managing Editor, *SAIL* Magazine, 98 North Washington Street, 2nd Floor, Boston, MA 02114.

Salt Water Sportsman Feature articles run 1,000 to 2,000 words. The average payment runs $500+, but may be more or less. *Salt Water Sportsman* buys fact-feature articles and short fillers dealing with marine sport fishing along the coast of the United States and Canada, the Caribbean, Central America, Bermuda, and occasionally South America and other overseas locations. Send a query first. Contact the editor in writing. Outline the article you want to write, detailing what you intend to cover, the peak season for that type of fishing, and what you will send as add-ons (photos, illustrations, etc.). "There is no taboo about naming charter skippers, lodges, airlines, guides, people, etc.," but do not name celebrities who might have gone along. "Emphasis should be on the how-to, where-to, when-to of salt water fishing." Articles should be computer-generated, double-spaced, and on white bond paper. Include the disk and a note identifying the software program in which the article was written. "The first page of your manuscript should include your name, address, and social security number at the top left. At top right, give us an estimate of wordage. Space down at least three or four inches and center the title of your choice. Beneath the title, center your byline as you wish it to appear in print." The publication wants 35mm color transparencies (slides) for feature and department articles. You may also send glossy, 5 x 7 or larger color prints. Send your article submissions to: *Salt Water Sportsman*, 2 Park Avenue, New York City, NY 10016. Alternatively, you may e-mail your submissions to: editor@saltwatersportsman.com.

Sky This is the Delta Airlines in-flight magazine. Authors may want to visit the Web site at www.Delta-Sky.com. It is expected that potential authors include writing samples and a self-addressed, stamped envelope with their freelance queries. Payment is based on assignment and experience.

The following are descriptions of the departments in *Sky* for which queries are accepted: Style + Value, "an eclectic miscellany of travel opportunities, including lodging, getaways, souvenirs, etc." (75 words); Proximity, "recommendations for what to do at or near the airport: restaurants, public golf courses, aerobic activities, or a bookstore that serves travelers well" (75 words); Long Weekend, "destinations and getaway ideas with an eye on affordability" (350 words); Le Shopping, "a shopping trip to a well-chosen city neighborhood full of unique boutiques, cafes, bars, and other fun places" (75 words); SpaHound, "tracking down the latest and greatest spa experiences, especially for the budget-conscious traveler" (500 words); Starbooks, "a conversation with an interesting and current author" (350 words); Good Looking, "focusing on great permanent art exhibitions from some of the world's best museums" (350 words); Fam Trip, "a local puts together a selective but wide-ranging itinerary on what to experience in his or her city" (600 words); Learning Curves, "a vacation where travelers seek to better themselves and/or improve the lives of others" (1,200 words); Vignette, "a short travel essay on a simple item or activity that will reveal volumes about a given culture" (500 words); Postcards, "a story of travel told in a portfolio of large, powerful photos paired with an essay on the 'one thing you must do while visiting this destination'" (500 words); Evidence of the Culture, "an in-depth travel essay on the cultural riches of destinations served by Delta and its SkyTeam partners" (1,200 words); and Quests, "a person's pursuit of a quest, whether it be sacred or secular, whimsical or profound" (1,200 words).

Travel & Leisure To submit a query, go to www.travelandleisure.com and click on *Contact Us* at the bottom of the page. Scroll down the left side of the page to *Editorial Submissions*. "About 95 percent of the magazine is written by freelance writers on assignment." Read the writer's guidelines, and then click on the *Click Here* tab to send your query. Compensation is negotiable.

Travel & Leisure Golf Go to www.travelandleisure.com/tlgolf/. Go to the bottom of the page, and click on Contact Us. Go to the fifth paragraph in the middle of the page, and click on submission guidelines. "About 95 percent of the magazine is written by freelance writers on assignment." Send a query letter that briefly outlines the ideas being proposed. Query letters also can be sent via e-mail. "In most cases, e-mail queries will receive the fastest responses." "The best sections to start with are departments in the front of the magazine." Use the e-mail link on the Web site. For mail, try the following address: *Travel & Leisure Golf*, Editorial Department, 1120 Avenue of the Americas, New York City, NY 10036. The phone number is (212) 536-2012.

Texas Highways Go to www.texashighways.com, click on Submission Guidelines at the top of the page, and then click on "Speaking of Texas" Submission Guidelines in the middle of the page. Send the spec article itself, not a query. Two to four articles are run each issue. The word count is 50 to 200 words per article, the shorter the better and no more than one double-spaced page. Articles should be about Texas. To get a good idea of the types of articles that are published, study recent issues and review the listing of topics (article titles) in the annual index (published in each December issue). Use "lively and interesting verbs in active voice." Photocopies of at least two primary sources must be included with each article. Pay is 40–50 cents per word on acceptance. Send articles to Ann Gallaway, *Texas Highways*, Box 141009, Austin, TX 78714-1009.

Transitions Abroad Go to www.transitionabroad.com. To access the magazine's writer's guidelines, click on *Travel* Writing in the left column on the home page under *Travel Abroad*. Scroll down to *Travel Writing Resources*. The guidelines provide details of what the magazine wants and what it does not want. There are many different sections and types of articles sought. The maximum length of articles is 1,500 words, but the average length is 800 to 1,000 words. "Manuscripts should be sent electronically and addressed to editor@transitionsabroad.com." Attach only Microsoft Word documents. Payment is on publication at the rate of $2 per column inch (50–55 words). The postal address is *Transitions Abroad*, P.O. Box 745, Bennington, VT 05201.

Washingtonian Magazine Editorial address is 1828 L Street, N.W. Washington, D.C. 20036; phone (202) 296-3600. Send article query ideas or stories to the assistant to the publisher at editorial@washingtonian.com. Send travel articles to Senior Editor Sherri Delphonse at sdalphonse@washingtonian.com with information on weekend getaways. Compensation is negotiable.

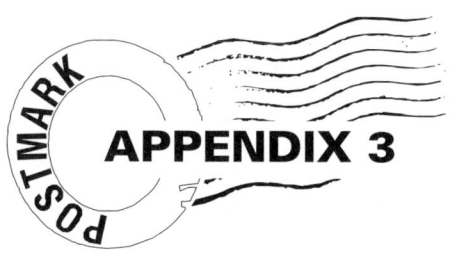

APPENDIX 3

Travel Article Leads

Reviewing publications yourself can provide a solid understanding of what each publication expects from travel writers from whom they purchase articles. Many authors rely only on a publication's writer's guidelines. And these can be most beneficial in narrowing down the publications to which you might want to submit an article. However, there is no substitute for a close review of a current (and sometimes two recent past) issues of the magazine to tell you exactly what the publication is currently buying.

This appendix identifies leads (the first sentence) of articles from a selection of consumer and trade travel publications. It also provides a word count, the number of photos, sidebars, and other add-ons. All of these give a picture of the unique requirements of each magazine.

The following are leads (first sentences of first paragraphs) of selected freelance authored and featured travel articles that appeared in various publications.

Number of Words and Add-ons	Article Title, Author & Lead
From the November 2005 edition of *Condé Nast Traveler*:	
2,773 WORDS + 3 boxed quotes + 4 sidebars + 10 photos + 2 graphic art pieces + 1 chart	**The Great Escape by Barbara S. Peterson** "It was not a miracle, but what happened to Air France flight 358 at Toronto's Pearson International Airport on August 2, 2005, could profoundly change the way most people think about large-scale airplane accidents."
2139 WORDS + 10 photos	**Pick a Card by Alex Robertson Textor and S.E. Kramer** "Almost every popular urban destination offers a city card or pass for free entry or reduced admission to museums and other attractions."
374 WORDS + 1 graphic art piece + 1 sidebar	**E-zzz to Swallow by Dr. Richard Dawood** "In the 1950s, a flight from New York to London on a Boeing Stratocruiser could take 15 hours—ample time for a meal and a game of bridge, followed by a full night's rest in one of the aircraft's luxury berths."
2,705 WORDS + 2 sidebars + 1 map + 5 photos	**Hidden Delights by Kevin Doyle** "Trust me."

Travel Article Leads

Number of Words and Add-ons	Article Title, Author & Lead
4,045 WORDS + 2 bold quotes + 5 photos + 2 maps + 1 boxed referral	**Extreme North by Rob Buchanan** "I'm walking down an empty street in a city I've never seen before."
222 WORDS + 2 photos	**The Way It Was (and Is Again) by Matthias Tener** "In no other city in the world are the tops of buildings more enticing and elusive than in New York."

From the Spring/Summer 2005 edition of *Specialty Travel Index*:

1,147 WORDS + 1 sidebar + 7 photos	**Italy's Po Valley: Timeless Beauty, Ageless Bikers by Andy Alpine** "Twenty-three of us sat outside our country hotel around a large table, some sipping wine, as the September sun reflected off the yellowing rice fields that surrounded us."
1813 WORDS + 1 sidebar + 7 photos	**Gardens of Ireland by Anne de Verteuil** "Perfect peace and a clear blue sky."

From the May 2005 issue of Arthur Frommer's *Budget Travel*:

2,564 WORDS + 4 sidebars + 49 photos + 3 photo grid charts	**My Paris Is Better Than Yours by Clotilde Dusoulier** "When I left Paris to live and work in the San Francisco Bay Area at the height of the Internet euphoria, there were some things that I expected—sunshine, freeways, a cool job in a start-up company—and some that I didn't.

Number of Words and Add-ons	Article Title, Author & Lead
1,527 WORDS + 6 photos + 6 boxed fact statements	**Will the Next Prague Please Stand Up? by Peter S. Green** "In the early 1990s, Prague drew young Americans with its aura of romantic adventure, as Hemingway wanna-bes plugged in their PowerBooks, sipped Pilsners, and traded notes on their screenplays."

From the April/May 2005 issue of *Travel Professional:*

1,195 WORDS + 3 sidebars + 3 photos + 1 boxed reference statement	**After the Tsunami: Response, Remembrance, and Recovery by Fred Gebhart** "People were strolling along the headland near the hotel after a late breakfast when these tremendous waves suddenly sent spray shooting like geysers 20, 30 meters (100 feet) into the air."
1,828 WORDS + 2 sidebars + 2 bold quotes + 1 graphic art illustration	**The Next Big Thing? by Michele McDonald** "Watch out, here they come."

From the July 25, 2005 issue of *Travel Weekly:*

2,274 WORDS + 1 sidebar + 5 photos + 2 blocked quotes	**Burma's Past, Myanmar's Future by Eric Marx** "Somerset Maugham compared it to 'a sudden hope in the dark night of the soul'."

Travel Article Leads

Number of Words and Add-ons	Article Title, Author & Lead
624 WORDS + 1 photo + 1 blocked description	**Agents Must Wield Their Influence by John Dalton** "Based on the actions of the airlines and automation suppliers, it is apparent that the way travel agencies book their clients will be changing."
356 WORDS + 1 photo + 1 blocked descriptor	**From Bordeaux to Basque Country by Lisa Lindblad** "Clients are accommodated at the sixteen-room Hostellerie de Plaisance in St. Emilion, a former monastery."

From the Fall 2005 edition of *Travel 50 & Beyond:*

848 WORDS + 6 photos + 1 sidebar	**The Glacier Express by Sam Cage** "At more than a mile above sea level, the sun reflecting off the deep snow is so bright that even the sky looks white."
1,175 WORDS + 5 photos + 1 sidebar	**Vocation Vacations by Joseph B. Frazier** "At a case or so a minute, the bottles come rattling off the filling and corking machine at Amity Vineyards in Oregon."

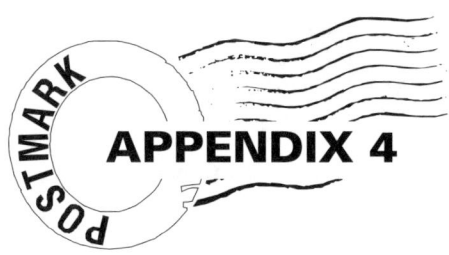

APPENDIX 4

Resources

2005 Writers Market
Kathryn S. Brogan and Robert Lee Brewer (Editors)
Writers Digest Books, 2004
1178 pages

The Best American Travel Writing 2003
Ian Frazier (Editor), Jason Wilson (Series Editor)
Houghton Mifflin, 2003
384 pages

The Best American Travel Writing 2004
Pico Iyer (Editor), Jason Wilson (Series Editor)
Houghton Mifflin, 2004
368 pages

Columbia Journalism Review
"The Travel Section: Roads Not Taken"
Tom Swick
May/June 2001

Lonely Planet Guide to Travel Writing
Don George
Lonely Planet Publications, 2005
272 pages

The Poynter Institute
801 Third Street South
St. Petersburg, FL 33701
Phone: 888-769-6837
www.poynter.org

Reporting & Writing: Basics for the 21st Century
Christopher Scanlan
Oxford University Press, 1998
656 pages

Shorthand Pitman 2000
Teach Yourself, 2003
192 pages

The Teeline Gold Course Book
Jean Clarkson, Stephanie Hall, Celia Osborne, and Ulli Parkinson
Heinemann Educational Books, 1991

The Travel Writer's Handbook: How to Write and Sell Your Own Travel Experiences
Louise Purwin Zobel
Surrey Books, 5th edition, 2002
322 pages

Travel Writing
L. Peat O'Neil
Writer's Digest Books, 2000
256 pages

The Writers Handbook 2005
Elfrieda Abbe
Writer, Inc., 69th edition, 2004
1003 pages

Writing for Story: Craft Secrets of Dramatic Nonfiction
Jon Franklin
Plume; Reprint edition, 1994
288 pages

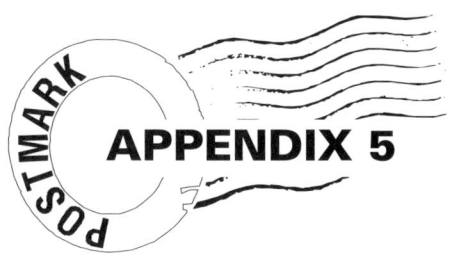

APPENDIX 5

Instructor Comment Sheets

As a benefit to both students and educators, this appendix is composed of nineteen Instructor Comment Sheets, one for each end-of-chapter writing assignment. These sheets provide instructors with a uniform place to make overall comments regarding the writing assignments received from each student. They also provide a place to record the grade earned for each assignment.

If your professor asks for you to attach Instructor Comment Sheets to your written assignments, please first complete the written assignment and then PRINT or TYPE your name at the top of the appropriate Instructor Comment Sheet. Then attach the Instructor Comment Sheet to your written assignment before turning in the assignment to your professor. In some cases, you will have a number of pages of papers. To keep them together, you might staple all of them with the Instructor Comment Sheet on top. Alternatively, you might place all of them into a manila envelope with your name printed on the outside of the envelope. If you are in doubt as to how your professor prefers for you to turn in assignments, ask your professor.

Name: _____

INSTRUCTOR COMMENT SHEET

**Descriptive or Factual Travel Writer
Writing Assignment One**

Assignment: _____

Instructor's Comments:

_____
_____
_____
_____
_____
_____
_____
_____
_____
_____
_____
_____
_____
_____

Points have been deducted from the score indicated below for the following reasons:

_____ days late   − _____ points

Assignment not computer generated   − _____ points

Other _____   − _____ points

Points

01	02	03	04	05
06	07	08	09	10
11	12	13	14	15
16	17	18	19	20

Name: _____

INSTRUCTOR COMMENT SHEET

**Small Points—Big Picture
Writing Assignment Two**

Assignment: _____

Instructor's Comments:

_____
_____
_____
_____
_____
_____
_____
_____
_____
_____
_____
_____
_____
_____

Points have been deducted from the score indicated below for the following reasons:

_____ days late   − _____ points

Assignment not computer generated   − _____ points

Other _____   − _____ points

Points

01	02	03	04	05
06	07	08	09	10
11	12	13	14	15
16	17	18	19	20

Name: _____

INSTRUCTOR COMMENT SHEET

Article Analysis
Writing Assignment Three

Assignment: _____

Instructor's Comments:

_____
_____
_____
_____
_____
_____
_____
_____
_____
_____
_____
_____
_____
_____

Points have been deducted from the score indicated below for the following reasons:

_____ days late	– _____ points
Assignment not computer generated	– _____ points
Other _____	– _____ points

Points

01	02	03	04	05
06	07	08	09	10
11	12	13	14	15
16	17	18	19	20

Name: _____

INSTRUCTOR COMMENT SHEET

Third-Person Writing
Writing Assignment Four

Assignment: _____

Instructor's Comments:

_____
_____
_____
_____
_____
_____
_____
_____
_____
_____
_____
_____
_____
_____

Points have been deducted from the score indicated below for the following reasons:

_____ days late	− _____ points
Assignment not computer generated	− _____ points
Other _____	− _____ points

Points

01	02	03	04	05
06	07	08	09	10
11	12	13	14	15
16	17	18	19	20

Name: _____

INSTRUCTOR COMMENT SHEET

**Postcard Brevity
Writing Assignment Five**

Assignment: _____

Instructor's Comments:

_____
_____
_____
_____
_____
_____
_____
_____
_____
_____
_____
_____
_____
_____

Points have been deducted from the score indicated below for the following reasons:

_____ days late − _____ points

Assignment not computer generated − _____ points

Other _____ − _____ points

Points

01	02	03	04	05
06	07	08	09	10
11	12	13	14	15
16	17	18	19	20

Name: _____

INSTRUCTOR COMMENT SHEET

**Selecting Article Ideas
Writing Assignment Six**

Assignment: _____

Instructor's Comments:

_____
_____
_____
_____
_____
_____
_____
_____
_____
_____
_____
_____
_____
_____

Points have been deducted from the score indicated below for the following reasons:

_____ days late — _____ points

Assignment not computer generated — _____ points

Other _____ — _____ points

Points

01	02	03	04	05
06	07	08	09	10
11	12	13	14	15
16	17	18	19	20

Name: _____

INSTRUCTOR COMMENT SHEET

**Your Travel Journal
Writing Assignment Seven**

Assignment: _____

Instructor's Comments:

_____
_____
_____
_____
_____
_____
_____
_____
_____
_____
_____
_____
_____
_____

Points have been deducted from the score indicated below for the following reasons:

_____ days late   − _____ points

Assignment not computer generated   − _____ points

Other _____   − _____ points

Points

01	02	03	04	05
06	07	08	09	10
11	12	13	14	15
16	17	18	19	20

Name: _____

INSTRUCTOR COMMENT SHEET

Writing With Your Five Senses
Writing Assignment Eight

Assignment: _____

Instructor's Comments:

_____
_____
_____
_____
_____
_____
_____
_____
_____
_____
_____
_____
_____

Points have been deducted from the score indicated below for the following reasons:

_____ days late — _____ points

Assignment not computer generated — _____ points

Other _____ — _____ points

Points

01	02	03	04	05
06	07	08	09	10
11	12	13	14	15
16	17	18	19	20

Name: _____

INSTRUCTOR COMMENT SHEET

Writing Sidebars
Writing Assignment Nine

Assignment: _____

Instructor's Comments:

_____
_____
_____
_____
_____
_____
_____
_____
_____
_____
_____
_____
_____

Points have been deducted from the score indicated below for the following reasons:

_____ days late — _____ points

Assignment not computer generated — _____ points

Other _____ — _____ points

Points

01	02	03	04	05
06	07	08	09	10
11	12	13	14	15
16	17	18	19	20

Name: _____

INSTRUCTOR COMMENT SHEET

First Draft of Your Spec Article
Writing Assignment Ten

Assignment: _____

Instructor's Comments:

_____
_____
_____
_____
_____
_____
_____
_____
_____
_____
_____
_____
_____

Points have been deducted from the score indicated below for the following reasons:

_____ days late — _____ points

Assignment not computer generated — _____ points

Other _____ — _____ points

Points

01	02	03	04	05
06	07	08	09	10
11	12	13	14	15
16	17	18	19	20

Name: _____

INSTRUCTOR COMMENT SHEET

Selecting Targeted Magazines For Your Contract Article Writing Assignment Eleven

Assignment: _____

Instructor's Comments:

_____
_____
_____
_____
_____
_____
_____
_____
_____
_____
_____
_____
_____
_____

Points have been deducted from the score indicated below for the following reasons:

_____ days late   – _____ points

Assignment not computer generated   – _____ points

Other _____   – _____ points

Points

01	02	03	04	05
06	07	08	09	10
11	12	13	14	15
16	17	18	19	20

Name: _____

INSTRUCTOR COMMENT SHEET

Sophisticating the Target Magazine Search
Writing Assignment Twelve

Assignment: _____

Instructor's Comments:

_____
_____
_____
_____
_____
_____
_____
_____
_____
_____
_____
_____
_____
_____

Points have been deducted from the score indicated below for the following reasons:

_____ days late   − _____ points

Assignment not computer generated   − _____ points

Other _____   − _____ points

Points

01	02	03	04	05
06	07	08	09	10
11	12	13	14	15
16	17	18	19	20

Name: _____

INSTRUCTOR COMMENT SHEET

Draft Two of Your Spec Article
Writing Assignment Thirteen

Assignment: _____

Instructor's Comments:

_____
_____
_____
_____
_____
_____
_____
_____
_____
_____
_____
_____
_____

Points have been deducted from the score indicated below for the following reasons:

_____ days late — _____ points

Assignment not computer generated — _____ points

Other _____ — _____ points

Points

01	02	03	04	05
06	07	08	09	10
11	12	13	14	15
16	17	18	19	20

Name: _____

INSTRUCTOR COMMENT SHEET

Selling Your Contract Article and Writing the Outline
Writing Assignment Fourteen

Assignment: _____

Instructor's Comments:

_____
_____
_____
_____
_____
_____
_____
_____
_____
_____
_____
_____
_____
_____
_____

Points have been deducted from the score indicated below for the following reasons:

_____ days late — _____ points

Assignment not computer generated — _____ points

Other _____ — _____ points

Points

01	02	03	04	05
06	07	08	09	10
11	12	13	14	15
16	17	18	19	20

Name: _____

INSTRUCTOR COMMENT SHEET

**The Final Draft of Your Spec Article
Writing Assignment Fifteen**

Assignment: _____

Instructor's Comments:

_____
_____
_____
_____
_____
_____
_____
_____
_____
_____
_____
_____
_____

Points have been deducted from the score indicated below for the following reasons:

_____ days late — _____ points

Assignment not computer generated — _____ points

Other _____ — _____ points

Points

01	02	03	04	05
06	07	08	09	10
11	12	13	14	15
16	17	18	19	20

Name: _____

INSTRUCTOR COMMENT SHEET

**Photos and the First Draft of Your Contract Article
Writing Assignment Sixteen**

Assignment: _____

Instructor's Comments:

_____
_____
_____
_____
_____
_____
_____
_____
_____
_____
_____
_____
_____
_____

Points have been deducted from the score indicated below for the following reasons:

_____ days late — _____ points

Assignment not computer generated — _____ points

Other _____ — _____ points

Points

01	02	03	04	05
06	07	08	09	10
11	12	13	14	15
16	17	18	19	20

Name: _____

INSTRUCTOR COMMENT SHEET

**Packaging and Submitting Your Spec Article
Writing Assignment Seventeen**

Assignment: _____

Instructor's Comments:

_____
_____
_____
_____
_____
_____
_____
_____
_____
_____
_____
_____
_____
_____

Points have been deducted from the score indicated below for the following reasons:

_____ days late   – _____ points

Assignment not computer generated   – _____ points

Other _____   – _____ points

Points

01	02	03	04	05
06	07	08	09	10
11	12	13	14	15
16	17	18	19	20

Name: _____

INSTRUCTOR COMMENT SHEET

**Completing and Submitting Your Contract Article
Writing Assignment Eighteen**

Assignment: _____

Instructor's Comments:

_____
_____
_____
_____
_____
_____
_____
_____
_____
_____
_____
_____
_____

Points have been deducted from the score indicated below for the following reasons:

_____ days late   – _____ points

Assignment not computer generated   – _____ points

Other _____   – _____ points

Points

01	02	03	04	05
06	07	08	09	10
11	12	13	14	15
16	17	18	19	20

Name: _____

INSTRUCTOR COMMENT SHEET

Your Individual Development Plan
Writing Assignment Nineteen

Assignment: _____

Instructor's Comments:

_____
_____
_____
_____
_____
_____
_____
_____
_____
_____
_____
_____
_____
_____

Points have been deducted from the score indicated below for the following reasons:

_____ days late — _____ points

Assignment not computer generated — _____ points

Other _____ — _____ points

Points

01	02	03	04	05
06	07	08	09	10
11	12	13	14	15
16	17	18	19	20

Index

Adams, Ansel 234
Advances 269, 294
Adventure articles 201–2
Adventure travel 161
Advice articles 202
Africanus, Leo 47
Agee, James 196
Agreement letters 212
Amundsen, Roald 56–57
Anthologies 21
   growing popularity of 72
Art
   as source of story ideas 84
Assignment letters 132–33

Bad Trips 161
Baldridge, Aimee 245
Ballard, Robert D. 61
Barrington, Judith 199
Bird, Isabella 54
Bly, Nellie 56
Bond, Mary Beth 72
Book proposals
   for guidebooks 264–65
Borrow, George 156
Bosanquet, Mary 62
Bowles, Paul 157
Brenan, Gerald 157
Brosnahan, Tom 72–73
Brown, Paul 57
Bryson, Bill 70, 157, 195
Buffet, Jimmy 60
Buford, Bill 157
Burkett, Elinor 64
Burton, Richard 156
Burton, Robert 51, 52

Business of travel writing 6–7, 304–18
   developing home page 316
   file keeping 310–12
   filing tax returns 304
   professional associations 317
   selecting office equipment 314–17
   types of business entities 304–5
Busselle, Michael 234, 237
Byron, Robert 37–39, 64, 165

Cahill, Tim 24, 72
Capa, Robert 233
Capote, Truman 196
Carey, James 194
Chaos commodity 200
Chatwin, Bruce 72, 157, 161
Cherry-Gerrard, Apsley 57
Clark, Edward 50
Clark, Roy Peter 85, 88, 196
Clichés
   avoiding 166
Cobb, Jodi 235
Commentary 195–98
   destination piece 198–99
   essays 199–200
Compensation
   flat fee 266
   for how-to travel books 284–85
   in the travel writing industry 322–23
   royalties 266–67, 273, 279, 295
Consumerism
   as source of story ideas 84

Contracts 10, 178, 305
  for guidebooks 268–72, 279
  for how-to travel books 293–96
Convention and visitors bureaus 129
Cook, James 49
Copyright ownership 268
Coryate, Thomas 48
Coster, Graham 60
Cousteau, Jacques 61
Cover letters
  writing 225
Creative nonfiction. *See* Narrative writing
Cripps, John Morton 50
Cruise articles 12
Culture
  as source of story ideas 84
Curzon, Robert 51

Dampier, William 47
D'Ancona, Cyriaco 46
Darwin, Charles 52
Davidson, Robyn 62
Day trips 205–6
de Botton, Alain 71
de Maistre, Xavier 51
de Vartheme, Lodovico 47
Deadlines 271, 295
Defining moment 200
Defoe, Daniel 50
Destination articles 11, 198–99
  including the negatives 223
Deutsch, Brad 117
di Pordenone, Odoric 45
Dickens, Charles 156
Didion, Joan 196
Dineson, Isak 63
Donner, Marcus 233
Doughty, Charles M. 51
Douglas, Norman 156
Durrell, Lawrence 157

Earhart, Amelia 60
Eberhardt, Isabelle 55
Ecotourism
  effect on travel writing 64–65
Eddy, Jerome 58
Egeria 45
Espey, David 20
Essays 199–200
Expenses 271, 272–73
  mileage 309–10

Fa-Hsien 45
Factual verification 147
Fadtan, Ibn 45
Fermor, Patrick Leigh 164
Field notes 105–9
Fielding, Henry 50
Finne, Ranulph 57
Fisher, M.F.K. 157
Flannery, Tim 65
Flavor articles 200–1
Fogel, Yossi 244
Food/dining articles 204
Fortney, Richard 61
Franklin, Jon 197
Frazier, Ian 92
Freebies 271
Freelancers
  use of press trips 131–33
Frommer, Arthur 72, 73
Frost, Lee 240
Fussell, Paul 170

Galton, Sir Francis 52
Gargan, Edward A. 62
Gargarin, Yuri 60
Gellhorn, Martha 157, 200
George, Don 71
Gilpatrick, Guy 61
Glenn, John 60
Granta 157
Greene, Graham 63, 159

Index 395

Guidebooks 14, 23, 31
  book proposals for 264–65
  building author recognition 279–80
  compensation 266–67, 323
  contracts 268–72
  electronic 74
  finding a publisher 263–66
  first 48
  growing popularity of 72
  list of publishers 260–63
  the series market 260
  tips about tools to use 276–77
  writing 149–50, 259–80

Hart, Jack 196–97
Hemingway, Ernest 196
Herodotus 44
Heyerdahl, Thor 62
Hilton, Isabel 157
History articles 204–5
Hoagland, Edward 63
Holland, Patrick 21, 70
Homer 25
Hook 219
How-to articles 13
How-to travel books 283–97
  buyers 285–87
  choosing a title 290
  compensation 284–85, 323
  idea concepts for 285–86
  selling the idea to a publisher 289–93
  types of 283
Howell, David 284, 286, 323
Huggan, Graham 70
Humor 200, 201, 223
  in travel writing 14, 148
Hurn, David 237

I'Anson, Richard 239, 240, 241
Imagination
  vs. invention 165

Indexing 296
Internet
  as source of story ideas 90–91
  impact on travel writing 21, 73–74
Interviews 213–15
  "off the record" 215
  recording 214
  using shorthand to take notes 214
Inverted pyramid style 149, 194–98
Invoices 226
Iyer, Pico 69, 72, 87, 157, 200

Johnson, Samuel 50, 92
Jones, Ann 63
Jones, Christie 113
Journaling
  recollections 111–12
Joyce, James 25
Jubaya, Ibn 45

Kane, Joe 62
Karesh, William 65
Kazantzakis, Nikos 157
Kerouac, Jack 59
Khusro, Nasiri 45
Kinglake, Alexander 51, 156
Kingsley, Mary 55
Knight, Sarah Kemble 50
Kramer, Mark 196
Krist, Bob 231–32
Kron, Karl 58

Langford, Michael 240
Language
  learning before you travel 159
Lawrence, T.E. 51
Leads 219
  attention-grabbing 146
Least Heat-Moon, William 59
Leddy, Dana 101, 114, 116, 119, 121

Leo, Jen 74, 90
Leonowens, Anna 55
Lewis, Norman 64, 157
Liebling, A.J. 196
Lindbergh, Charles A. 60
List management 312–14
Lithgow, William 48
Lodewycksz, Willen 46
Logs 105–9
Lonely Planet 72
Lopez, Samantha 113

Magazines
  as source of story ideas 96
  compensation 323
  kinds of travel writing they buy 176
  selling contract articles to 177
  selling spec articles to 187–88
  travel writing for 74, 149, 156, 157
Magellan, Ferdinand 47
Mailer, Norman 196
Maps 276
  as resources 160
  in guidebooks 270
Markam, Beryl 63
Marketing
  how-to travel books 296
Marketing and sales analysis 292
Marquise de Sevigne 48
Marx, Robert 61
Matthiessen, Peter 65, 70, 72
Mawson, Douglas 56–57
Mayes, Frances 72
Mayle, Peter 72
McCartney, Susan 232, 233, 240
McCormick, John 195
McMurtrey, Larry 59
McPhee, John 196
Media kits
  as source of story ideas 89
Messner, Reinhold 57

Miller, Herb 87
Mitchell, Joseph 196
Montague, Mary Wortley 48
Morris, James Humphrey 65
Morris, Jan 65, 72, 167, 195
Morris, Mary 60
Moryson, Fynes 48
Muggleton, Kevin 63
Murphy, Dervla 58

Nabokov, Vladimir 168
Naipaul, V.S. 64
Nansen, Fridtjof 53
Narrative writing 196–98
  flavor articles 200–1
New Journalism 197
Newby, Eric 59
Newman, Bernard 58
Newspapers
  as resources 159
  as source of story ideas 96
  compensation 322–23
  selling spec articles to 176–77
  travel writing for 74, 149, 155–56, 157
Noncompeting books clause 270
North American Travel Journalists Association 317
Nzenza-Shand, Sekai 64

Observation
  as source of story ideas 82
O'Connor, Flannery 164
Olesky, Walter G. 61
O'Neil, L. Peat 91, 199
O'Rourke, P.J. 169

Packaging and delivering articles 225–26
Park, Mungo 51
Parkes, Carl 73, 90
Paul, Elliot 157

Index

Peck, Annie Smith 55
Perec, Georges 165
Perelman, S.J. 169
Photo equipment
  and depth of field 240
  digital 244–45
  f-stop in 240
  film 242–43
  filters 241
  flash 241
  selecting 238–42
  selecting lenses 240–41
  slides 242–43
  tripod 241
Photos
  airline 252
  composition tips 232–36
  cruise 252
  from stock photo libraries 251
  from tourist bureaus 251
  getting releases 216
  in guidebooks 270
  including with articles 148
  mailing 226
  photojournalism vs. snapshots 237–38
  provided by resorts 252
  providing good travel photography 231–47
  sample model release 238
Pierce, Gordon 285
Plot
  in travel writing 147
Poetry
  as source of story ideas 81
Point of view 166
  selecting 218
Political and social issues
  as source of story ideas 83
Polo, Marco 45
Postcards 110
Pott, Rolf 74
Pound, Ezra 159

Pratt, Mary Louise 43–44
Preparing for trips 158–60
Press releases
  as source of story ideas 88
  getting onto press lists 88
Press trips 125–39
  and tourism 127
  as source of story ideas 89–90, 126
  benefits to host 127
  definition of 126
  etiquette 136
  individual vs. group 130–31
  networking with editors and writers 138
  relieving travel expenses 126–27
  schedules 135
  sources of news on 134
  sponsors of 129–30
  subsidized 70, 89–90, 136–38
  timing of 134
  transportation costs 133
  used by freelancers 131–33
  vs. vacations 134–36
Prince Henry the Navigator 46
Prince, Nancy 54
Project Receipts and Disbursements Record 306, 307
Proust, Marcel 231
Public relations firms
  relationship with travel writers 128–29
Publisher's liability insurance 272
Pyle, Ernie 196

Query letters 184
  sample 185–86
  vs. telemarketing 180–81, 186

Raban, Jonathan 62, 157, 170
Rae, John 53
Raleigh, Sir Walter 47
Reader demographics 212–13

Reader evaluators 292–93
Readership of travel articles 193, 198
Receipts and Disbursements Statement 308
Religion and spirituality
  as source of story ideas 84
Research 92–96, 159, 213
  guidebooks 95, 273–76
  on-site 160–63
  pre-trip planning 275
  publications before pitching articles 178
  travelogues 93–95
  writer's guidelines 179–80
Resort marketing offices 129
Returns 272, 295
Reviews 13
Reynolds, Joshua 158
Ricci, Father Matteo 47
Right of first refusal clause 268
Rights (publication) 305–6
  exclusive 305–6
  local or regional 306
  North American 305
Ross, Lillian 196
Roundup articles 13, 206
Royall, Anne Newport 54

Sacks, Oliver 70
Said, Edward 37
Sain, Vanessa 112
Salby, Betinna 58
Sample chapters 291
Sample copies
  requesting 92
Sand, Georges 54
Sander, Nick 58
Scanlan, Christopher "Chip" 194–95, 214
Scoresby, William 53
Scott, Robert Falcon 56–57
Sedgwick, Catharine Maria 54

Selecting locations 159
Sensory experiences
  as source of story ideas 82
Shackleton, Ernest 56–57
Shaw, Irwin 157
Shelley, Mary Wollstonecraft 54
Shepherd, Alan 60
Sidebars 216
  including with articles 148
Slocum, Joshua 62
Smith, John 47
Smollett, Tobias 50
Society of American Travel Writers 317
Solomon, Susan 57
Spano, Susan 70, 95
Speake, John Hanning 52
Specialist articles 202–3
Stanley, Henry Morton 52
Stark, Freya 156
Stegner, Will 57
Steinbeck, John 59, 157, 196
Stephens, Mitchell 194
Sterne, Lawrence 50
Stevens, Stuart 60
Stevens, Thomas 58
Steves, Rick 72
Story ideas
  coming up with angle 85–86
  from guidebooks 95
  from Internet research 90–91
  from media kits 89
  from newspapers and magazines 96
  from press releases 88
  from press trips 89, 126
  from spotting trends 87–88
  from trade publications 91–92, 96
  from travelogues 93–95
  generating 81–85
  how editors evaluate 85
  timing of 85

Index

write what you know 86–87
Storytelling
  and travel writing 82
Stylebook 146
Subcontracting 270, 276
Swick, Tom 201
Syndicates
  compensation 323
  targeting 324

Tear sheets 310
Technology
  as source of story ideas 84
Telemarketing
  parameters of 181–84
  vs. query letters 180–81, 186
Tellam, Austin 116
The Elements of Style 146
The Road to Oxiana 37–39, 64
"The World of Travel Writing"
  map 26–27
Theme 147, 169
Theroux, Paul 24, 59, 71, 157,
  164, 165, 195
Thompson, Hunter 196
Thubron, Colin 64, 157, 164, 169
Tickler file 310
Toffler, Alvin 239
Tour articles 12–13
Tourisitic writing 20
Tourism
  vs. travel writing 32
Tourism offices 129
  directory 139
Tourist information centers 278
Trade publications
  as source of story ideas 91–92, 96
  compensation 323
  targeting 324
  writing for 11
Transport articles 203
Travel and tourism bureaus 274

Travel books
  as resources 159
  contracting for 176
  growing popularity of 71–73
  self-publishing 72
  vs. travel journalism 155–58
Travel journalism 170
  vs. travel books 155–58
Travel journals 24, 101–20, 200,
  207, 213
  as source of story ideas 81, 102
  character commentaries in
    112–13
  incorporating local materials into
    109–11
  referring to when writing 219
  reflective 115–25
  selecting the form for 103
  titling entries 111
  workshopping 119
Travel literature 20, 32–33, 195
  analytical nature of 170
  autobiographical perspective in
    34
  theme of loss in 35–36
Travel memoirs 20, 24
Travel news articles 207
Travel novels 26–27, 33, 50
Travel Weekly 96
Travel writing
  and scientific travel 49
  Antarctic adventures 56–57
  Arctic adventures 53
  benefits of 65
  broadest literary genre 39
  by air 60
  by automobile 58
  by boat 62
  by railroad 59
  by women 53–56
  criteria for contemporary 22–24
  definition of 20, 69–70

expected information 148
growing industry 322
hallmarks of quality 146–47
history of 24–26, 43–66
importance of details 22
in Africa 63
in eighteenth century 48–49
in fifteenth century 46
in nineteenth century 156
in seventeenth century 47–48
in sixteenth century 46–47
in twentieth century 156–57
narrative 146–47
on bicycle 57
outer space 60
popularity of 71
renaissance in 20–22
seven missing elements of 164–71
strategies for increasing income in 324
ten sins of 164–71
types of 31–32
undersea exploration 61
Travelers' Tales 72
Traveling
  done by Americans 158
  with companions 162–63
Traveling incognito 274–75
Trollope, Anthony 156, 164
Turnley, Peter 238
Twain, Mark 196

Urquhart, Cath 10

Voice 164
  first person 165

Warranties and indemnities 272
Waugh, Evelyn 64, 167, 168
Wells, Ken 195
West, Rebecca 64
Wharton, Edith 58
Wheeler, Sara 57
Willard, Emma Hart 55
Wolfe, Tom 196
Workman, Fanny Bullock 56
Writer-for-hire 266
Writer's Guidelines 179
Writer's guidelines
  researching 179–80
Writing
  act of 163–71
  contract 172, 176, 177–78
  final draft 224–25
  first draft 216–23
  lead paragraph 195
  narrowing process 212
  nut graf in 195
  on speculation 172, 176, 187–88
  parameters for contract articles 188, 212
  process 211–27
  second draft 223–24
  selecting a title 217
  selecting tense 218
  "Show, don't tell" 167
  using an outline 218

Young, Arthur 50

Zobel, Louise Purwin 89, 243